The Baby Boom

The Lexington Books Special Series in Libraries and Librarianship

Richard D. Johnson, General Editor

The Parliament of Great Britain: A Bibliography
Robert U. Goehlert and Fenton S. Martin

Prizewinning Books for Children
Jaqueline Shachter Weiss

The Feminization of Librarianship in France
Mary Niles Maack

The Public Library in the 1980s
Lawrence J. White

International Business Reference Sources
Cynthia C. Ryans

Vietnam War Bibliography
Christopher L. Sugnet and John Hickey

The Electronic Library
Hugh F. Cline and Loraine T. Sinnott

Archival Choices
Nancy E. Peace

Contracts, RFPs, and Other Procurement Documents for Library Automation
Edwin M. Cortez

The Baby Boom: A Selective Annotated Bibliography
Greg Byerly and Richard E. Rubin

The Baby Boom

A Selective Annotated Bibliography

Greg Byerly
Kent State University

Richard E. Rubin
Akron–Summit County Public Library

Lexington Books
D.C. Heath and Company/Lexington, Massachusetts/Toronto

Library of Congress Cataloging in Publication Data

Byerly, Greg, 1949–
    The baby boom.

    Includes indexes.
    1. United States—Social conditions—1945-   —Bibliography. 2. United States—Economic
conditions— 1945-   —Bibliography. 3. United States—Population—Bibliography.
4. Marketing—United States—Bibliography. I. Rubin, Richard E. II. Title.
Z7164.S66B925   1985   016.3046'32'0973   84–47904
[HN59.2]
ISBN 0–669–08903–6 (alk. paper)

Published simultaneously in Canada
Printed in the United States of America on acid-free paper
International Standard Book Number: 0–669–08903–6
Library of Congress Catalog Card Number: 84–47904

Contents

Introduction

Over one-third of the present population of the United States was born during the nineteen years between 1946 and 1965. This bulge in the birthrate, known as the baby boom, has significantly affected our schools, economy, and lifestyles for more than three decades. Now, in the eighties, the baby boomers have reached maturity and they are spending money, changing tastes, managing businesses, and electing candidates. For the next fifty years, this generation will have a major say in determining the character of our society.

It is not surprising, then, that the baby boomers have been the source of both popular and scholarly discussion. For example, *Business Week's* cover story for July 2, 1984, explored the "Baby Boomers['] Push for Power." The great success of books like Landon Jones's *Great Expectations: America and the Baby Boom Generation*, and movies like *The Big Chill* attest to America's preoccupation with trying to understand this generation. Marketing strategists, in their attempt to harness the wealth of the baby boom, regularly produce articles in marketing periodicals. Television networks and advertisers, anxious to employ the marketing strategies, orient their TV programs and commercials to the baby boomers.

Scholars have also tried to grasp the impact of this generation. Demographers, especially, have actively researched this topic and found it of such significance that *American Demographics* has declared 1984 "The Year of the Baby Boom" and devoted its entire May 1984 issue to the topic. Clearly, interest in the baby-boom generation shows no sign of abating.

While much has been written on the topic, poor bibliographic control has made it difficult for researchers, marketing executives, and scholars to locate specific materials or to identify similar research studies. For example, it is difficult enough to find general marketing information relating to the baby boom. However, locating references to specific products or brand names is virtually impossible, given the current state of marketing literature. No standardized subject headings for the baby boom have been established and, consequently, it has been frustrating and time-consuming to identify publications on this topic.

This book is a selective, annotated bibliography on the American baby boom. Over seven hundred references are identified and annotated in eight chapters covering demographic, economic, marketing, managerial, sociological, and popular aspects of the baby boom. Monographs, dissertations, documents, and journal articles published in English are included. All journal articles were assigned to one of seven chapters. Although some of the articles were multidisciplinary in scope, each article was placed in only one chapter. A detailed subject index is provided to facilitate access to specific or unique topics, regardless of chapter placement. For example, while two chapters deal with marketing to the baby boom, the subject index also identifies relevant marketing information in articles whose main emphasis places them in other chapters.

Items selected for inclusion in this bibliography had to focus primarily on the baby boom, defined as the generation of Americans born between 1946 and 1965. Chapters on the baby boom from books of a broader scope were typically excluded. Although historical items were included, the publications chosen had to illuminate contemporary discussion of the baby boom in the United States. In addition, the publications had to serve as accessible and useful research tools. Except for dissertations, unpublished materials (such as conference papers) are excluded, as are materials not generally available in the United States. Private surveys produced by professional associations (e.g., the American Council of Life Insurance's 1983 study entitled "Baby Boom Generation Settling Down") or by marketing research organizations (e.g., the *House & Garden* Louis Harris study, "How the Baby Boom Generation Is Living Now") are similarly excluded because of their general unavailability.

This is not an exhaustive bibliography of the baby boom. There are many related topics which, although they bear a peripheral relationship to the topic, are not covered. The following topics are specifically excluded.

1. Works that deal with broad cultural and social issues and which do not substantially focus on the baby boom, such as Margaret Mead's *Culture and Commitment: A Study of the Generation Gap*.
2. Works that explain demographic procedures or techniques, such as Guillaume Wunsch's *Introduction to Demographic Analysis*.
3. Works that discuss fertility patterns only tangentially related to the baby boom, such as Wilbur Cohen's *Demographic Patterns in America* or Michael Haines's *Fertility and Occupations: Population Patterns in Industrialization*.
4. Works that deal with general population studies, issues and forecasts, such as Bernard Berelson's *The Great Debate on Population Policy*, Tomas Frejka's *The Future of Population Growth: Alternative Paths to Equilibrium*, Robert Snyder's *The Biology of Population Growth*, and Simon Kuznets's *Growth, Population, and Income Distribution*.
5. Government and census statistics, such as the Census Bureau's *Current Population Reports*.
6. Fictional accounts of the baby-boom generation.
7. Studies of population booms in other countries. Articles on the Canadian baby boom have been included when they illuminate baby-boom issues in the United States.

Bibliographic citations were initially retrieved through both manual and online searches of appropriate indexes and databases. All items selected were personally examined and annotated by the compilers. One exception was dissertations unavailable for inspection. *Dissertation Abstracts International* was used as a source for abstracts for these items, and the volume and year of the index used are in parentheses at the end of each abstract. All entries are descriptively annotated, and standard bibliographic information (author, title, place of publication, publisher, dates, and pages) is given for each. Reviews are listed where available for all books. Subject and personal name indexes are included, as are an author index and a periodicals cited index.

The book is divided into eight chapters. Chapter 1 includes books, dissertations, ERIC documents, and government publications. The remaining seven chapters list journal articles reflecting demographic, economic, managerial, educational/psychological/sociological, popular, and marketing perspectives. Because of the substantial focus of marketers on automobiles, housing, and insurance, a separate chapter combining these three marketing targets has been included in addition to the general marketing chapter. The chapter containing popular articles is the only chapter for which relevant articles were selected based on the type of magazine in which they were published. Articles on broad topics from popular magazines, such as those commonly available at newsstands or indexed in *Readers' Guide to Periodical Literature*, were generally placed in this separate chapter.

One area of special interest is the inclusion of reports and statements made during the hearings of the U.S. House of Representatives Select Committee on Population in 1978. Volume 2 of the committee hearings, "Consequences of Changing U.S. Population: Baby Boom and Bust," contains twenty-five prepared statements not reprinted or indexed elsewhere. These statements are separately annotated in chapter 1.

The American baby boom is a constantly evolving demographic phenomenon. Our purpose in this book is to provide direct bibliographic access to the materials published on the baby boom. This topic should be of interest to a wide range of researchers, including advertisers, business and marketing executives, sociologists, demographers, educators, librarians, and psychologists. This bibliography should enable such researchers to quickly and effectively investigate the baby boom from their individual perspectives and to avoid the duplication of effort inherent in searching various indexes.

1
Books, Dissertations, and Documents

1. Alden, Alison. "Delayed Childbearing: Issues and Implication." Ph.D. dissertation, Harvard University, 1981.

   Explores the contemporary trend of delayed childbearing by baby-boom women. A secondary analysis of various demographic statistics was conducted to determine the extent of this trend and to discover the reasons for this delay in family formation. Well-educated young women are the most likely to be childless, but this may be a "transitory" condition that will change after age thirty. Age, career satisfaction, and psychological development are factors that affect a woman's fertility decisions as she grows older. Three different types of delayers are identified and analyzed. (DAI XLII [1982])

2. Anderson, Joseph M. "Population Change and the American Labor Market: 1950–2000." U.S. Congress, House, Select Committee on Population, Hearings on the Consequences of Changing U.S. Population: Baby Boom and Bust, 95th Congress, 2nd Session, 2 June 1978, pp. 781–804.

   Asserts that the changes in the labor force in this century have been caused primarily by fluctuations in the birthrate and changes in the pattern of age-sex structure. Discusses three major topics: (1) the "possibilities for substitution among the various age groups"; (2) demographic composition of unemployment; and (3) forecasting labor market variables, using an econometric model. Predicts dramatic rise in the labor force for individuals between twenty-five and fifty-four as the baby-boom generation enters that age group, and a similar rise in women entering the work force.

3. Barabba, Vincent P. "Effects of Population Change on Voting Behavior and Other Aspects of Lifestyle." U.S. Congress, House, Select Committee on Population, Hearings on the Consequences of Changing U.S. Population: Baby Boom and Bust, 95th Congress, 2nd Session, 23 May 1978, pp. 369–83.

Notes that in the recent past attention has focused primarily on rising birthrates and the future size of the population. Contends that analysis must now shift from birthrates to the composition and distribution of the population. Applies this analysis to projected voting trends. Observes that with fewer children, the older population will have considerable effect on the political climate. Other aspects studied include the political effects of the baby-boom population, the black population, and migration of population from metropolitan to nonmetropolitan areas. Concludes with observations about the effects on education and health activities. Extensive references are appended.

4. Berger, Mark Charles. "The Effects of Labor Force Composition on Earnings and Earnings Growth." Ph.D. dissertation, The Ohio State University, 1981.

Investigates whether the entry of the baby boom into the labor force can explain the changes observed in the earnings among male workers. Models of the production process, earnings, and earnings growth are developed to yield "estimates of elasticities of complementarity between schooling, experience and sex groups." Concludes that the shifts in the work force caused by the baby boom did substantially affect the structure of male earnings. Consequently, predictions based on these findings indicate "considerable persistence of lower earnings of college graduates relative to other groups and a lifetime depression in earnings for the members of the large baby-boom cohorts." (DAI XLII [1982])

5. Berry, Mary F. "Statement." U.S. Congress, House, Select Committee on Population, Hearing on the Consequences of Changing U.S. Population: Baby Boom and Bust, 95th Congress, 2nd Session, 25 May 1978, pp. 604–14.

Notes that, traditionally, schools have tried to deal with the problem of increasing school enrollments. Contends that current demographic trends have forced schools to consider declining enrollments. Cautions that these trends are complex and that members of the post–World War II baby boom will begin to have their children in the 1980s. Asserts further that enrollment rates may vary on a regional basis because of out-migration from the Northeast and North Central part of the United States to the South and Southwest. Recommends school finance reform, encouragement of schools to attract nontraditional school-age populations, flexible use of school facilities for other social purposes, and teacher retraining.

6. Bienstock, Herbert. *New and Emerging Occupations: Fact or Fancy.* Arlington, Va.: ERIC Document Reproduction Service, ED 208 256, 1981. 16 pp.

> Describes three demographuc changes since World War II that have caused labor surpluses: (1) migration from the rural South to the urban North; (2) increase in the number of women in the work force; and (3) the post-war baby boom. Notes that although high school dropouts in the baby boom caused a brief increase in youth unemployment, college graduates of this generation have created a significantly larger labor surplus. These changes will have a dramatic effect on higher education in the 1980s. The need for continuing education and retraining will be strong. However, jobs that are projected to be in demand in the future may not require a college degree. Based on a paper presented in 1981 at the National Center for Research in Vocational Education Staff Development Seminar.

7. Bowman, Robyn. *Aging in the Modern World.* Arlington, Va.: ERIC Document Reproduction Service, ED 156 145, 1978. 30 pp.

> Provides a selective annotated bibliography of government publications dealing with aging. The significance of the trend toward an aging population is emphasized. Notes that "In 1900 only 4% of the American population was elderly. 1977 brought that figure up to 10%; by the year 2025 gerontologists have projected that 20% of our population will be 65 years of age or older." Increased life expectancy and the baby-boom generation are cited as the causes of this increased aged population. Public libraries are urged to serve as referral and information sources for the elderly.

8. Butler, Robert N. "Statement." U.S. Congress, House, Select Committee on Population, Hearings on the Consequences of Changing U.S. Population: Baby Boom and Bust, 95th Congress, 2nd Session, 1 June 1978, pp. 722–40.

> Addresses health issues that affect the aging population in the United States. Notes that by 2030 the sixty-five-year-old population will peak at 52 million and that women will live longer and hence have multiple health and social problems. Indicates that the National Institute on Aging is pursuing research in such areas as metabolism, endocrinology, pharmacology, biochemistry, and nutrition, particularly with respect to the aging of the body. Includes numerous charts on control of childhood diseases, reduction in maternal mortality, life expectancy, population in nursing homes and institutions, and life expectancy.

9. Chase, Richard Allen. "A Choice, a Voice, and a Piece of Property: The Culture of Neighborhood Renovation and Displacement." Ph.D. dissertation, University of Minnesota, 1983.

Presents "a myth and symbol field study of the origins, meanings, and effects of self-help housing rehabilitation in a Minneapolis neighborhood." The incoming home owners were identified as young, affluent members of the baby-boom generation. They were also considered to be "self-serving individuals, motivated by a search to satisfy personal preference that found fulfillment in the ongoing parochial search for community." Self-help neighborhood rehabilitation frequently preserves the neighborhood only by displacing the original inhabitants who sought to save it. (DAI XLIV [1983])

10. Clark, Robert L. "Impact of Retirement Age on the Social Security System." U.S. Congress, House, Select Committee on Population, Hearings on the Consequences of Changing U.S. Population: Baby Boom and Bust, 95th Congress, 2nd Session, 1 June 1978, pp. 705–21.

Discusses the impact of an aging population on the Social Security system. Points out that low fertility rate increases the proportion of the population in older age groups while providing a smaller base of wage earners to support the older population. Recommends an increase in the retirement age and a systematic review by the federal government to establish a "national retirement policy."

11. Corey, Del et al. "What's On the Horizon? Trends Impacting Higher Education." Arlington, Va.: ERIC Document Reproduction Service, ED 231 270, 1983. 27 pp.

Examines two major demographic trends that will affect the future of education: the baby boom and the migration from the Northeast to the South. Notes that members of the baby boom historically "overload every societal system and intrastructure, and then leave a void in their wake." Emphasis is on community college survival. Various factors affecting college curriculum are listed.

12. Cronin, Joseph M. "Statement." U.S. Congress, House, Select Committee on Population, Hearings on the Consequences of Changing U.S. Population: Baby Boom and Bust, 95th Congress, 2nd Session, 25 May 1978, pp. 653–57.

Observes that the baby-boom years produced families in which three children were common, and the Illinois education system built its schools with this in mind. Asserts that ten years later such factors as the zero population growth (ZPG) movement, birth control, and the decision to delay children produced a serious decline in school enrollment. Contends that declining enrollments present challenges as well as problems. Recommends that schools respond to the needs of adults through literacy, GED, and other adult education programs. Suggests that schools can be used for historical and cultural centers as well as for senior-citizen centers.

13. DeMagistris, Robin Carlson. "Measuring the Impact of Demographic Change on Aggregate Personal Saving and Consumer Debt." Ph.D. dissertation, Purdue University, 1982.

Suggests that the decline in savings rate and the increase in consumer installment debt can be partially explained by analyzing demographic changes. Theorizes that "If consumers with different demographic characteristics demonstrate different economic behavior, as the distribution of demographic characteristics changes within society, aggregate behavior will change." The aging of the large baby-boom generation is the primary demographic factor that must be considered. A "microeconomic model of savings and debt" is used to demonstrate that demographic factors do directly affect individual economic behavior. (DAI XLIII [1982])

14. de Marcellus, Robert X. "Impact of Continued Low United States Fertility on Defense Capability." U.S. Congress, House, Select Committee on Population, Hearings on the Consequences of Changing U.S. Population: Baby Boom and Bust, 95th Congress, 2nd Session, 23 May 1978, pp. 438–55.

States that the high birthrates recorded in the fifties have now dropped dramatically and that this drop may have drastic consequences on the military. Predicts that the manpower pool of eighteen-year-olds will drop 15% by 1985 and that this will cause serious recruitment problems for a volunteer army. Observes that with the aging of the U.S. population, a higher percentage of the federal budget will go to needs of the aging and will adversely affect the defense budget. Contends that the decline in birthrates is affecting European countries as well, particularly England and West Germany—NATO allies. Recommends an increase in fertility rates.

15. Derzon, Robert A. "Statement." U.S. Congress, House, Select Committee on Population, Hearings on the Consequences of Changing U.S. Population: Baby Boom and Bust, 95th Congress, 2nd Session, 1 June 1978, pp. 658–74.

Discusses demographic factors that will determine future health-care policies, particularly Medicare and Medicaid. Reviews briefly the historical basis for these programs. Points out that early in the twenty-first century the baby boom will become a "senior boom" and that this senior boom will be followed by a decline in the elderly population. Warns that the wage-earning population will decrease as the elderly of the baby boom increase in number, placing a severe burden on the wage earners. Cautions, however, that too many modifications of the Medicare–Medicaid system for the baby-boom population may lead to serious problems as the baby-bust population ages.

16. Easterlin, Richard Ainley. *The American Baby Boom in Historical Perspective.* New York: National Bureau of Economic Research, 1962. 60 pp.

Laments the ambivalent attitude of economists toward population growth and argues that economists must come to understand the causes of this growth. Identifies the baby-boom generation as a fruitful object of study to determine the nature of fertility behavior. Analyzes three populations: foreign born, native-born urban, and native-born rural. Examines population growth in the context of Kuznets Cycles. Concludes that (1) the baby boom runs counter to the historical trend of declining fertility in this century; (2) fertility is related to labor market conditions; and (3) the cycle of high fertility and low fertility may continue for decades as labor market conditions change. Includes numerous tables on birthrates and fertility ratios. Includes references. Also available in *American Economic Review* 51 (December 1961): 869–911.

17. Egbert, Robert L. *Demography in the United States: Some Twentieth Century Myths.* Arlington, Va.: ERIC Document Reproduction Service, ED 216 439, 1982. 15 pp.

Assesses the validity of five demographic myths concerning education. The first myth incorrectly claims that the baby boom was caused by the return of soldiers following World War II. Claims that the baby boom actually began in 1939. Statistics to support this hypothesis are presented and their significance is interpreted. Incorrect assumptions concerning the start of the baby boom "can cause major misinterpretations of related trends and events." The four other myths discredited are that (1) the Great Depression decreased both birthrates and fertility rates; (2) the birthrate continues to decline; (3) the current burden of the dependent population is high; and (4) over half of all children live in one-parent families. Based on a paper presented in 1982 at the Annual Meeting of the American Educational Research Association.

18. Eisenberger, Katherine E. "Some Demographic Factors Influencing Elementary and Secondary Schools." U.S. Congress, House, Select Committee on Population, Hearings on the Consequences of Changing U.S. Population: Baby Boom and Bust, 95th Congress, 2nd Session, 25 May 1978, pp. 557–67.

> Identifies three demographic factors that are affecting elementary and secondary schools: (1) increases or decreases in enrollment; (2) rates of birth, death, and fertility; and (3) changes in the family and women at work. Notes that the fertility rate has been declining since 1957, leading to a population that is older. Predicts numerous changes, including (1) increased demand for nursery preschool and day-care centers; (2) inclusion of a broader age group in the schools; (3) increases in special support services for children of one parent or dual working families; and (4) curricular revisions at all levels.

19. Espenshade, Thomas J. "The Economic Consequences of Sustained Low Population Growth in the United States." U.S. Congress, House, Select Committee on Population, Hearings on the Consequences of Changing U.S. Population: Baby Boom and Bust, 95th Congress, 2nd Session, 23 May 1978, pp. 384–437.

> Notes that the recent decline in U.S. fertility rates has sparked interest in the effects of slow or zero population growth (ZPG). Reviews the empirical and theoretical research in this area, particularly as it exhibits economic ramifications. Included are discusssions of (1) demographic research; (2) theoretical models; (3) empirical studies, especially in the areas of Social Security, education, space, labor force, and consumption; and (4) policy implications for a stationary population. Suggests several research topics for study.

20. Fishlow, Harriet. *A Demographic Overview of Postsecondary Education.* Arlington, Va.: ERIC Document Reproduction Service, ED 228 935, 1982. 17 pp.

> Examines various demographic trends and forecasts concerning postsecondary education. The tremendous growth in college enrollment between 1955 and 1970 was caused by the number of college-age students in the baby boom and the increased rate of college participation. The latter is judged "the more important cause of growth." The future outlook is relatively bleak until at least the late 1990s because of the decline in college-age youth. Contrary to some opinions, increased enrollments by older adults "do not appear probable." Regional variations are noted. Private institutions will probably be affected most by the projected declines in enrollment.

21. Fishlow, Harriet. "Demography and Changing Enrollments." U.S. Congress, House, Select Committee on Population, Hearings on the Consequences of Changing U.S. Population: Baby Boom and Bust, 95th Congress, 2nd Session, 25 May 1978, pp. 568–93.

Predicts significant fluctuations in school enrollments due to demographic conditions. Observes that although the 1970s saw a general decline in enrollment, the baby-boom babies will start producing children by 1980, so elementary enrollment will increase while high-school enrollment will continue its decline. Asserts that a "flexible" response is necessary, particularly in dealing with excess physical plant, retraining of teachers, and certification programs. Emphasizes the need to project future enrollments in order to plan for demographic changes.

22. Forrest, David Kerr. "Age-Structure and Unemployment: Some Consequences of the Post War Baby Boom." Ph.D. dissertation, University of Western Ontario, 1983.

Investigates the effects of various demographic factors on the rate of Canadian unemployment. Multiple regression techniques were used to help predict participation rates, and eight equations were tested for their ability to explain "the unemployment rate of a specific demographic group, defined by age and sex." Results indicate that the increase in number of young people in Canada as a result of the baby boom "had only a small effect on the overall unemployment rate but a major effect on the structure of unemployment." A brief analysis for the United States is also presented. (DAI XLIV [1984])

23. Freeman, Richard B. "The Effect of the Youth Population on the Wages of Young Workers." U.S. Congress, House, Select Committee on Population, Hearings on the Consequences of Changing U.S. Population: Baby Boom and Bust, 95th Congress, 2nd Session, 2 June 1978, pp. 767–80.

Analyzes the significance of the increase in young workers in the labor force of the sixties and seventies. Explores such issues as the economic impact of this infusion of workers, especially the age-earnings profile. Examines how the market responds to changes in the age composition, and discusses potential consequences for the labor market as the subsequent baby bust provides fewer young workers in the future. Includes tables on the age structure of the U.S. population.

24. Glick, Paul C. "The Future of the American Family." U.S. Congress, House, Select Committee on Population, Hearings on the Consequences

of Changing U.S. Population: Baby Boom and Bust, 95th Congress, 2nd Session, 23 May 1978, pp. 287–306.

Studies the American family by examining such areas as (1) changes in family life cycle; (2) postponement of marriage; (3) marriage and divorce rates; (4) one-parent families; and (5) unmarried persons. Notes that declines in the birthrate and enrollment rates, coupled with a stabilization of the number of women in the work force, should lessen the amount of change in family life. This is contrasted with the significant change that occurred in the recent past. Observes that "underlying many of the Nation's family problems during the 1950s and 1970s has been the difficulty of coping with the tremendous task of absorbing into the social system the massive number of young adults who were born during the period of high birth rates after World War II."

25. Hodgkinson, Harold L. *Guess Who's Coming to College: Your Students in 1990.* Arlington, Va.: ERIC Document Reproduction Service, ED 234 882, 1983. 4 pp.

Discusses briefly the maturing of the baby boom in terms of its impact on college enrollments in the 1980s. The closing of elementary schools and then high school in the sixties and seventies, as the baby-boom generation grew up, established a pattern that may lead to the closure of colleges in the 1980s. Difficulties in predicting future enrollments are described. The decline in birthrates after the baby boom was "almost completely a Caucasian (and probably middle class) phenomenon." Regional and age factors in determining future enrollments are also noted.

26. Hodgkinson, Harold L. *"Terrain Paper" on Demography and Higher Education.* Arlington, Va.: ERIC Document Reproduction Service, ED 228 938, 1982. 19 pp.

Considers various demographic trends that affect higher education. Notes that the baby boom has "sequentially put exorbitant demands on every age level as it moves through, like a mouse in a snake." As this generation ages it may cause a revolt in postsecondary education by dramatically expanding the number of "lifelong learners" actively continuing their education. Racial and regional variations are also enumerated. Emphasizes that colleges and universities "will have to plan for a decline in the size of the cohort graduating from high school."

27. Hofferth, Sandra L. "Family Structure Changes and Child Care." U.S. Congress, House, Select Committee on Population, Hearings on the

Consequence of Changing U.S. Population: Baby Boom and Bust, 95th Congress, 2nd Session, 25 May 1978, pp. 525–56.

Observes that there has been a marked increase in the number of mothers entering the labor force. Consequently, many more children experience alternative care for twenty hours a week or more. Focuses on the following questions: "What is the magnitude of this phenomena? What kinds of care do different types of working mothers choose? Is there enough care? What will be the need for child care by 1990? What might alter the supply of day care or the needs of working mothers by 1990? . . . What, if anything, should or could be done at the federal level?" Numerous tables providing statistical information on day-care centers and children of working mothers are included.

28. Hollander, T. Edward. "The Impact of Enrollment Trends on the Role of State Coordinating Boards." U.S. Congress, House, Select Committee on Population, Hearings on the Consequences of Changing U.S. Population: Baby Boom and Bust, 95th Congress, 2nd Session, 25 May 1978, pp. 623–52.

Analyzes projected declines in enrollment, particularly on the college level. Subjects covered include (1) statistical projections on college enrollment into the 1990s; (2) analysis of enrollment decline by type of institution; (3) identification of characteristics of institutions least vulnerable to enrollment decline; (4) the role of coordinating boards to maintain cooperation among institutions; and (5) the role of the state during periods of enrollment decline. Special emphasis is placed on New York State.

29. Jones, Landon Y. *Great Expectations: America and the Baby Boom Generation.* New York: Random House, 1980. 380 pp.

Examines in depth the nature and impact of the post-World War II baby boom on American society. Among topics covered are (1) defining and understanding the causes of the baby boom; (2) exploring the influence of baby boomers as young people, particularly with regard to social phenomena such as jobs, crime, and the Vietnam War; (3) understanding the maturing baby boomers as they become parents and consumers; and (4) predicting the future for this generation. Argues that baby boomers will change society in different ways as they age. Points out that this generation was raised with great optimism but has become pessimistic and skeptical of fundamental institutions such as government, church, and the military as it has encountered numerous difficulties. Includes index, notes, and bibliography.

(Reviews: *Choice*, February 1982, p. 823; *New York Times Book Review*, September 27, 1981, p. 41; *Chronicle of Higher Education*, October 14, 1980, p. 30; *Business Week*, November 3, 1980, p. 18; *Population and Development Review*, 1981, pp. 131–34.)

30. Kamerman, Sheila B. "Projected Needs for Child Care Services in the 1980s." U.S. Congress, House, Select Committee on Population, Hearings on the Consequences of Changing U.S. Population: Baby Boom and Bust, 95th Congress, 2nd Session, 25 May 1978, pp. 615–22.

    Examines three topics: (1) the inability to confront directly the inevitable consequences of the baby-boom cohort as they age; (2) the complexity and lack of clarity in current discussions of day care in the United States; and (3) a prediction of day-care needs based on an analysis of labor market trends, demographic patterns, and parental wants and needs. Asserts that attention to the baby boom has focused on the effects it will have as it reaches retirement age, but that little attention has been paid to its middle years. Notes that there has been a significant rise in the number of married women entering the labor force and that the impact of this trend on day care services and pre-primary school programs cannot be ignored.

31. Kettle, John. *The Big Generation.* Toronto: McClelland and Stewart Limited, 1980. 264 pp.

    Examines the impact of the Canadian baby boom from birth to future maturity and retirement. Covers such areas as (1) growth of the baby-boom generation and expectations of the parents; (2) effects of baby boomers on the education system; (3) effects of consumer demands on the marketplace; (4) impact of the baby boomers on the labor market and on promotional opportunities; (5) political impact on baby boomers; and (6) effects of the aging baby boomers on the retirement system. Includes detailed notes and index.
    (Review: *MacLeans*, December 29, 1980, p. 48.)

32. Ladsburg, David L. *The Business of Adult Education: Open Season in the Marketplace.* Arlington, Va.: ERIC Document Reproduction Service, ED 212 333, 1982. 17 pp.

    Notes the growing market for adult education and considers which institutions can best meet this demand. The baby boom is the prime factor in this increased demand because of its sheer numbers, higher educational levels, preponderance of working women, and increasing job dissatisfaction. Notes that "As that group grows, the demand for adult education will continue to grow." Competing institutions for these adult students are identified. Community colleges will have to fight for adequate funding to continue to provide appropriate adult education.

33. Lazar, Joyce Barham. *The Status of Research on Women in the 70s.* Arlington, Va.: ERIC Document Reproduction Service, ED 156 579, 1978. 24 pp.

Reviews the current status of women and identifies areas for further research. The importance of demographic analysis is stressed: "Whereas once it was thought that anatomy was destiny, it now appears that demography may be destiny." The maturing of the baby boom will mean (1) more mid-life crises; (2) large numbers of households headed by women, especially over the age of sixty-five; (3) increased number of separated, divorced, or widowed women; and (4) later marriage and childbearing for many women. Areas of research needed on women of all ages are broadly defined. A bibliography is also included. Based on a report of the President's Commission on Mental Health, Task Panel on Special Populations.

34. Lewis, Raymond J., Jr. *Lifelong Learning in America: An Overview with Implications for Secondary Education. Education and Work Program Project Report.* Arlington, Va.: ERIC Document Reproduction Service, ED 235 324, 1980. 32 pp.

Predicts that recent expansion of adult education will continue and will intensify in the 1980s. The aging of the baby boom is the "most obvious factor affecting adult learning patterns." In addition, job stagnation and limited upward occupational mobility will force many workers to consider furthering their education. Postsecondary institutions are urged to "focus increasing attention on adult learners in the next fifteen years in efforts to fulfill their missions and avoid substantial retrenchment due to loss of traditional clientele."

35. Loewenstein, Gaither Drake. "The New Underclass: Downward Mobility in the Post Baby Boom Generation." Ph.D. dissertation, University of Delaware, 1983.

Claims that because younger members of the baby boom have found it difficult to enter the labor market, their reduced career potential has depressed their aspirations and life-styles. Labor market statistics are presented to illustrate the impact of the baby boom on the labor force. Personal interviews and case studies are used to demonstrate the loss of motivation among young, unskilled workers. Broad policy implications are described, and various recommendations, such as a federally funded, neighborhood-based jobs program, are presented. (DAI XLIV [1983])

36. McDonald, Scott Camerson. "Human and Market Dynamics in the Gentrification of a Boston Neighborhood." Ph.D. dissertation, Harvard University, 1983.

Investigates the process of "gentrification" in an inner-city section of Boston. Results of a survey of buyers in this area and some expensive Boston suburbs are compared with respect to demographic, market, and life-style characteristics. Concludes that "gentrification stems from the demand-side pressures on urban housing markets stimulated by the maturation of the postwar baby boom." Briefly considers the viability of gentrification in other cities. (DAI XLIV [1983])

37. Michaels, Joanne. *Living Contradictions: The Women of the Baby Boom Come of Age.* New York: Simon and Schuster, 1982. 238 pp.

Explores the significance of being a female baby boomer in contemporary society. Observes that the size of this generation automatically creates a focus on its activities and notes that women are entering the work place in significant numbers. Discusses the values and behaviors of baby-boom women as they mature, touching on such topics as (1) the place of career; (2) living arrangements; (3) motherhood; and (4) political activism. Cites case histories to explicate each chapter. States that "growing up female as part of the first wave of the baby boom is what this book is all about . . . " Includes notes and recommended readings.
(Reviews: *Library Journal*, April 1, 1982, p. 740; *Booklist*, April 15, 1982, p. 1050; *Kirkus Review*, February 15, 1982, p. 259.)

38. Moore, Charles Guy. *Baby Boom Equals Career Bust.* Washington, D.C.: U.S. Department of Health, Education and Welfare. Office of Education, 1977. 18 pp. Also available from Arlington, Va.: ERIC Document Reproduction Service, ED 145 411, 1977. 21 pp.

Analyzes the social implications of the baby boom, particularly as they relate to the job market. Points out that the job market is flooded with young baby boomers, who have severely increased competition for jobs. Contends that this has led to a "career bust" for the college-educated, who were raised with the expectation that their degrees would produce jobs. Analyzes the impact of women on the labor force as their participation increases significantly. Notes that the job market is especially poor for liberal arts graduates. Recommends more realistic expectations, better guidance techniques, and use of the baby-boom surplus to deal with our social problems.

39. Morrison, Peter A. "New York State's Transition to Stability: The Demographic Outlook." U.S. Congress, House, Select Committee on Population, Hearings on the Consequences of Changing U.S. Population: Baby Boom and Bust, 95th Congress, 2nd Session, 23 May 1978, pp. 329–68.

Observes that New York State is experiencing a transition in population pattern from steady growth to near stability. Notes that this transition will result in a redistribution of population in metropolitan and nonmetropolitan areas. Pays particular attention to the effect on college and school enrollments and on the distribution of the elderly. States as the purpose of the article: "To distill the basic information on current population trends in the state and highlight economic and social problems that those trends are likely to create." Maps and tables are provided for regional population changes in the United States and annual migration rates for New York State.

40. Morrison, Peter A. "The U.S. Population's Changing Regional Distribution: Trends and Implications." U.S. Congress, House, Select Committee on Population, Hearings on the Consequences of Changing U.S. Population: Baby Boom and Bust, 95th Congress, 2nd Session, 23 May 1978, pp. 307–28.

Examines effect of the dramatic decline in the birthrate, especially with respect to migration of the U.S. population. Observes that a stabilization of the U.S. population is occurring and that some regions will feel the impact much more severely than others. Asserts that "in the metropolitan sector, population is shifting away from the mature industrial subregions toward subregions in the South and West. In the nonmetropolitan sector, there has been a strong and pervasive revival in all subregions." Recommends assisting localities with problems encountered from growth and decline, and recognizing the national responsibilities of solving these problems. Includes tables and charts on U.S. migration.

41. Plotkin, Manuel D. "Future Size and Growth Rate of the U.S. Population." U.S. Congress, House, Select Committee on Population, Hearings on the Consequences of Changing U.S. Population: Baby Boom and Bust, 95th Congress, 2nd Session, 23 May 1978, pp. 273–86.

Reviews demographic conditions that may arise in the next fifty years. Observes that the baby-boom population will be the largest population group throughout their lives. Provides tables that project total population, annual births and deaths, and average annual percent change in the U.S. population from 1950 to 2025. Notes that it may be a period of zero population growth or increasing fertility rates. Asserts that "it will be a period of boom and bust for age-related institutions—schools and colleges, housing, retirement, pension plans, and even the undertaking business—as the baby-boom generation pursues its course through the age structure of the U.S. population."

42. Quistwater, J.M.R. *General Education for the Too Late Generation.* Arlington, Va.: ERIC Document Reproduction Service, ED 180 569, 1979. 24 pp.

Focuses on changes in community-college enrollments that will be induced by various demographic factors, most notably the aging of the baby-boom generation and the increased number of women in the work force. The cyclical pattern of age-group distribution is noted: "At the same time that we are witnessing the passing of the tail of the post war baby boom through our high schools, colleges and universities, local hospitals record birth rates unparalleled in recent years— the beginning of what is known as the 'echo' of the post war baby boom." Factors affecting career prospects and suggestions for program planning are identified. The maturing of the baby boom will influence not only community colleges, but also other aspects of society such as the work force and retirement plans.

43. Ruff, Richard D. *A Study of the Future of Vocational Education: Implications for Local Planning.* Arlington, Va.: ERIC Document Reproduction Service, ED 199 563, 1981. 13 pp.

Recounts the results of the first two years of a study involving future research conducted by the National Center for Research in Vocational Education. The future of vocational education in the 1980s is analyzed. The baby boom is judged "the dominant source of demographic change in the 1980s." Both the number of available students and public support for vocational education may decline in the future. Study concludes, "The educational and training implications of the loss of traditional clients and the rise in importance of new populations is a trend to which local vocational education planners must be extremely sensitive during the 1980s."

44. Russell, Louise B. *Baby Boom Generation and the Economy.* Washington, D.C.: Brookings Institution, 1982. 183 pp.

> Provides a detailed analysis of the baby-boom generation and its impact on basic economic factors. Among areas covered are (1) a statistical analysis of the fertility patterns from 1900 to the present; (2) the effects of baby boomers on the education system, including the drop in enrollments in the late 1960s; (3) the implications of the baby boomers' entrance into the labor market and the relationship of age structure to the unemployment rate; (4) the consumer demands of baby boomers, particularly for housing and durable goods; and (5) the effects of the aging baby boomers on the retirement and Social Security systems. Concludes that baby boomers have had some influence on the economy but not necessarily a major one. Includes numerous tables and appendices, and an index.
> (Reviews: *Choice*, March 1983, p. 1027; *Journal of Economic History*, 1984, pp. 224–26; *Political Science Quarterly*, 1983, p. 727; *Population and Development Review*, 1983, pp. 375–77.)

45. Sawhill, Isabel V. "Women in the Labor Market: Prospects and Policies." U.S. Congress, House, Select Committee on Population, Hearings on the Consequences of Changing U.S. Population: Baby Boom and Bust, 95th Congress, 2nd Session, 2 June 1978, pp. 741–66.

> Studies potential effects on the economy and structure of the family as more and more women enter the labor force. Notes that only one-third of the adult women were in the labor force in 1950, but by 1978 almost one-half were part of the work force. Observes that the concept of "women's place" is breaking down and that women are seeking jobs for continuous employment. Contends that the double burden of women to care for both the home and job puts women at a competitive disadvantage. Indicates that governmental policies involving Social Security, child custody, protective labor laws, credit practices, and military service must be adapted to new sex roles.

46. Simon, Julian L. "Additional People Improve the Standard of Living Through Knowledge Creation and Productivity Increases." U.S. Congress, House, Select Committee on Population, Consequences of Changing U.S. Population: Baby Boom and Bust, 95th Congress, 2nd Session, 2 June 1978, pp. 805–84.

> Asserts that contrary to popular belief, increased population in more developed countries (MDCs) is beneficial to the country. Notes that the conventional Malthusian model does not recognize that more people create more new knowledge, and that this new knowledge creates

greater productivity. Presents numerous tables demonstrating population growth and growth in output. Proposes a modification of the Malthusian model that adds peoples' "inventive and adaptive capacities." Recommends an end to concern over population growth in the United States and an encouragement of immigration. Also includes Simon's article, "The Only Impending Shortage Is a Shortage of Bad News," and chapters from his book, *The Economics of Population Growth*.

47. Simon, Julian L. "The Only Impending Shortage Is a Shortage of Bad News." U.S. Congress, House, Select Committee on Population, Consequences of Changing U.S. Population: Baby Boom and Bust, 95th Congress, 2nd Session, 2 June 1978, pp. 831–35.

Reviews the proliferation of false statements concerning high population and its alleged harmful consequences. Examines assertions made by Kurt Waldheim and Paul Erlich, *Newsweek*, the *New York Times*, and others. Counters these assertions by analyzing the sources of the statements and inadequacies of the underlying models. Argues that negative conclusions about population growth may be well received because they (1) foster research money by way of government grants; (2) sell newspapers, magazines, and so forth; (3) serve the self-interest of conservation groups; and (4) concern our strong beliefs about human life.

48. Smith, Elmer W. "Statement." U.S. Congress, House, Select Committee on Population, Hearings on the Consequences of Changing U.S. Population: Baby Boom and Bust, 95th Congress, 2nd Session, 1 June 1978, pp. 675–704.

Analyzes the effects of the baby-boom and baby-bust populations on the Social Security system. Notes that currently 31 people get Social Security benefits for every 100 workers; by the turn of the century there will be 50 beneficiaries per 100 workers. Asserts that as the baby-boom population reaches retirement age, the baby-bust population will be responsible for supporting the Social Security system, resulting in sharply increased costs. Contends that factors such as decreased mortality and birthrates and increasing participation of women in the labor force will also affect the system. Proposes continued analysis of demographic projections and predicts long-range deficits for the Social Security system.

49. Spencer, Robert C. "The Management of Decline in Higher Education." U.S. Congress, House, Select Committee on Population, Hearings

on the Consequences of Changing U.S. Population: Baby Boom and Bust, 95th Congress, 2nd Session, 25 May 1978, pp. 594–603.

Discusses the plight of Sangamon State University in Illinois, which was built in 1970 and was confronted with enrollments that were much lower than originally projected. Reviews the growth of educational opportunities, particularly for students attending community or state collges. Notes that external forces influenced the management of these institutions. Most prominent among these forces were campus constituencies demanding participation in decision-making, and technical report-writing requirements that placed an overemphasis on quantitative measures. Recommends a reexamination of our national priorities.

50. Steinberg, Ira S. *The New Lost Generation: The Problems of the Population Boom.* New York: St. Martin's Press, Inc. 1982. 160 pp.

Uses both philosophical and sociological methods to analyze the baby-boom generation. Contends that the baby boom is actually two separate population explosions: the first occurred as the post-World War II soldiers returned home; the second, which the author calls the "super boom" because of its size, occurred in the fifties and sixties. Identifies the baby boomers as the "New Lost Generation" destined to endure overcrowded schools, severe job competition and unemployment, and a questionable life in retirement. Points out that this will lead to continual and serious frustration and demoralization among a significant portion of the U.S. population. Examines various policy alternatives that could alleviate this problem. Argues that a need exists to develop a strong, expanding economy. Includes index.
(Reviews: *Choice*, December 1982, p. 616; *Sociology: Reviews of New Books*, February 1983, p. 11; *Population and Development Review*, 1982, pp. 849–50.)

51. Stoddard, Karen Marie. "The Image of the Aging Woman in American Popular Film, 1930–1980." Ph.D. dissertation, University of Maryland, 1980.

Focuses on the image of aging women in popular films. Changes in the role of women as mothers are noted and analyzed in detail. In the 1940s and 1950s women who did not marry and produce children typically experienced "devastating consequences" in films. The baby boom can be partly explained by these constant reminders that women should become mothers. The 1960s were also greatly affected by the members of the baby boom. The "sexual attractiveness and procreative abilities" of women were stressed in films and on television. Nontraditional and radical roles for women began to be presented in the 1970s. Concludes that the "gradual de-mythologizing of maternity as a necessary role for a woman's self-actualization helped focus greater attention on the alternatives available to women as they age." (DAI XLI [1980])

52. Sullivan, Kathleen McCann. "Meeting Educational Needs of Women in Midlife Through Postsecondary Institutional Planning." Ph.D. dissertation, University of Mississippi, 1981.

Summarizes opinions and suggestions of continuing education practitioners from fourteen postsecondary institutions concerning the educational needs of maturing baby-boom women. Participants in the study expect these female "middle-aged learners" to be interested in career advancement courses and to be disadvantaged by financial problems and lack of adequate academic preparation. Continuing education programs must emphasize "diversity, responsiveness and flexibility in academic programming." Various survey instruments and models were developed for this project. (DAI XLI [1981])

53. Van Horn, Susan Householder. "Women's Roles: Work and Fertility for American Women Between 1900 and 1980." Ph.D. dissertation, Carnegie-Mellon University, 1980.

Explores the roles of women as mothers and paid workers in the twentieth century. Three time periods are analyzed. The first forty years of the century witnessed significant declines in fertility and a small increase in the participation of women in the work force. The second period, 1940 to 1960, demonstrated substantial increases in both fertility and work. These mothers of the baby boom frequently exhibited a "serial dual role" by working, having children, and then returning to work. The third period, 1960 to 1980, has reverted to the pattern established early in the century of an inverse relationship between fertility and work-force participation. Women are working, but not producing children. Concludes that "the century may well end as it began." (DAI XLI [1981])

54. Vaughan, Jerry L. "The Major Impacts of the Baby Boom Upon American Life, 1845–2050." Arlington, Va.: ERIC Document Reproduction Service, ED 230 478, 1983. 24 pp.

Provides an overview of the baby boom's impact on society and predicts how it will affect the future. A brief history of the baby boom is given and possible causes identified. Past effects on unemployment, consumer markets, crime, television and entertainment, households, and geographic population distribution are summarized. Future consequences for households, consumer patterns, politics, education, employment, and social welfare are then forecast. Concludes that the United States "appears to have embarked upon a 20 year cycle of boom and bust economics and demographics."

55. Weiner, Nella Fermi. "Baby Bust and Baby Boom: A Study of Family Size in a Group of University of Chicago Faculty Wives Born 1900 to 1934." Ph.D. dissertation, University of Chicago, 1981.

Summarizes a study conducted by the author of sixty University of Chicago faculty wives, thirty born between 1900 and 1914 and thirty born between 1920 and 1934, to determine the reasons for their fertility behavior. Study notes that women of the earlier generation had few children, while the later generation produced the post-war baby boom. Tests four hypotheses, including the Easterlin hypothesis of remembered poverty and Ryder's theory of unintended fertility. Concludes that Ryder's theory is supported by the data—that the mothers of the fifties had many more accidental pregnancies than did the previous generation. (DAI XLII [1981])

56. Whaley, Charles E. *The Major Impacts of the Baby Boom Cohort Upon American Life, Past, Present and Future.* Arlington, Va.: ERIC Document Reproduction Service, ED 231 709, 1983. 35 pp.

Describes the impact of the baby-boom generation in broad terms. The baby boom has "to a great degree shaped marketing strategies, educational and government policies, given birth to billion dollar enterprises and generally reshaped our thinking toward a number of aspects of American life." Causes of the baby boom are identified and its effects on such realms as television, advertising, and suburban populations are outlined. Two areas of concern are future health-care costs and the Social Security system. Numerous predictions are made based on the "growing sophistication and political clout of the baby boom."

57. Wray, Joe D. "Population Pressure on Families: Family Size and Child Spacing." U.S. Congress, House, Select Committee on Population, Consequences of Changing U.S. Population: Baby Boom and Bust, 95th Congress, 2nd Session, 25 May 1978, pp. 456–524.

Reprinted from volume 2, chapter 11, of *Rapid Population Growth: Consequences and Policy Implications.* Notes that there is an alarming population explosion at global and national levels. Covers such areas as (1) current knowledge about the effects of family size and birth interval; (2) health consequences of family size; (3) health consequences of birth interval; and (4) the implications of the evidence. Among the effects of increased family size are increased illness and child mortality, less satisfactory intellectual growth, and economic and emotional stress. Notes also that "excessive *crowding* of children . . . will produce the same effects quickly that excessive *numbers* of children will produce . . . " Provides numerous tables and references.

2
Demographic Articles

58. "ACLI. Analysis Shows Effect of Maturing Members of Baby Boom."
    The National Underwriter: Life and Health Insurance Edition 85 (August
    29, 1981): 5.

    Summarizes the report issued by the American Council of Life In-
    surance on the aging of the U.S. population. Stresses the following
    points: (1) key demographic factors are influenced by the enormous
    population produced by the post-war baby boom; (2) one-third of the
    population will be between the ages of twenty-five and forty-four by
    1990; (3) the labor pool will, as a consequence of aging, be older and
    more experienced; (4) households will increase in number but many
    will be nontraditional; and (5) future birthrates will be significantly af-
    fected by the baby-boom mothers and their childbearing decisions as
    they reach the prime fertility ages.

59. "Aging Baby Boom Affects Labor Pool, Household Growth." *Best's Re-
    view: Life/Health Insurance Edition* 82 (September 1981): 147.

    Summarizes an analysis of demographic trends indicating that there
    will be fewer teenagers, more older workers, more minority immi-
    gration, and an increase in older Americans in the 1980s. However,
    the most dramatic changes will occur further in the future. Contends
    that "it is not the graying of America, but the aging of the baby boom
    that should have the greatest impact." Both household growth and the
    overall labor pool will be significantly affected by the aging of the
    baby boom.

60. "America on Verge of New Baby Boom." *Intellect* 107 (August 1978): 7.

    Outlines the theory expressed by Ronald D. Lee, a University of
    Michigan economist and demographer, that "America is on the verge
    of a new baby boom, which will peak in the 1990's at more than one-
    and-one-half times the current birth rate." The theory is adapted from

the method of population forecasting begun by Richard Easterlin and is based on two concepts: one, both size and age distribution greatly affect relative economic status, and two, relative economic status effectively determines fertility. If the 1980s and 1990s are prosperous, as predicted, then Lee predicts that young adults will "marry earlier and have more children."

61. "Another Baby Boom?" *Science Digest*, October 1965, p. 38.

Explores briefly the prospects for another baby boom in the late 1960s and 1970s. Points out that there will be a 40 percent increase in the number of women in prime childbearing years during the next five years. Notes that a baby boom could produce a population of 400 million by 2005. Notes a general decline in fertility rates since 1957, and observes tht the cost of raising children may inhibit a sharp increase in the birthrate.

62. "Babies Bottom Out: A 'Maybe Boom'." *Science News* 112 (August 13, 1977): 101.

Discusses a report by the *National Center for Health Statistics* indicating a rise in the birthrate. Attributes this rise to an "echo" baby boom. This "echo" boom is a consequence of the post-World War II baby-boom women, who are entering their prime fertility period. Points out that overall this trend is beneficial in preventing a disproportionately old population. Also notes, however, that the increase in teenage pregnancy is disturbing and is a consequence of inadequate sex education. Contends that it is too early to determine whether this is the start of another baby boom.

63. "Baby Boom Families." *American Demographics* 4 (April 1982): 46–47.

Forecasts the number and income of baby-boom families through 1990. In 1990 over half of all families will be headed by baby boomers. Among the fastest growing family groups will be those with incomes between $50,000 and $70,000 that are headed by persons between the ages of thirty-five and forty-four. This is attributed to the anticipated trend toward two-income families and to the earning capacity of baby boomers entering their peak earning years. Graphs and tables are used to demonstrate these predictions statistically.

64. "Baby Boom Generation Productive." *Advertising Age* 55 (May 31, 1984): 3.

Notes U.S. Census Bureau figures indicating that "the baby boom generation has reversed the declining fertility rate." There were 1.1

million more children under five years of age on July 1, 1983, than on April 1, 1980. This represents a fifteen-year high in this age bracket. Also notes that "as the baby boomers moved through the life cycle, the 25 to 34 age segment, with 29.5 million, was up 14.8%."

65. Baker, Ross K. "Demogaffes: In Bust We Trust." *American Demographics* 1 (July/August 1979): 48.

Observes, in a humorous fashion, the proclivity of demographers to label a trend as either a "bust" or a "boom." Extreme possibilities and interrelationships are presented. For example, it is suggested that "what lurks behind the 'baby bust' may be a 'lust bust.' " Concludes that the baby boom could have been more accurately named the "womb bomb."

66. Barabba, Vincent P. "How Demographics Will Shape Decade." *National Underwriter: Life and Health Insurance Edition* 84 (January 12, 1980): 2.

Analyzes key demographic elements that will affect society in the next decade. Identifies four prominent trends: (1) the changing age structure due to the aging of the post-World War II baby boom; (2) changing patterns in family structure and marriage statistics; (3) changes in the work-force composition; and (4) changes in the role of women. Also analyzes migratory trends, especially the increasing population in the Sunbelt and the movement from metropolitan to nonmetropolitan areas. Notes critical age bracket of baby boomers, aged twenty-five to forty-four, who are entering their primary years for home purchase and career development.

67. Bean, Frank D. "The Baby Boom and Its Explanations." *Sociological Quarterly* 24 (Summer 1983): 353–65.

Examines numerous theories that attempt to explain fertility behavior resulting in the post-war baby boom, including those of Richard Easterlin, Norman Ryder, and Charles Westoff. Separates the explanations into four categories: (1) sociocultural; (2) economic; (3) social-psychological; and (4) relative economic status. Singles out the increase in average family size as a particular point for sutdy. Finds that the baby boom had many causes and that no one theory can explain it in its entirety. Pays special attention to the concept of unintended fertility.

68. Buyz, William P., and Michael P. Ward. "Baby Boom and Baby Bust: A New View." *American Demographics* 1 (September 1979): 11–17.

Offers explanations for the substantial decline in the fertility rate since 1975. Various reasons for this baby bust are examined. Baby-boom women in their childbearing years seem to be influenced most by two considerations in determining whether to have children: one, family income, and two, the opportunity cost of their time. Other elements influencing their decision include economic conditions, attitudinal and societal changes, and contraceptive devices. Various charts plot these influences over the period 1947 to 1975.

69. Campbell, Arthur A. "Baby Boom to Birth Dearth and Beyond." *Annals of the American Academy of Political and Social Scientists.* 435 (January 1978): 40–60.

Presents a detailed statistical analysis of fertility changes in the United States. Different measures of fertility are identified, and statistics of completed fertility among young cohorts are examined to predict future trends. Contends that past upward and downward movements in annual rates of fertility have been exaggerated by the overall patterns of fertility. In reality, the actual trend is toward low completed fertility rates. No evidence exists to support a return to the high rates of the 1950s.

70. Clare, James L. "The Canadian Marketplace in the 1980s: Part 2—Demographic Changes." *Canadian Insurance* 85 (August 1980): 28–35.

Considers the Canadian baby boom and its effect on the Canadian marketplace. While the baby boom caused high unemployment in the 1970s and will create serious economic problems when its members retire in the next century, its immediate impact will be a "major factor of growth in the economy as this group joins the labor force and matures into a highly productive unit." Other demographic constituents that influence marketing in Canada are considered: (1) death rates; (2) immigration; (3) population; (4) marriage and divorce; and (5) families and households.

71. Cosmatos, D.; D.B. Brock; and J.A. Brody. "Effect of the Post World War II 'Baby Boom' on the Aging Population." *Journal of Clinical and Experimental Gerontology* 4 (1982): 109–13.

Presents a historical overview of fertility, then projects effects of baby boom on the elderly population in the next century. A graph shows the percentage of population over sixty-five years of age as reported at decimal intervals from 1900 to 1970, and as projected to 2050. The percentage of persons over eighty-five years of age will dramatically increase until the percentage of the elderly gradually levels off around the middle of the twenty-first century.

72. Cutler, Neal E. "Population Dynamics and the Graying of America." *Urban and Social Change Review* 10 (Summer 1977): 2–5.

> States that the purpose of the article "is to introduce some of the basic information and concepts underlying the population dynamics which are resulting in the graying of America." Employs the concepts of fertility, mortality, migration, and dependency ratio and birth cohort to provide an understanding of the "graying" process. Points out that the baby-boom generation will eventually become the "Gerontology Boom," and that the ratio of working people to retirees will be significantly affected as this occurs. Cautions that the baby-boom cohort, as with all birth cohorts, is not just of similar age but possesses unique generational values that must be considered in future social planning. Includes tables on age composition of the population from 1930 to 2050, life expectancy, and dependency ratios.

73. David, Henry P., and Wendy H. Baldwin. "Childbearing and Child Development: Demographic and Psychosocial Trends." *American Psychologist* 34 (October 1979): 866–71.

> Considers how childbearing and fertility-regulating behavior influences child development and the general well-being of children. Historical trends of American fertility are delineated, and the baby boom is identified as an "unusual period of our demographic history." Three characteristics of childbearing that affect child development are identified: (1) "wantedness of births"; (2) family size preferences; and (3) differences in the demographic characteristics of mothers. Trends toward smaller families and adolescent childbearing are also noted, as are international policy considerations.

74. "Demographic Budget." *American Demographics* 2 (July/August 1980): 32–35.

> Points out that the president's budget analysis includes for the second time a section on demographics. Notes that the budget report attributes declining productivity to the youth and inexperience of the baby-boom cohort entering into the labor force. Asserts that the baby boomers will have a significant impact on the budget for years to come as their needs develop and change. Such areas as housing, jobs, health care, and pensions will also be affected. Reviews in detail the impact of baby boomers on education, housing productivity, national defense, retirement, and health.

75. "Demographic Forecasts: Americans in Midlife." *American Demographics* 4 (June 1982): 46–47.

28 • *The Baby Boom*

Forecasts the number of families headed by persons aged forty-five to
sixty-five in the 1980s. The percentage of such families will decline
because "the baby boom generation as it enters the family-formation
years, will head a higher proportion of families." Income figures both
for families and unrelated individuals in the forty-five-to-fifty-four and
fifty-five-to-sixty-four age groups are given and are illustrated in
graphs and tables.

76. "Demographic Forecasts: Families and Income." *American Demographics*
4 (February 1982): 46.

Predicts that the number of consumer units consisting of unrelated
adults will increase rapidly during the first five years of the 1980s, but
that families should increase faster for the second half of the decade.
This demographic shift is attributed to "the expansion of the family
building age groups, 25-34 and 35-44, as they are filled with baby
boomers." Incomes of unrelated individuals are predicted to grow
faster than those for families throughout the decade. Statistical tables
and a graph are included.

77. "Demographic Forecasts: Families by Size and Income." *American Demographics* 4 (March 1982): 46–47.

Presents a brief analysis of family size and income through 1995.
Families of four or five persons will be the fastest growing category,
but two-person families will gain the most in absolute numbers "as the
baby boom generation marries but delays having children." Larger
families will have greater incomes, mainly because they are headed
generally by older adults and have more active earners. The projected
increase in the number of families in the middle- and upper-income
ranges by 1995 is based on the "large proportion of familes—of all
sizes—that will be headed by baby boomers approaching their peak
earning years." Statistics and bar graphs are provided.

78. "Demographic Forecasts: Family Futures." *American Demographics* 6 (May
1984): 50.

Forecasts the financial future of families for the last years of this century. A graph and a table are used to illustrate family income from
1980 through 1995 in five-year intervals. More and more families will
be considered affluent, primarily because of the increased number of
dual-earner families. Families earning over $50,000 will grow fastest,
up 137 percent by 1995.

79. "Demographic Forecasts: Household Size and Income." *American Demographics* 4 (January 1982): 46–47

Attempts to forecast household size and income throughout the 1980s. Observes that single-person households grew in the 1970s because of the influx of baby boomers in their early twenties. Notes that this trend will slow significantly as the baby boomers get married and raise families. Argues that this will produce a significant rise in four-person households. Predicts, as well, that as size of household increases, income will increase because more potential wage earners are present. Includes tables both for households with incomes of $30,000 and over, and for one- to five-person households by income.

80. "Demographic Forecasts: Households and Income in 1995." *American Demographics* 6 (April 1984): 50.

Revises early household projections downward because of continuing inflation. A table and graph are used to show projected households by income from 1980 through 1995 in five-year intervals. Median household income will continue to rise, and the fastest-occurring increases will be in households with incomes over $50,000. Annual growth in households may have peaked in 1984, but increases will continue as the baby-boom population ages.

81. "Demographic Forecasts: Income of Young Householders." *American Demographics* 5 (June 1983): 46–47.

Traces the number of householders under age twenty-five through 1995. An increase is forecast between 1980 and 1985, followed by a decline between 1985 and 1995, and then another increase between 1990 and 1995. These fluctuations will be caused by the "tail-end of the baby boom generation moving into this age group during the 1980s, then out of it, and the baby boom's own children entering adulthood during the early 1990s." Charts and tables present figures for households headed by persons under twenty-five by size and income for 1980 through 1995.

82. "Demographic Forecasts: Single-Person Households." *American Demographics* 5 (April 1983): 50–51.

Projects the number of single-person households from 1980 to 1995. These households will increase by 52 percent, to a total of 30 million. Predicts that the major source of this rise will come from the thirty-five-to-forty-four-year-old age bracket because "the number of persons in this age group living alone should more than double between 1980 and 1995, as the baby-boom generation enters middle age, and divorce breaks up families." Includes numerous tables on single-person households by age and income, and by age of householder.

83. "Demographic Forecasts: Thinning Banks, Rising Fortunes." *American Demographics* 4 (September 1982): 46–47.

> Studies the impact the baby-bust generation will have on the under-twenty-five age group in the 1980s. Significant declines are forecast in the number of consumer units headed by persons under twenty-five. Notes that the baby bust's small numbers will make jobs "easier for them to find and their incomes relatively greater than for members of the baby boom." Graphs and tables are presented for families headed by persons under twenty-five and for unrelated individuals under twenty-five, ranked by income, for 1980, 1985, and 1990.

84. "Demographic Forecasts: Young Householders." *American Demographics* 6 (June 1984): 46.

> Profiles the under-twenty-five-year-old householder and predicts income levels through 1995 for these households. In 1980, householders under age twenty-five are still members of the baby-boom generation, but by 1995 this group will be comprised of the smaller baby-bust cohorts born in the early 1970s. Income levels are forecast to increase dramatically. A table and bar graph are used to illustrate these trends.

85. "Demographics: Population Up 4½ Million Since 1980: Baby Boom Families, Income Growing." *Zip* 5 (May 1982): 59.

> Notes specific demographic forecasts made by Data Resources, Inc., in 1982. The number of households headed by baby boomers is projected to account for one half of all families by 1990. Income levels will also grow dramatically. The number of people living alone is also expected to increase dramatically in the 1980s because of "the baby boomers' tendency to delay marriage, to divorce, and to live alone with unmarried mates."

86. Easterlin, Richard A. "On the Relation of Economic Factors to Recent and Projected Fertility Changes." *Demography* 3 (1966): 131–53.

> Points out that the author had previously proposed a theory of fertility behavior to explain the post-war baby boom. Attempts to test this theory—that fertility behavior is determined by labor market conditions for persons when they are young—on the present decline in fertiliy rates. Reviews fertility behavior since 1940 and notes that recent economic conditions are significantly worse for individuals of child-bearing years, which accounts, at least in part, for the fertility decline. Acknowledges the need to develop improved population projections with the cohort approach. Includes numerous tables on fertility and birthrates, incomes, heads of households, and labor-force participation rates.

87. Easterlin, Richard A.; Michael L. Wachter; and Susan M. Wachter. "The Coming Upswing in Fertility." *American Demographics* 1 (February 1979): 12–15.

     Proposes an analysis of fertility behavior based on an analysis of labor supply. Argues that when young adults enter a labor market where supply is short, their wealth is greater and they have more children; when young adults enter a labor market where workers are plentiful, their wealth is less and they have fewer children. Notes that the post-World War II baby boom was a consequence of the short supply of labor two decades earlier and that the subsequent baby bust resulted from the oversupply of baby boomers. Predicts continuing cycles of baby boom and bust over the next decades.

88. Easterlin, Richard A.; Michael L. Wachter; and Susan M. Wachter. "Democracy and Full Employment: The Changing Impact of Population Swings on the American Economy." *Proceedings of the American Philosophical Society* 122 (June 1978): 119–30.

     Advances a theory to explain fertility behavior following World War II. Argues that this behavior is significantly influenced by the condition of the labor market as individuals of childbearing years enter it. When the supply is low, the market is good for the workers and increases their prosperity; when the market for labor is poor, economic conditions are not good. Contends that high fertility reflects good labor markets. The baby boom following World War II can be accounted for in this manner; similarly the subsequent baby bust is predicted as well based on this theory. Observes that this high-low fertility cycle may be repeated. Includes tables on crude birthrates, population growth, and unemployment rates.

89. Easterlin, Richard A.; Michael L. Wachter; and Susan M. Wachter. "Demographic Influences on Economic Stability: The United States Experience." *Population and Development Review* 4 (March 1978): 1–22.

     Analyzes the effect on American labor force trends of the end to open immigration in the 1920s and the beginnings of a "full-employment" economy in the years after World War II. New types of long-term trends, or "Kuznet's cycles," are identified. The entry of the baby-boom generation into the work force has not only increased unemployment, but also decreased fertility. However, if current trends continue, there should be increased fertility and a decline in unemployment in the future.

90. "End of the Baby Boom." *Science Digest*, September 1967, p. 81.

     Contends that the current birthrate indicates that the baby boom is over. Notes that the rate has been declining since 1958 and has reached a level as low as the 1930 Depression rates. Projects a population of 300 million by the year 2000. Cautions that the declining birthrate may soon be reversed as the baby boomers reach prime childbearing years. Challenges the current theory that oral contraceptives have caused the low birth rate and cites the Depression period as a counter example.

91. Flaim, Paul O. "The Effect of Demographic Changes on the Nation's Unemployment Rate." *Monthly Labor Review* 102 (March 1979): 13–23.

Analyzes the effect of major demographic shifts since the 1950s. A key factor is the post-war baby-boom population, which infused a large number of teenagers into the labor market. Discusses the comparative impacts of participation rates and age composition. Concludes that the participation rates have had only a small impact and that "the demographic effect on the unemployment rate over these two decades can be traced primarily to the gradual entry into the labor force of millions of youths born during the baby boom that began in the mid-1940s and peaked at the end of the 1950 decade." Includes tables on labor-force composition and participation.

92. Glick, Paul C. "How American Families Are Changing." *American Demographics* 6 (January 1984): 21–25.

Examines household formation trends. Notes that the "lifestyle decisions of members of the baby-boom generation will in large part determine trends in marriage and divorce during the 1980s." Rates of both marriage and divorce should slow in the 1980s as birthrates, employment levels, and educational levels gradually stabilize. Tables and charts statistically show projected household changes and how children will live. Family ties are considered likely to remain strong, although family composition may frequently change because of divorce, single parenting, and lifelong single status.

93. "Go West Small Fry." *American Demographics* 4 (November 1982): 12.

Summarizes a forecast made by Dennis Ahlburg of the University of Minnesota at an American Statistical Association conference on forecasting. Regional variations in the expected baby boomlet are detailed. A significant decline in births is forecast for the Northeast and a surprising decline is anticipated in the South. The West will gain the most in population. A graph shows regional shares of births for 1980 and offers projections for 1990.

94. Goldman, Eric F. The Emerging Upper American." *American Demographics,* 3 (July/August 1981): 20–23.

Coins the term "Upper Americans" to describe a distinct segment of the baby-boom generation. While hard to define, Upper Americans are "relatively youthful, educated in a particular type of college, affluently moving along in a service occupation." Their most distinguishing characteristic, however, is their desire not to be considered Middle American. While judged to be only 15 percent of the adult population, the Upper Americans are shown to be "influential far beyond their sheer numbers." Concludes that while they have many commendable traits, it is "also clear that Upper Americans are not exclusively a healthy force."

95. Greider, William. "The Unlucky Cohort." *American Demographics* 1 (October 1979): 2–3.

Distinguishes between two generational groups—the "lucky cohort" and the "unlucky cohort." The latter is the large baby-boom generation. Argues that the baby boom's sheer size overwhelmed many social programs designed to aid it, such as youth programs of the Great Society in the 1960s. Significant changes will occur in the economy as state governments spend less on education and other services associated with young people and the federal government is forced to increase expenditures for the elderly and sick. However, any economic stagnation will result in political pressures "as the 'baby boom' children reach middle age."

96. Happel, Stephen K., and Timothy D. Hogan. "Birth Rate Trends: Implications for the Future." *Arizona Business* 27 (November 1980): 3–10.

Outlines demographic trends in Arizona and the United States and looks at projected birthrates. Census statistics are used to present an overview of the effect of the baby boom on the state and the entire country. Two conflicting explanations of these birthrates, the Chicago-Columbia Approach and the Easterlin Hypothesis, are compared. Contends that future birthrates will depend on the economy, the number of working women, and changing household pattern. A continuation of a "cyclical pattern of birth rates" is forecast.

97. Hu, Joseph. "Household Projections: An Alternative Approach." *American Demographics* 2 (October 1980): 22–25.

Discusses current techniques for predicting household formation. Notes that household formation has significant impact for marketers of consumer products. Points out that the Census Bureau employs a demographic analysis and argues that economic conditions also influence household formation. Employs a new model that takes economics into account. Predicts significant growth in household formation, particularly in the twenty-five-to-thirty-four-year-old age bracket if economic conditions are right. Contends that the baby-boom generation is entering this age bracket in the 1980s, which could create "dramatic shifts" in household formation. Includes table on household forecasts by age.

98. Huber, Joan. "Will U.S. Fertility Decline Toward Zero?" *Sociological Quarterly* 21 (Autumn 1980): 481–92.

Examines nineteenth-century fertility trends and compares them to twentieth-century trends. Conditions that will contribute to an ongoing fertilty decline are as follows: (1) direct cost of child rearing continues to rise; (2) psychic cost of child rearing is high; (3) economic benefits of children are declining; (4) opportunity costs of staying at home are increasing; (5) two-earner families are becoming commonplace; (6) divorce rate has dramatically increased; and (7) lack of adequate day care is a serious obstacle. Conditions that brought about the baby boom are not present and, consequently, "the most probable long-term fertility trend is continued decline, not just to ZPG [Zero Population Growth] but toward zero." Concludes that the "U.S. is structurally antinatalist."

99. Hyatt, James. "The Future of Business." *American Demographics* 2 (January 1980): 25–29.

Stresses the importance of demographics and provides an overview of population trends. The baby boom is held responsible for "many of the present and future aches to be faced by business." While the maturing of the baby boom may bring strong housing demands in the 1980s, it is important to realize that this generation is very different from the preceding one. Changes in the labor force are detailed and the long-range problems that will occur when the baby boom reaches retirement age are outlined. Urges business managers to "keep in mind the location of that bulge from year to year, just as they pay attention to other economic indicators."

100. Johnson, Willard. "Population Growth in the United States of America—1972." *Population Review* 15 (January/December 1971): 18–23.

Discusses recent prediction by U.S. Census Bureau that the United States is reaching Zero Population Growth. Reviews the trends in birthrates and notes that the eleven-year period from 1954 to 1964 produced 4 million births annually and that this high rate derives from the post-war baby boom. Contends that predictions of ZPG fail to recognize that as baby-boom mothers enter childbearing years, the birthrate will be significantly affected. Provides a historical perspective on birthrate declines and analyzes the causes of these declines. A discussion of Zero Population Growth, Inc., is included.

101. Johnston, Denis Foster. "The Aging of the Baby Boom Cohorts." *Statistical Reporter* 76 (March 1976): 161–65.

Examines the impact of the baby-boom cohort as it passes through various age groups. Notes that the earliest effects were felt in the school systems. Currently the impact on the labor force is evident as baby boomers enter jobs. Predicts that these employees will soon be developing careers and seeking housing, which will place new demands on the work place and housing market. Discusses in detail baby boomers' attitudes toward education and contends they will pursue adult education and will pay for it with substantial discretionary income. Includes tables on population projections from 1945 to 2035, college enrollment rates, and dependency ratios.

102. Jones, Landon Y. "Catch 35—and the Survival of the Species." *Conference Board* 19 (February 1982): 2–8.

Recounts the immediate and profound effects of governmental pressure to promote fertility, and then considers the predictability of the birthrates of America's baby-boom mothers. The biggest question is how many baby-boom women will never have children. Pressures of the "biological clock" may spur many baby-boom women to have babies as they approach thirty-five. Conflicting views of demographers concerning future American fertility rates are compared. Excerpted from Jones's *Great Expectations: America and the Baby Boom Generation* (see no. 30).

103. Jones, Landon Y. "The Emerging Superclass." *American Demographics* 3 (March 1981): 30–35.

Profiles the "Superclass," young affluent members of the baby-boom generation in the 1980s. As the entire baby boom matures in the eighties and enters its peak earning years, it will "have the wealth and power to bend America to its will." Members of the Superclass are typically wealthy, college educated, anti-authoritarian, and self-absorbed. A new work ethic that stresses self-fulfillment is developing. Based on the author's *Great Expectations: America and the Baby Boom Generation.* (see no. 30). One of a three-part series (see also nos. 192 and 180).

104. Jones, Landon Y. "The Middle-Aging of America." *Executive* 7 (Spring 1981): 24–27.

> Notes that the baby boom will turn the United States into a "middle-aged nation" in the last two decades of this century. This group of thirty-five-to-forty-five-year-olds will be better educated, but may face a "promotion squeeze." Life-styles for middle age will change and the role of women will similarly be altered. A "Superclass" of affluent baby boomers will arise. Politically, baby boomers will "age into the biggest and most politically powerful interest group ever assembled." Concludes that a maturing baby boom will "continue to reshape the values and goals of society."

105. Kahley, William. "Migration: Changing Faces of the South." *Economic Review: Federal Reserve Bank of Atlanta* 67 (June 1982): 32–42.

> Examines the trends that have caused and influenced the substantial Southern migration patterns since 1970. Detailed statistics are presented to analyze various characteristics of these Southern migrants. Employment opportunities in the South combined with the predicted mobility of the baby boom's young workers to produce a large increase in the region's population. Two conditions will affect Southern migration in the future: declining fertility, and aging of the baby boom. The former should slow the rate of migration; but the latter may mean that more experienced older workers will move South.

106. Kahley, William. "The Southeast in the 1980s." *Economic Review: Federal Reserve Bank of Atlanta* 66 (May 1981): 4–11.

> Predicts that the Southeast will continue to experience above-average economic growth in the 1980s, but that population growth will decline as the baby boom matures. Changes in employment, income, and population for the entire area are analyzed in detail. Concludes that all predictions "depend upon the individual and collective choices made by baby boomers and their relatives." A state-by-state analysis of individual employment, income, and population-change forecasts for the 1980s is appended.

107. Kendrick, John W. "Ripples in Birth Rate Cause Waves in Future Decades." *Commerce America* 1 (December 20, 1976): 2–3.

> Presents a concise overview of the "prominent population wave that will be moving through successive age groups for the next 50 years" as the baby boom ages. The changes in birthrates that resulted in the baby boom are considered "only temporary deviations in long-estab-

lished trends." Graphs include: (1) Birth and Death Rates and Natural Increase, 1900–75; (2) Population growth in 5-year Periods, 1900–2025; and (3) Age Composition of the Population, 1940–2025.

108. Kloppenburg, Jack. "The Demand for Land." *American Demographics* 5 (January 1983): 34–37.

Argues that rapid population growth in nonmetropolitan areas identified by the 1980 census will continue as the baby boom ages. The availability of jobs and the trend toward early retirement are seen as reasons for this "demographic reversal." Mobile-home occupancy is increasing, especially among young married couples in rural areas. The flow of population to nonmetropolitan areas should not be surprising, since the "idea of a home on a small acreage in pastoral setting, debt-free, has always held a powerful appeal for Americans."

109. von Koschembahr, John C. "Bracing for Another Baby Boom: A National Gleam-in-the-Eye Could Lead to Profits." *Financial World* 148 (April 15, 1979): 50.

Concludes that a substantial increase in the birthrate is likely as baby-boom women reach childbearing years in large numbers. The "better-have-one-before-it's-too-late" syndrome is expected to produce a flurry of births among older baby-boom women in the early 1980s. Investment opportunities, especially in the baby and preschool markets, are individually examined. A table provides investment figures for nine "baby-boom stocks." Notes that "merchants plying the children's market are standing just outside the delivery room, waiting to light their cigars."

110. Lee, R.D. "Aiming at a Moving Target: Period Fertility and Changing Reproductive Goals." *Population Studies* 34 (July 1980): 205–26.

Attempts to develop a theory relating fertility to reproductive goals, by using data provided by the post-war baby boom and subsequent baby bust. Abandons the "fixed target model" in favor of the new theory called the "moving target model," which provides greater responsiveness to changing reproductive goals over time. Nine propositions implied from the theory are stated. Argues that new model explains many aspects of fertility change, although further refinement is required.

111. Linden, Fabian. "Echoing." *Across the Board* 18 (November 1981): 76–78.

Notes that the "echo birth boom" of babies born to baby-boom women has finally begun. Reasons for its arrival later than anticipated and estimates of its magnitude are outlined. The delay in increased fertility was caused by baby-boom women's postponing both marriage and children. This boomlet is expected to be of a "low order," i.e., many first and/or only child births. A significant economic impact is predicted. A graph shows ages for marriage and motherhood.

112. Linden, Fabian. "From Here to 1985." *Across the Board* 14 (June 1977): 21–25.

Traces the "extensive chain reaction" caused by the baby boom. Trends involving income, family formation, place of residence, educational attainment, labor force participation, and population characteristics are presented statistically and analyzed individually. Notes that the baby boom is "now in its final act" and concludes that "Tomorrow's America will be different from yesterday's, but most likely less turbulent."

113. Linden, Fabian. "Markets: The Age of Growth." *American Demographics* 6 (June 1984): 4–5.

Profiles the characteristics of households in the thirty-five-to-forty-four age bracket. Such households typically have (1) children; (2) working wives; (3) higher-than-average incomes; (4) higher levels of education; and (5) relatively affluent incomes. During the 1990s, this age group, "which today represents the front line of the baby-boom generation," will account for most of the growth in the consumer market. A statistical profile of householders aged thirty-five to forty-four is presented in a table.

114. Linden, Fabian. "Markets: Families with Children." *American Demographics* 6 (April 1984): 4–6.

Provides statistics that identify families with children as a special segment of consumer-oriented businesses. A table compares families by age and income. Parents' income in families without children typically peaks earlier—between ages thirty-five and forty-four—than in families with at least one child, where it peaks between forty-five and fifty-four. Baby-boom adults are both marrying and having children later. Stresses the economic importance of the large number of women expected to have their first child in the 1980s.

115. Long, Harry H. "What the Census Will Tell Us About Gentrification." *American Demographics* 2 (September 1980): 18–21.

Analyzes two seemingly incompatible trends: a movement of city residents into rural areas, and an influx of young affluents into the cities.

Discusses the causes of this "rural renaissance" and "neighborhood gentrification." Partly attributes the increasing numbers of young people in city neighborhoods to the generation of baby boomers, who are in the age groups when city life is particularly appealing. Cautions, however, that "the housing choices of the baby boom generation . . . are difficult to anticipate." Warns further that if these baby boomers have children, they are likely to find the suburbs more appealing.

116. McCue, Julia. "Baby Boom's New Echo." *Editorial Research Reports* 1981 (June 26, 1981): 471–88.

Discusses prospects for a new baby boom created by the post-war baby-boom mothers' now deciding to have children. Includes sections on (1) reasons for the fertility decline in the last two decades; (2) problems of postponing pregnancy; (3) facts concerning the original post-war baby boom; (4) effects of the population bulge; and (5) future population growth. Includes tables on U.S. births since World War II, live births and fertility rates, birthrates by age of mother, and U.S. population projections to the year 2000. Also includes a selected bibliography.

117. Melko, Matthew, and Leonard Cargan. "The Singles Boom." *American Demographics* 3 (November 1981): 30–31.

Notes that there are "more singles in America than ever before." Three categories used by the Census Bureau are considered: (1) the never-married; (2) the widowed; and (3) the divorced. The baby boom is responsible for the statistical increase in the never-married population, but other societal factors, especially changing attitudes, are blamed for the increase in divorces. Widowed people are living longer, but are also remarrying more frequently. Future increases in number of singles will depend primarily on the number of divorces.

118. Morrison, Peter A. "Demographic Links to Social Security." *Challenge* 24 (February 1982): 44–49.

Deals with demographic factors that will directly affect the future of Social Security. Five trends are considered: (1) aging population; (2) employed wives; (3) longer life expectancy; (4) changing retirement age; and (5) future immigration. The baby-boom generation will play a significant part in all these trends except the rate of immigration. Recommends that demographic trends, especially fertility rates, be more closely followed, and that the Social Security system's long-term financial viability be closely examined.

119. "New Baby Boom on the Way?" *Metropolitan Life Insurance Company Statistical Bulletin* 51 (May 1970): 2–3.

Notes a significant upswing in births, beginning in October 1968. The median age of mothers at birth is presented in a table and is shown to be declining in 1968. Moderate-sized families of two or three children remain popular, and larger families are not considered likely. Concludes that these fertility trends should continue through the 1970s.

120. "New Baby Boom Predicted." *Juvenile Justice Digest* 3 (September 26, 1975): 3.

Reports on a study conducted by two California demographers concluding that the "unprecedented decline in the nation's birth rate is ending and a new baby boom is on the way." California birth statistics for 1974 are analyzed and compared with statistics from other states in formulating this opinion. Neither the availability of contraception nor economic uncertainty seems to be deterring women from having children. Although births are increasing in California in the mid-1970s, there is no corresponding increase in marriage rates.

121. Newitt, Jane. "Behind the Big-City Blues." *American Demographics* 5 (June 1983): 26–29, 38–39.

Analyzes population trends in the twenty largest U.S. cities and metropolitan areas. Dramatic declines occurred in these areas in the 1970s because there was "little space to house the baby boom children who were leaving home." While some statistics indicate a back-to-the-city movement in the 1980s, its long-term impact will be marginal. Nevertheless, "big cities have been benefiting from the sheer size of the baby boom generation, and its record-breaking proportion of college graduates." Tables document the retention and attraction ratios for young adults in the twenty largest cities.

122. Newitt, Jane. "How to Profit from Demographic Forecasting." *American Demographics* 4 (May 1982): 26–31.

Recounts dramatically incorrect demographic forecasts involving births, women's employment, and geographical mobility made in the 1960s and early seventies. However, demographic trend analysis should remain an indispensable part of business and market planning. The baby boom has moved the United States "into a new demographic era, in which every decade's age composition differs significantly from the previous decade's." Notes that hindsight explains much of the baby-boom generation's impact on society in the young adult years of the seventies. Migration and mortality are two significant variables affecting long-range demographic forecasts.

123. Newitt, Jane. "What the Northeast Was Doing Right . . . And What Went Wrong." *American Demographics* 4 (September 1982): 26–29.

Argues that conventional analyses of why the Northeast experienced a sharp out-migration of both people and money in the 1970s are "distorted." While various economic attributes combined with the appeal of the Sunbelt to attract young people from the Northeast, the most important factor was more basic: "The Northeast did not build for its young adults." Contends that a scarcity of appropriate housing "pushed" baby boomers out of the metropolitan areas in the Northeast. Urban suburbs, however, could not expand sufficiently to accommodate the needs of baby-boom cohorts. Consequently, cities of the Northeast are not "foredoomed to decline," but can be revived by inner-city renewal and planned suburban expansions.

124. "1980 Baby Boom Predicted by Census." *Jet* 59 (October 2, 1980): 36.

Reports briefly on the increasing number of births in the United States in 1980. Indicates that 3.5 million births are predicted, the greatest number since 1971. Notes that the Census Bureau believes the large number of women entering childbearing age accounts for the increase.

125. Norton, Arthur J. "Keeping Up with Households." *American Demographics* 5 (February 1983): 16–21.

Surveys the patterns of household formation and size from 1970 to 1982 and offers predictions for the eighties. Two types of households are identified: family and nonfamily. The rapid growth in nonfamily households is attributed to (1) delayed marriages on the part of many baby boomers; (2) increased likelihood of divorce; and (3) tendency for older singles to keep their own homes after the death of a spouse. Notes that the trend toward marriage may actually result in fewer divorces and greater marital stability. Statistics are presented in graphs and tables.

126. Norton, Arthur J., and Paul C. Glick. "What's Happening to Households?" *American Demographics* 1 (March 1979): 19–22.

Details notable changes in household compositions. The number of households has grown faster than the population since 1970 for a variety of reasons: (1) the baby boom; (2) smaller families; (3) more singles; and (4) longevity. Notes that the baby boom will have a significant effect on future household characteristics as its members make decisions concerning marriage, divorce, and children. It is extremely difficult to predict accurately how members of the baby boom will form households. Concludes that the "baby boom generation, because of its numbers alone, does not behave like other generations."

127. "Openers: America at 2000." *American Demographics* 5 (January 1983): 11.

Reports new projections by the U.S. Census Bureau concerning national population growth. No return to the high birthrates that caused the baby boom is anticipated. As the baby boom ages and fertility declines, the median age of the population will increase. Different-sized age groups will continue to affect all areas because of the ongoing cycle of baby boom and baby bust. Population estimates for most age groups are given for both 1990 and 2000.

128. "Openers: Surprise, Surprise." *American Demographics* 5 (January 1983): 11–12.

Suggests that budget cuts by the Reagan administration could "leave the nation unprepared to cope with another baby boom." While another baby boom is considered unlikely by most demographers, changes in the frequency of gathering various fertility data could significantly obscure the beginning of a new baby boom. Based on a report to the House Subcommittee on Census and Population by University of Wisconsin demographer Halliman H. Winsborough.

129. "Openers: The Insurance Agent Boom." *American Demographics* 3 (January 1983): 12–13.

Demonstrates a direct correlation between fertility data from the baby-boom years and recruiting data for new insurance agents. A factor of twenty-three years between birth and recruitment is noted. Further analysis can predict long-term and intermediate-term indicators of potential membership in the Million Dollar Round Table. These analyses were prepared by John P. Bell, director of information services for the Million Dollar Round Table.

130. "Plan Now to Meet Consumer Needs of the Future." *D & B Report* 31 (December 1983): 14.

Observes that by 1995 the number of households with real income of over $50,000 will triple from the 1980 level. This increase will "be in response to the maturing of the big baby boom generation in the prime labor force stage, a high proportion of them being college-educated men and women holding upper-level managerial, professional and technical jobs." Members of this "new income elite group" will have smaller families, both spouses working, and significantly greater discretionary income. Based on analyses and findings published in Consumer PROSPECTS,® a two-volume report prepared by the Futures Group.

131. "Population Pyramids." *American Demographics* 1 (February 1979): 36–37.

Explains the uses of "population pyramids" and demonstrates how they are to be interpreted; they are commonly used in comparing various cohorts within the baby boom. Comparisons of different geographic areas or time periods are easy when population pyramids are used. These bar graphs serve as both a representation of the present and a projection of the future.

132. Preston, Samuel H. "Family Sizes of Children and Family Sizes of Women." *Demography* 13 (February 1976): 105–14.

Provides a detailed statistical analysis of the relationship between the number of children born to a mother and the average size of the mother's family. A "simple and exact relation" is shown to exist. It is important to note that the baby boom resulted from more couples having few children, not from significantly larger families. Consequently, baby-boom women "must, on average, bear substantially fewer children than were born into their own family of orientation merely to keep population fertility rates constant."

133. Reynolds, Reid T.; Bryant Robey; and Cheryl Russell. "Demographics of the 1980s." *American Demographics* 2 (January 1980): 11–19.

Provides an overview of demographic trends that will influence the 1980s. The following areas are statistically described: (1) population growth; (2) fertility; (3) mortality; (4) immigration; (5) age structure; (6) households; (7) labor force; (8) minorities; (9) migration; and (10) country versus city. The two greatest uncertainties are where Americans will live and how many children they will have. Concludes that the "1980s are likely to be a decade of challenges."

134. Rindfuss, Ronald R., and Larry L. Bumpass. "How Old Is Too Old? Age and the Sociology of Fertility." *Family Planning Perspective* 8 (September/October 1976): 226–30.

Assesses the effects of age on fertility. Related demographic and social components that influence a couple's decision to postpone or stop childbearing are also evaluated. Analysis of statistics compiled by the National Fertility Study shows that, quite simply, "later means fewer."

Women who postpone bearing a child are less likely to ever have a child at a later time. Stresses that the most significant considerations are sociological, not biological. Age relative to others in similar circumstances is what most directly affects fertility.

135. Robertson, Matthew, and Arun S. Roy. "Fertility, Labor Force Participation and the Relative Income Hypothesis: An Empirical Test of the Easterlin-Wachter Model on the Basis of Canadian Experience." *American Journal of Economics and Sociology* 41 (October 1982): 339–50.

Tests the relative income hypothesis, using Canadian data. The theory that fertility and labor force participation are directly influenced by relative income is supported by empirical evidence in this study. However, desired income level was based on the income of current peer groups, not on past parental income levels. Concludes that "the entry of the post war baby boom cohort into the labor market during the late 60s and early 70s increased significantly the supply of young adults, resulting in a decline in their income and living standards relative to other cohorts."

136. Robey, Bryant. "Age in America." *American Demographics* 3 (July/August 1981): 14–19.

Studies the age distribution of the United States as revealed in 1980 census figures. All evidence indicates that "America is aging rapidly." Implications for companies currently marketing to preteen groups are emphasized. Regional, sex, and racial differences in age distribution are considered in detail. A population pyramid and numerous bar graphs are used to illustrate various age profiles.

137. Robey, Bryant. "A Guide to the Baby Boom." *American Demographics* 4 (September 1982): 16–21.

Provides an overview of the baby-boom generation. Basic demographic figures are presented to describe the influence this generation has had and will continue to have on all aspects of society. Demonstrates that the baby boom "remains America's most influential age group." Various statistics are illustrated in tables, population pyramids, and graphs.

138. Robey, Bryant. "Profile: A Youthful Look." *American Demographics* 4 (October 1982): 36–38.

Proclaims that "good times are ahead," primarily because the number of teenagers is dropping sharply. However, the recent slight increase in fertility will result in another large group of teenagers in the 1990s. The effects of this demographic cycle on families, schools, marriages, and death rates are statistically presented. A table lists population under twenty-five years old by state for various age brackets.

139. Robey, Bryant, and Cheryl Russell. "How America is Changing: 1980 Census Trends Analyzed." *American Demographics* 4 (July/August 1982): 16–27.

Examines the preliminary data from the 1980 census reported by the Census Bureau in "Provisional Estimates of Social, Economic, and Housing Characteristics, State and Selected Standard Metropolitan Statistical Areas" (PHC80-51-1, March 1982). The following areas are analyzed: (1) age and marital status; (2) nativity and language spoken; (3) rising educational levels; (4) labor force changes; (5) employment and occupations; (6) transportation; (7) disabilities; and (8) housing. The impact of the baby-boom generation on these population characteristics is noted where appropriate.

140. Robey, Bryant, and Cheryl Russell. "The Year of the Baby Boom." *American Demographics* 6 (May 1984): 18–21.

Examines the demographic characteristics of the baby-boom generation, particularly as they relate to age, education, income, and occupation. Notes that by 1995, the thirty-one-to-fifty-six-age cohort will increase by over 20 million and that this cohort makes major contributions to productivity in the economy. Observes that (1) baby boomers are the best-educated generation; (2) baby-boom women are much better educated and will expand their participation in the labor force in general and in careers requiring college educations; (3) baby boomers share traditional views toward family and marriage; and (4) baby boomers have made fundamental changes in America.

141. Russell, Cheryl. "Demographics of the Dominion." *American Demographics* 2 (July/August 1980): 18–23.

Reviews the general demographic characteristics of Canada. Similarities with the United States are noted, but the emphasis is on the differences. Canada experienced a post-war baby boom that is similarly affecting Canadian household formations and the housing market in the 1980s. Canada has a very concentrated population divided into two contrasting cultures, British and French. Statistics are provided for Canadian households, migration, immigration, and linguistic composition.

142. Russell, Cheryl. "Inside the Shrinking Household." *American Demographics* 3 (October 1981): 28–33.

> Reviews 1980 Census statistics showing that average household size fell below three during the 1970s. Three influences in this decline are considered: (1) more people living alone before and after marriage; (2) smaller families because of decreased fertility; and (3) more elderly widows. The baby boom has delayed family formations, and this has contributed to the "singles boom." Regional variations are studied in detail. Charts list states and large metropolitan areas ranked by average household size in 1980. Graphs illustrate changes in household size, 1790 to 1980; the top ten states in rate of household growth, 1970 to 1980; and the ten states that gained the most households during the 1970 to 1980 increase.

143. Russell, Cheryl. "Rocky Mountain Highs." *American Demographics* 4 (June 1982): 24–27, 44.

> Profiles the phenomenal population growth in the eight Mountain States as revealed in the 1980 census. Migration to the Mountain States, especially by members of the baby-boom generation, accounts for much of this growth. Since these new residents are young and are in the family formation years, population growth is projected to continue increasing in the eighties. Detailed analyses of the characteristics of the population of these Mountain States are provided.

144. Russell, Cheryl. "Who's Having Those Babies?" *American Demographics* 4 (January 1982): 36–38.

> Describes the Census Bureau's new series called the Current Population Survey, which reports on the demographic patterns of women currently giving birth. Notes that the data will be especially useful to marketers because of the timeliness of the information. Points out that the fertility behavior of baby-boom women is particularly important because of the size of this group. Observes that (1) the number of births are increasing; (2) fertility rates are increasing as baby boomers reach childbearing age; (3) fertility is highest as income or education decreases; (4) women's birth expectations remain low, so the number of children in a family will be relatively small. Includes tables on fertility and birth expectations.

145. Samuelson, Paul A. "An Economist's Non-Linear Model of Self-Generated Fertility Waves." *Population Studies* 30 (July 1976): 243–47.

> Points out that classical economists viewed population analysis as an important aspect of economics but that modern economists have generally

ignored it. Notes that Richard Easterlin is an exception and that his attempt to analyze baby-boom fertility rates provided a mathematical model for explaining future fertility trends. States that "the purpose of this paper is to give an oversimplified version of the Easterlin theory, and subject it to rigorous analysis, both in the large and in the neighborhood of equilibrium." Cautions demographers on the misapplication of the linear Lotka-Bernardelli model to a nonlinear population analysis.

146. "Second Baby Boom Seen for 80s." *American Banker* 145 (March 10, 1980): 12.

Reports that a "sequel to the postwar baby boom" is quite likely, based on the increase of babies born in 1979 and the rapidly expanding number of women in the childbearing years. This boom is "attributed to those women who postponed child bearing in the 1960s for reasons of career or financial security and independence." The offspring of these baby-boom mothers could have a significant impact on industries and services that depend on babies.

147. Serow, William J. "The Best and Worst of Times." *American Demographics* 1 (November/December 1979): 21–25.

Considers the immediate and long-range effects of the projected population slowdown for the last three decades of the century. Effects on five areas are considered: (1) labor; (2) income and prices; (3) consumption; (4) government spending; and (5) federal expansion. The aging of the baby boom and the entry of the smaller baby-bust generation into the labor force will produce both a shortage of workers and a slowdown in overall economic growth.

148. "Sloppier Contraception, Not More Wanted Births, Caused 1950s Baby Boom, NFS Researcher Says." *Family Planning Perspectives* 10 (November/December 1978): 369.

Reports a radical theory that the baby boom was the result of failed contraception, not an increased desire for children. N.B. Ryder expressed this belief in a paper presented at the annual meeting of the Population Association of Atlanta in 1978. Based on an analysis of data from the 1965 and 1970 National Fertility Studies, Ryder's theory contends that during the baby-boom years, women "were having more children not because they wanted more, but because they were experiencing more accidental pregnancies." Only two considerations were found to affect the total number of children: a couple's fertility intentions, and the extent and effectiveness of contraception use.

149. Small, Lawrence P. "Unraveling the Maze of Demographics." *Canadian Business Review* 5 (Summer 1978): 32–34.

> Analyzes age-specific demographic trends and shows how they have affected Canadian society since World War II. The relationship between population in selected age groups and infant and old-age dependency ratios is considered in detail. The baby boom has seriously affected Canadian education, work-force, and household growth. A final significant impact will be felt after the year 2000, when the baby boomers will "have the position, power and resources to pave the way for their movement into old age."

150. Smith, David P. "A Reconsideration of Easterlin Cycles." *Population Studies* 35 (July 1981): 247–64.

> Characterizes the Easterlin cycle by using four hypotheses that attempt to explain the relationship between income and family formation, especially with respect to the baby-boom cohort. Provides an alternative to the Easterlin cycle by emphasizing "secular and period effects . . . Fertility, in this interpretation, is a social process in which members of different age groups follow similar courses." Concludes, after considerable mathematical analysis, that fertility in the United States "is best understood . . . without recourse to Easterlin theory."

151. Spencer, Gregory, and John F. Long. "The New Census Bureau Projections." *American Demographics* 5 (April 1983): 24–31.

> Describes various national population projections made by the Census Bureau and analyzes several future implications based on these figures. The 1980 census forced changes in various assumptions that influence projections. For example, predictions concerning fertility, mortality, and immigration had to be revised. Trends identified include (1) slower future population growth; (2) more elderly; (3) larger group of adults aged thirty to forty-four "as the baby boom continues to age"; and (4) continued rate of 3.7 million births annually through the mid-1990s.

152. Stockwell, Edward G. "The Changing Age Composition of the American Population." *Social Biology* 19 (March 1972): 1–8.

> Points out that the age composition of a population affects many key elements in society, such as political attitudes, tastes, consumption patterns, labor force efficiency, productive capacity, the educational system, and treatment of the elderly. Discusses the trends in aging and notes that the baby-boom generation caused a reversal of the downward trend in the birthrate since 1900. Analyzes two population tools:

the index of aging and the dependency ratio. Argues that as the baby-boom mothers reach childbearing years, the population age may again begin to drop. Contends that the future age composition of the U.S. population will depend on the fertility behavior of these baby-boom mothers.

153. Stockwell, Edward G. "Some Notes on the Changing Age Composition of the Population of the United States." *Rural Sociology* 29 (1964): 67–74.

Observes that the age distribution of a population has a major effect on income, labor force composition, psychological attitude, and career. Notes that the baby boomers reversed what had been a constant decline in the U.S. birthrate. Argues that these baby boomers will create a younger population overall and that the society may have to respond to their needs. Examines age composition, particularly its effects on urban and rural environment, and contends that the younger population resides primarily in urban areas.

154. Sweezy, Alan. "The Economic Explanation of Fertility Changes in the United States." *Population Studies* 25 (July 1971): 255–68.

Analyzes in detail the theory proposed by R.A. Easterlin to explain the increase in fertility during the post-war period. Provides a description of the Easterlin viewpoint and exposes defects in it, particularly its inability to explain the fertility rates of the 1920s. Contends that economic "considerations have been relatively minor in their influence and that changes in fertility have for the most part been the result of changes in attitudes—changes in 'tastes' rather than in the constraints of income and price." Includes numerous tables on birthrates.

155. Taeuber, Conrad. "A Changing America." *American Demographics* 1 (January 1979): 9–15.

Reviews six demographic trends that have significantly transformed the United States: (1) the baby boom; (2) households; (3) mobility; (4) migration; (5) metropolitan areas; and (6) population growth. Statistics and graphs are used to illustrate these changes. One table provides an overview of the baby-boom generation. Emphasizes the extent to which the baby boom influences "planners, politicians and producers of consumer goods alike."

156. Taeuber, Conrad. "A Changing America." *Real Estate Appraiser and Analyst* 45 (May/June 1979): 23–29.

Discusses the challenges facing America as the baby-boom cohort passes through American society. The effect of the baby boom is projected for each decade from 1980 to 2030. Focuses on such areas as (1) impact on education; (2) effect on competition in the work place; (3) family size and consumer spending; (4) earnings; (5) health care as baby boomers age; and (6) retirement and its impact on Social Security. Includes tables on birthrates, median age over time, growth in households, migration, and population projections. Concludes that a better understanding of baby-boom demographics is required if business is to succeed.

157. Treas, Judith. "The Great American Fertility Debate: Generational Balance and Support of the Aged." *Gerontologist* 21 (February 1981): 98–103.

Stresses that future fertility rates greatly influence the ability of society eventually to support the aged. Projections of the over-sixty-five population resulting from various fertility assumptions are given in a table and analyzed in detail. The need for a "demographic balance of generations" is emphasized, but shown to be statistically impossible between 2010 and 2030, when the baby-boom generation will retire. Only a higher rate of fertility in the 1980s and 1990s can restore balance. Since future rates of fertility cannot be accurately predicted, "the ongoing debate over fertility trends should command the attention of everyone who is interested in the status of older people over the long haul."

158. Van Der Tak, Jean., ed. "U.S. Population: Where We Are; Where We're Going." *Population Bulletin* 37 (June 1982): 1–50. Also available from Arlington, Va.: ERIC Document Reproduction Service, ED 231 709, 1983.

Examines in considerable detail the changing demographic character of the U.S. population. Among the areas explored are (1) population growth to the present; (2) fertility rates; (3) marriage and divorce rates; (4) mortality and life expectancy; (5) immigration; (6) population distribution and migration; (7) age composition, education, employment, and work-force composition. Notes that the annual number of births is rising because baby-boom women are reaching prime ages of fertility. Discusses the causes of the original baby boom and observes that demographers expected a greater increase in the birthrate of the seventies but baby-boom women delayed having children. Includes numerous tables of birthrates, households, mortality, marriage rates, immigration, mobility, earnings, and education. Extensive bibliography.

159. Velie, Lester. "Made in Bed—Much of Our National Distress." *Across the Board* 18 (January 1981): 38–43.

Summarizes the economic and demographic theories of Richard A. Easterlin. Easterlin's "law of numbers" is explained and analyzed. This theory concludes that "the number of babies in any given generation will markedly affect our economy and social institutions when the babies mature and seek to do the world's work." Easterlin feels that the impact on the economy of the baby-boom "jumbo generation" confirms his theory. If Easterlin is right, it may be true that "for economic health, birth restraint is as powerful as budget restraint."

160. Wachter, Michael L., and Susan M. Wachter. "Here Comes Another Baby Boom." *Wharton Magazine* 3 (Summer 1979): 29–33.

Predicts that the birthrate will begin to increase in the 1980s, creating a smaller version of the baby boom. Theorizes that birth cohort size depends on the size of the childbearing population and the experiences that cohort faces in the labor market. Argues that large cohorts face more difficult and competitive work environments and, therefore, they delay marriage and childbearing. Reviews the experiences of the post-World War II baby boomers and argues that their children will have an easier time getting jobs because they are part of a smaller cohort. Contends that children of baby boomers will consequently have more children. Attempts to refute a divergent position taken by Charles F. Westoff, director of Princeton University's Office of Population Research.

161. Watson, Ripley. "Firms Take Note: Data Indicate a 2nd Baby Boom Is Under Way." *Journal of Commerce* 353 (July 15, 1982): 1A–5A.

Notes that an evident increase in births may have significant impacts on a wide variety of businesses. Paradoxically, this "maternity momentum" is not from increased fertility, but because "the baby-boom invaders are currently in command of the child bearing years." The extent of this baby boomlet is considered, and evidence seems to indicate that it will peak in 1986. However, statistics vary regionally, and final figures will not be available until the baby-boom generation leaves the childbearing years behind.

162. Weiner, Nella Fermi. "Baby Bust and Baby Boom: A Study of Family Size in a Group of University of Chicago Family Wives Born 1900–1934," *Journal of Family History* 8 (Fall 1983): 279–91.

Attempts to test two differing theories of fertility behavior—those of Richard Easterlin and Norman Ryder. Studies the fertility behavior of sixty faculty wives born between 1900 and 1914 or 1920 and 1934.

Concludes that Easterlin's theory of post-war affluence is not borne out; however, study tends to confirm Ryder's hypothesis that unintended fertility led to the baby boom. Points out that the post-war environment was more pleasure-oriented, which made planning both more difficult and less important.

163. Westoff, Charles F. "The Decline of Fertility." *American Demographics* 1 (February 1979): 16–19.

Excerpts portions of a chapter in *Demographic Dynamics in America* by Wilbur J. Cohen and Charles F. Westoff. Reasons for the historical decline of fertility are identified and the likelihood of a new baby boom is evaluated. Various factors, such as delayed marriage, the changed status of women, and contraceptive advances, all point to continued low birthrates, not to another baby boom. Concludes that "low fertility at one level or another seems here to stay."

164. Westoff, Charles F. "Fertility Decline in the West: Causes and Prospects." *Population and Development Review* 9 (March 1983): 99–104.

Points out that rapid population growth gets much more attention than the trend toward declining birthrates occurring in the western world. Notes that the baby boom was an anomaly and that birthrates have been steadily declining for the past two centuries. Contends that it is important to understand the sociological basis of low fertility and reviews various theories including (1) Richard Easterlin's argument that cohort size determines future labor market prospects, which in turn determine fertility behavior; and (2) the view that declines in religious authority and a rise in equality for women cause low fertility. Predicts low fertility for years to come.

165. Westoff, Charles F., and Elise F. Jones. "The End of 'Catholic' Fertility." *Demography* 16 (May 1979): 209–17.

Compares Catholic and non-Catholic fertility patterns since World War II. Data from five national fertility surveys conducted between 1955 and 1975 are compared. Notes that during the baby boom, "contrary to expectations, disproportionately greater increases in fertility occurred in the Catholic population." However, since the end of the baby boom, Catholic fertility rates have declined to the point that they now closely approximate those of non-Catholics. Explanations for this decline focus on birth control used and on societal pressures for small families.

166. "Working Women and the 'Baby Bust.'" *Rand Research Review* 3 (Spring 1979): 3–5.

Reports on the demographic analysis of William Butz and Michael P. Ward, who attempt to explain the declining fertility rate. Reviews the historical birthrates since 1900 and identifies the recent fertility decline as a "baby bust." Analyzes the current bust by explicating the concept of "opportunity costs" of women's time, which argues that because women's work-force participation is increasingly valuable in terms of earnings, there is less motivation to raise a family, since the cost is too great. Predicts that the baby bust will probably continue.

3
Economic Articles

167. Andreassen, Arthur. "Changing Patterns of Demand: BLS Projections to 1990." *Monthly Labor Review* 101 (December 1978): 47–55.

   Analyzes four long-term trends: (1) personal consumption; (2) investment; (3) net exports; and (4) government purchases. Predicts that personal consumption will remain a high portion of the GNP; private investment will constitute a greater percentage of the GNP; foreign trade accounts will be balanced; and government purchases will decline as a share of the GNP. Baby boomers will particularly affect residential housing demand as they mature into middle age. Predicts expansion of rental units and mobile homes for the same reasons. Includes tables on personal consumption, private domestic investment, net exports, and governmental purchases.

168. Berger, Mark C. "Changes in Labor Force Composition and Male Earnings A Production Approach." *Journal of Human Resources* 18 (Spring 1983): 177–96.

   Develops a translog model of aggregate production to estimate the impact of changes in labor force composition on the earnings of male workers. Detailed statistical analyses are presented. Earning changes among male workers in the early 1970s are attributed to entry of the baby boom into the labor force, the higher educational levels of many workers, and the increase in the number of women in the work force. Notes that "within the baby boom cohorts, the earnings of college graduates relative to other workers may remain depressed throughout their lifetimes."

169. Blake, Larry J. "The Manpower Surplus Myth Revisited." *Community College Review* 10 (Spring 1983): 5–11.

   Notes that increased need for labor in the past thirty years was met by three forces: (1) automation of much farm labor; (2) increased number of women in the work force; and (3) absorption of the baby-boom generation. The inaccuracy of most manpower demand forecasts is demonstrated. Other influences on the labor supply, such as unemployment and migration, are briefly considered. Predicts that future growth in demand will "bring on a slight to severe labor shortage."

170. Browne, Lynn E. "Why the Mini-Skirt Won't Come Back." *New England Economic Review* (November/December 1981): 16–26.

Observes that while in previous decades the baby boomers dominated the youth market, they now have aged. Focuses on the economic effects of the baby boomers as they enter their thirties. Covers the following areas: (1) effect on education as overcapacity due to declining enrollments creates problems for schools; (2) impact of the baby boomlet as baby-boom mothers start having children; (3) effect on the labor force as baby boomers compete intensely for promotions; (4) effect on consumer spending, especially the impact on housing and alternative living areas such as condominiums and cooperatives.

171. "Counting on the Census." *Journal of American Insurance* 55 (Winter 1979–80): 13–15.

Stresses the importance of analyzing the 1980 Census statistics to determine what demographic trends will influence the insurance industry. As the fastest growing portion of the population, the baby boom requires special attention. Notes that in the 1980s the baby boomers will "enter their prime years in terms of earning and buying power, pumping up demand for both durable goods and housing, as well as property insurance to cover their investments."

172. Crichton, Sarah. "Self-Employment Comes of Age." *Venture* 3 (September 1981): 90–97.

Observes that there is a significant new trend toward self-employment in the United States. Cites among the reasons for this phenomenon: (1) a rise in the need for consultants among the increasing number of service industries; (2) increase of women in the labor pool; (3) feelings of frustration in the work environment; and (4) increase in the labor pool from the baby-boom generation. Presents case studies of self-employed individuals. Contends that the self-employment trend may be reversed as the baby-bust generation of the sixties and seventies enters the work force.

173. "Demographic Forecasts: Employment in the 1980s." *American Demographics* 4 (November 1982): 46–47.

Details projected changes in employment in the 1980s. The baby boom will be assimilated into the work force in the early years of the decade, and then employment growth will decline as the baby-bust generation enters the pool of beginning workers. Regional variations in employment are predicted, with the South and West expected to grow fastest. Individual state employment projections to 1990 are presented in a table. A graph details changes in employment by Census division for the period 1979 to 1990.

174. Dimmit, Michael, and Edward Renshaw. "A Note on the Government Employment Multiplier." *Nebraska Journal of Economics and Business* 16 (Summer 1977): 47–56.

Reviews briefly the background of the use of income and employment multipliers in predicting future economic trends. Advances the view that employment multipliers have been generally ignored but could be useful in determining public policy. Examines the outlook for employment for the end of the 1970s. Points out that the post-World War II baby boomers are entering the labor force in great numbers and predicts very high levels of unemployment. Contends that employment multipliers lead to the conclusion that public-service jobs will be necessary to achieve full employment.

175. Dooley, Martin D., and Peter Gottschalk. "Does a Younger Male Labor Force Mean Greater Earnings Inequality?" *Monthly Labor Review* 105 (November 1982): 42–45.

Discusses earnings inequality among men between 1959 and 1977. Challenges the idea that this inequality can be explained completely by the introduction of baby-boom males into the work force. Concludes that "even within education-experience cells, the variance of log annual earnings has been increasing. For men with less than 20 years of experience, the variance of log weekly earnings has also been rising."

176. Dooley, Martin D., and Peter Gottschalk. "Earnings Inequality Among Males in the United States: Trends and the Effect of Labor Force Growth." *Journal of Political Economy* 92 (February 1984): 59–89.

Investigates the increase in relative earnings inequality among male workers since 1958. Earlier analyses are briefly surveyed, and then a detailed statistical model is used to forecast the effect of changes in labor-force growth rates on the within-cohort variance of log earnings. Estimates concerning future earning patterns are presented. Concludes that "recent increases in male earnings inequality may have been caused in part by the post World War II baby boom and baby bust acting through the unprecedented large swings in labor force growth rates during the last half of the twentieth century."

177. Eagleton, Thomas F. "Runaway Public Pension Systems." *Conference Board Record* 13 (April 1976): 22–24.

Considers the ability of the local, state, and federal governments to meet future pension costs, and asks the question, Who will pay in 2001? The increased number of baby-boom retirees who must be supported by a significantly small baby-bust population of workers is viewed with alarm. Various structural changes, such as delayed retirement age, are briefly presented, and a plea for "fiscal discipline" is made. Notes that "unless we act now, in future years the classic question of economic priorities might well become 'guns or pensions?'"

178. Espenshade, Thomas J. "Demographics of Decline." *American Demographics* 3 (February 1981): 22–23.

Evaluates the effects an aging society will have on patterns of spending and consumption. Demographic elements such as family size seem to have minimal influence on consumption patterns. Consequently, a "major reorganization of the economy will probably not be required to accommodate a slower rate of population growth, because consumers will spend their money much as they have in the past." The aging of the baby boom should not unduly affect national patterns of consumption.

179. Ferguson, Brian S. "A Simulation Study of the Effect of an Aging Population in the Consumption-Loan Model." *Southern Economic Journal* 49 (July 1982): 45–61.

Applies Samuelson's Consumption-Loan Model to predict the future economic impact of aging on the economy. Concludes that this model may be useful in predicting economic impacts caused by demographic changes over the next several decades. Points out that distributional effects are detrimental to the baby-boom generation but that the subsequent baby-bust cohort will benefit.

180. Francese, Peter K. "Demographics: A Compass to Customers." *Credit and Financial Management* 86 (January 1984): 14–16.

Discusses the impact of changing demographic influences on the demand for credit. Points out that (1) the median age of the population is rising and older workers have high income; (2) the growth in upper-income families is partly due to the aging of the baby-boom population; (3) the entrance of baby boomers into the work force will flood the labor market and create a demand for new businesses; (4) changing roles of women have led to dramatic changes in work-force characteristics and household formations; and (5) there is increasing emphasis on recreational activities and life-styles that appeal to the older adult.

181. Fullerton, Howard N., Jr. "The 1995 Labor Force: A First Look." *Monthly Labor Review* 103 (December 1980): 11–21.

Provides a detailed analysis of the labor force in 1995, using revised estimates from the Bureau of Labor Statistics. Breaks down data using age, sex, and race as key variables. The major growth in the work force will come from women and minorities, with two-thirds of the labor force growth coming from women alone. Observes that between 1985 and 1995, baby boomers will enter the prime working ages and that this will increase the average age of the labor force. Argues that this growth in prime-age workers should increase productivity and reduce the burden of the retirement system. However, competition for career positions will increase. Includes tables on rate of growth of civilian labor force by age, sex, and race.

182. Fullerton, Howard N., Jr., and John Tschetter. "The 1995 Labor Force: A Second Look." *Monthly Labor Review* 106 (November 1983): 3–10.

Predicts that "during the 1982–1995 period, the number of persons of prime working age (25–54) in the labor force is expected to grow considerably faster than the total labor force. Young workers will decline in absolute numbers as the rate of growth of the total labor force slows markedly. These growth trends reflect the aging of the baby-boom generation and a subsequent sharp decline in birth rates." Notes that this revision adds an additional 3.8 million people to the work force, with two-thirds of the growth comprised of women. Tables on civilian labor force by sex, age, and race, projected to 1995, are presented. Includes projections based on alternative economic conditions.

183. Gamlin, Joanne. "Early Retirement Trend Wanes As Inflation Bites." *Busi-Insurance* 12 (April 17, 1978): 1.

Reports that early retirement is no longer as popular as it was. Inflation is seen as the major reason employees are not volunteering for early retirement. Employers are also less pressured by younger workers as the baby boom's entrance into the labor force is ending, and, consequently, they are less likely to encourage early retirement. A trend is predicted toward even later retirements as the baby-bust generation enters the labor force.

184. Geisel, Jerry. "Social Security: A Misunderstood Problem." *Business Insurance* 15 (July 13, 1981): 28.

Contends that plans suggested by the Reagan administration to save Social Security from disaster are totally insufficient to deal with the long-range problems confronting the program. The retirement of the baby boom and its replacement in the work force by the smaller baby-bust generation will result in "a demographic nightmare" that imperils the program. Some innovative solutions are briefly considered, but emphasis is on increasing awareness of the problem.

185. Ham, Joan. "Adhesive Bandages to Zippers." *Across the Board* 14 (June 1977): 45–53.

Evaluates the accuracy of the Consumer Price Index as an index of inflation. Two new indexes, a new Consumer Price Index for all urban households and a revised Consumer Price Index for urban wage earners and clerical workers, will be introduced in 1977 to more accurately reflect consumer spending habits. Changes were required because of the "coming of age of babies of the post World War II period who are currently in their mid-20s and 30s." These new consumers are shown to be more sophisticated, better educated, and more affluent. An alphabetical list of items in the old Consumer Price Index is appended.

186. Hayghe, Howard. "Marital and Family Characteristics of Workers." *Monthly Labor Review* 101 (February 1978): 51–54.

Analyzes the various forces that have affected the marital profile of the U.S. labor force. Points out that there has been a considerable increase in the number of wives and unmarried individuals in the work force since 1960. Attributes this increase primarily to the maturation of the baby-boom population. Probes specifically such categories as mothers in the labor force, husband-wife families, and Armed Forces families. Tables on marital status of work force by sex, age, and civilian status are presented.

187. Hayghe, Howard. "Marital and Family Patterns of Workers: An Update." *Monthly Labor Review* 105 (May 1982): 53–56.

Examines the labor force composition as of March 1981, with special emphasis on women workers. Reports a significant rise in the number and proportion of working mothers with young children. Attributes this to the impact of the World War II baby-boom women, who are now in their twenties and thirties and looking for work. Reviews the labor force composition in other categories as well, including single, divorced, or separated persons. Numerous tables are provided to examine the work force by age, marital status, sex, race, income, and national origin.

188. Holleb, Doris B. "Housing and the Environment: Shooting at Moving Targets." *Annals of the American Academy of Political and Social Scientists* 453 (January 1981): 180–221.

Studies the development of housing for all socioeconomic groups in the 1970s and projects the future of housing in the 1980s. Notes that attempts were made in the seventies to produce decent housing for all, but inflationary pressures disproportionately affected the poor. Observes that rental units in older Northern cities have been adversely affected by out-migration, which has also promoted the segregation of minorities. Expresses concern over the high percentage of total income taken up by housing. Asserts that there remains an "enormous pent-up demand for housing fed by the huge baby boom generation and the mushrooming of small adult households."

189. "An Improved Plan to Rescue Social Security." *Nation's Business*, February 1983, pp. 24–27.

Reports on congressional efforts to pass a Social Security bill that will restore solvency to the system. Reviews the major recommendations of the National Commission on Social Security Reform and proposals from the U.S. Chamber of Commerce. Explains both the short- and long-term problems in the system. Identifies a major long-term problem as the aging of the baby-boom population. Notes that when Social Security was initiated, there were sixteen workers for every retiree; by the time the baby boomers reach retirement age, the ratio will be about 2 to 1. Cites among the proposed solutions: (1) slowing the rate of benefit growth; (2) increasing retirement age; (3) raising taxes, including taxes of workers not presently paying Social Security; and (4) using general revenues to cover Social Security deficits.

190. Johnson, Beverly L., and Elizabeth Waldman. "Marital and Family Patterns of the Labor Force." *Monthly Labor Review* 104 (October 1981): 36–38.

Examines work-force composition, especially the marital status of workers. Notes that a greater percentage of nonmarrieds exists in the work force than in previous periods, and attributes this to the post-war baby boomers who have enterd the labor market. Baby boomers tended to delay marriage or decided not to marry at all. Points out that even when the baby boomers married, they were twice as likely to divorce. The percentage of working wives continues to increase, and there is also a trend toward multi-earning families. Includes numerous tables on labor force participation regarding number of wage earners, marital status, and sex.

191. Johnston, Denis Foster. "Population and Labor Force Projections." *Monthly Labor Review* 96 (December 1973): 8–17.

Analyzes the future work-force composition to 1985. States that "the movement of this baby boom generation through the population constitutes the most dynamic feature of the population projections to 1985 and beyond." Discusses fertility rates, especially the significant decline following the baby boom. Projects work-force size and age composition, noting that major growth will occur in the thirty-five-to-fifty-four-year-old group in the 1980s. The effects of more women in the labor force and the impact of educational status are examined. Includes tables on labor force participation, rates of change in population, and educational attainment of the civilian labor force.

192. Jones, Landon Y. "My Son, The Doctor of Cab Driving." *American Demographics* 2 (November/December 1980): 20.

Explores the frustrations of the baby-boom generation as it attempts to integrate its large numbers into the labor force. Points out that the baby boomers received lengthy educations that gave them high expectations of financial success. Asserts that the economy could not absorb them and even those that got jobs found the oversupply resulting in smaller raises, fewer promotions, and lower prospects for future earnings as they aged. Analyzes in detail the causes of unemployment, with emphasis on the black-white differences in teenage unemployment. Observes that the baby-boom generation is forever destined to "wait in line." Based on the author's *Great Expectations: America and the Baby Boom* (see no. 30). One of a three-part series (see also nos. 103 and 280).

193. Joyce, Libby. "A New Approach to the Unemployment Crisis: Ignore It Until It Goes Away." *Canadian Business* 51 (May 1978): 118.

Argues that unemployment is a serious problem in Canada and that simply waiting until the baby boom is finally absorbed into the work force is not a viable solution. Two diverse groups, "bleeding hearts" and "pro-growth economists," share this view. However, government officials view unemployment as a "problem that can fix itself if they leave it alone." Urges immediate action to train unskilled young people and to stimulate the economy.

194. Kettle, John. "The Retirement Puzzle." *Executive* 6 (November 1979): 10–11.

Analyzes the impact of the maturation of the baby-boom generation, particularly with respect to labor force and pension problems in Canada. Points out that the present influx of baby boomers will probably not be absorbed successfully, and thus will create unemployment. Notes as well that as they age, they will form a large middle-management class that will raise a barrier to upward movement by younger employees. Reflects that as the baby boomers reach retirement age, they will constitute 21 percent of the population and place a severe burden on the pension system.

195. Keyfitz, Nathan. "The Baby Boom Meets the Computer Revolution." *American Demographics* 6 (May 1984): 22.

Observes that previous generations of workers could usually be trained for one job that would be performed for an entire work life. Notes that today, technological change is so rapid that workers have to be much more adaptable. Identifies the baby-boom generation as the one that will have to adapt the most. Predicts that more and more repetitive tasks will be accomplished by the computer, freeing workers for service jobs. Contends that the baby-boom generation is so large that job competition is great and many are presently serving in jobs that will become obsolete. Argues that these individuals will have to adopt the attitude that reeducation is essential. Cautions that present social attitudes create an obstacle to people who need to learn when they are over forty.

196. Lecht, L. "The Labor Force Bulge Is Temporary." *Across the Board* 14 (December 1977): 15–22.

Claims that current levels of both unemployment and employment are distorted by the massive number of individuals in the labor force as a result of the baby boom. In addition, when the baby boom is fully absorbed, it will be followed by a much smaller baby-bust generation, which should lower labor force growth. Consequently, it is predicted that "in the decade ahead unemployment rate goals will revert to levels that would have been regarded as unattainable or inflationary in 1977."

197. Linden, Fabian. "The Business of Consumer Services." *Conference Board Record* 12 (April 1975): 13–17.

Reviews patterns of consumer spending for broad service industry areas. Categories analyzed include (1) shelter; (2) household operations; (3) transportation; (4) medical and personal care services; (5) education; and (6) foreign travel. Demographic factors relating to the baby boom are cited as influences on each of these categories. Overall, the relative demand for services has declined as a percentage of total personal consumption expenditures since 1967.

198. "Making a Career Choice, or Change?" *Materials Engineering* 95 (May 1982): 11.

Summarizes a report prepared by Scientific Manpower Commission concerning the job market for engineers, computer scientists, and other technical professionals. Notes that the number of science graduates has been declining since 1975 and that this decline will continue through 1989. Observes that this decline is due to the passing through of the post-war baby boomers.

199. Much, Marilyn. "Social Security: Who Pays for the Cure?" *Industry Week* 215 (November 15, 1982): 60–64, 68.

Emphasizes the need for both short-term steps and long-term plans to save the Social Security system from bankruptcy. Current problems are insignificant compared to the eventual crunch when the baby-boom generation retires. Notes that "the ranks of beneficiaries will swell when the post war 'baby boom' reaches retirement age—counting on support from a disproportionate number of workers from the 'baby bust' generation." Concludes that "employers, as well as employees, will have little choice but to accept reform gracefully."

200. Munnell, Alicia H. "Possible Responses to Social Security's Long-Run Deficits." *New England Economic Review* 1982 (January/February 1982): 25–34.

Reviews possible solutions to the long-term problems of the Social Security system. Notes that by 2010, the drain on the system will increase substantially as the post-World War II baby boomers reach retirement age. Two solutions have been proposed: lowering replacement rates, and increasing the age for retirement. Analyzes these alternatives in detail, with special attention to the effects of lowering benefits and raising taxes. Indicates that tax increases will be necessary and will probably account for about 17 percent of the future payroll.

Numerous tables on life expectancy, pension participation, and tax rates are included.

201. "Number of Non-agricultural Self-employed People." *Inc.* (March 1981): 34.

Summarizes a U.S. Department of Labor study showing that the number of self-employed workers increased significantly in the 1970s. Members of the baby boom were found to place a "higher premium on being able to work for themselves than did prior generations." A graph provides annual levels of nonagricultural, self-employed workers from 1971 through 1979.

202. "Openers: Job Jumping." *American Demographics* 2 (June 1980): 10.

Contends that "as the baby boom matures, the work force should become more stable." Young workers are typically more mobile than older workers. Therefore, as the baby boom ages, it is logical to expect that the length of time on a job will increase. A 1978 study by the Bureau of Labor Statistics indicates that the median length of time on a job was 3.6 years in 1978. Reservations about an increasingly static labor force are expressed: "But rigidity in the labor force can cause economic stagnation; a changing economy benefits from a work force that is willing to leave declining occupations for better opportunities."

203. Oppenheimer, Valerie Kincade. "Demographic Influence of Female Employment and the Status of Women." *American Journal of Sociology* 78 (January 1973): 946–61.

Explores patterns of female participation in the work force, and analyzes demographic and socioeconomic factors to explain this increased participation since the end of World War II. Demand for female occupations, such as clerical workers or teachers, increased at a time immediately after the war when young and unmarried women, the preferred female workers, were declining in number. Consequently, other women, i.e., older and married, were admitted into the work force to sustain continued economic development. Statistics are presented to support these contentions. An analysis of the projected demand and supply of female workers until the year 2000 leads to the conclusion that we have passed the "point of no return."

204. Oppenheimer, Valerie Kincade. "Structural Sources of Economic Pressure for Wives to Work: An Analytical Framework." *Journal of Family History* 4 (Summer 1979): 177–97.

Presents a detailed theoretical analysis of economic pressures that impel women into the labor force. Institutional elements, relative cohort size, and educational attainment are identified as "ingredients" in determining these pressures. However, the major component is the "relatively poor economic position of young men." If young males' earnings remain low, "economic stress such as marriage postponement and reduced or postponed fertility may well be a permanent feature of our society." However, favorable economic outlooks for the smaller baby-bust generation may result in increased fertility and reduced numbers of women workers.

205. Perloff, Jeffrey. "Labor and Productivity." *Executive* 7 (Fall 1980): 22–23.

Compares two suggested explanations for the declining productivity growth rate since the mid-1960s. Restrictive union practices are considered unlikely to have been a significant contributor to this productivity slowdown. However, demographic shifts within the labor force that were caused by the baby boom "would have led to a decline in average productivity due to the larger percentage of youths in the market." A demographically adjusted marginal productivity figure is proposed that takes into account differences among categories of workers.

206. Robey, Bryant. "Baby Boom Economics." *American Demographics* 5 (April 1983): 38–41.

Summarizes the findings of Louise B. Russell in her book *The Baby Boom Generation and the Economy* (see no. 44). Studies the effect of the baby-boom generation on education, the labor force, consumer spending, and the Social Security system. Points out that (1) baby boomers were not deprived educationally on account of their numbers; (2) the increases in unemployment in the 1970s were not due solely to the influx of teenage baby boomers—the economy absorbed a large proportion of these people; (3) real income growth was not as severely affected by baby boomers as generally thought; and (4) baby boomers have not demonstrably increased consumer demand except in the housing industry. Contends that overall the effect of the baby boomers has been exaggerated.

207. Robey, Bryant, and Cheryl Russell. "Trends: A Portrait of the American Worker." *American Demographics* 6 (March 1984): 17–21.

Describes shifts in the American labor force as "the baby boom generation becomes a larger share of the total labor force, with its better education and greater commitment to women's roles as workers." Statistics and graphs are used to demonstrate (1) changing occupations; (2) jobs of the 1980s; (3) an educated work force; (4) a baby-boom labor force; (5) women at work; (6) working mothers; (7) full-time versus part-time employment; (8) work hours; (9) black unemployment; (10) future trends; and (11) industry shifts.

208. Russell, Louise B. "The Baby Boom Generation and the Labor Market in the Next Decade." *World Future Society Bulletin* 17 (November/December 1983): 20–22.

Refutes various theories about the effect of the baby-boom generation on future job availability. Contends that neither overall unemployment nor earnings are unduly affected by the baby boom. Statistical evidence is briefly presented. Other influences, such as technological change and shifting foreign markets, are considered more important than the sheer numbers of the baby boom. Asserts that the "size of the baby boom generation has played, and will play, a part in shaping events in the labor market, but such a modest part that no one need fear that demography is destiny."

209. Samuelson, Robert J. "Look Closely, and the Recovery Starts to Make Some Sense." *American Banker* 149 (January 17, 1984): 8–10.

Assesses various aspects of the economic recovery in 1983–84. One major question is why unemployment has declined so substantially. Part of the answer "clearly reflects the aging of the post war baby boom generation." As the last members of the baby boom are absorbed into the work force, the number of new entrants will decline sharply. This will cause a direct decrease in unemployment. Banking regulations and federal deficits are also discussed in some detail.

210. Schmid, Gregory. "Productivity and Reindustrialization: A Dissenting View." *Challenge* 23 (January/February 1981): 24–29.

Argues that plans for reindustrialization are not needed to revive productivity growth rates. The fall in productivity rates during the 1970s was "a direct consequence of a revolutionary increase in the U.S. labor force which made labor cheap relative to capital." The baby boom simply overwhelmed the labor force with untrained young workers, which resulted in a decline in the cost of labor. This will change in the 1980s as the baby boom is totally absorbed into the work force and replaced by members of the smaller baby-bust generation. Therefore, no program of reindustrialization will be required to improve productivity.

211. Scott, Loren C. "Demographic Shifts and the Economy of the 1980s." *Louisiana Business Review* 44 (April 1980): 2–5.

Provides an overview of the factors that will influence the economy in the 1980s. The baby boom is cited as the most significant. The effects of the baby boom in the seventies are summarized and attributed to the large number of teenagers in the work force. An "admittedly optimistic" prediction is presented for the 1980s as the baby boom ages. Crime and unemployment rates should drop, housing and manufacturing are expected to prosper, and the country should become more conservative. Potential problems for the next century, as the baby boom grows old, are briefly noted.

212. Singell, Larry D. "Some Private and Social Aspects of Labor Mobility of Young Workers." *Quarterly Review of Economics and Business* 6 (Spring 1966): 19–28.

Investigates the process by which youths seek and obtain jobs in the labor market. Employs an empirical study based on a sample of high school students in Detroit. Notes that studying behavior of youth may prove valuable, particularly because the baby-boom generation will swell the youth labor ranks by almost 60 percent by 1975, and will play a major role in the work force. Examines how youths find job leads and what criteria they use to select jobs. Recommends establishing state employment agencies in high schools, special neighborhood job counseling centers, and special newspaper ads for youth employment. Argues that helping youths find jobs will benefit society.

213. Smith, James P., and Finis Welch. "No Time To Be Young: The Economic Prospects for Large Cohorts in the United States." *Population and Development Review* 7 (March 1981): 71–83.

Reviews the overall economic effect suffered by the baby boomers as they enter the labor force. Covers such topics as (1) demographic and labor market impact; (2) relationship between cohort size and economic status; (3) long-term prospects for the baby boomers; (4) relationship between cohort size and earning and employment; and (5) relationship of income and education level with respect to baby boomers. Concludes that employment problems are generally a result of overcrowding, not over-education, and that as baby boomers mature, the negative impact of their large numbers on employment and income will dissipate.

214. Spain, Daphne, and Suzanne M. Bianchi. "How Women Have Changed." *American Demographics* 5 (May 1983): 18–25.

Analyzes changes in the status of women as the baby boom is maturing. Census figures are used to demonstrate how increased divorces, lower birthrates, and delayed marriages have affected the American household. The most significant demographic change has been the increase of women in the work force. Contends that women "have taken their labor out of the delivery room and into the market place, with consequences that affect everyone—men and women, adults and children." Tables and charts provide various statistical evidence.

215. Stanley, Thomas J., and George P. Moschis. "America's Affluent." *American Demographics* 6 (March 1984): 28–33.

Profiles the "affluent American" and stresses the "impact the baby boom will have on the distribution of affluent income." While only about 8 percent of millionaires are under forty, this will change rapidly as the baby boom matures. Tables include: (1) Number of Households with Incomes of $475,000 or More By Age, 1981 and 1990; (2) U.S. Millionaire Population Trends, 1980; (3) Number of 1981 Income Tax Returns from Top Ten States Reporting Adjusted Gross Incomes of $50,000 and $1,000,000; (4) Households with Annual Incomes of $50,000 or More within Major SMSA's; and (5) Households with Incomes of $50,000 or More, 1975–1981.

216. Sternlieb, George, and James W. Hughes. "Running Faster to Stay in Place—Family Income and the Baby Boom." *American Demographics* 4 (June 1982): 16–19, 42.

Documents a decline in buying power since 1973 for American families. Inflation has eliminated any real gains in family income since that time. Notes that if large numbers of wives had not entered the work force, most American families "would have suffered substantial declines in real income." The arrival of the entire baby-boom generation into the twenty-five-to-forty-four-year-old age group in the late 1980s appears very "alluring," but their impact may be greatly overrated. Large housing costs, for example, may negatively affect discretionary income for most baby boomers in the 1980s. Concludes that "economic uncertainty and relatively high unemployment challenges the idea that things will get better simply because of changes in the baby boom generation's life cycle."

217. Tarter, Jeffrey. "The Baby Boom: Where Have All the Children Gone?" *Inc.* 2 (November 1980): 78–80.

Examines briefly the impact of the maturing baby boom on the economy in the 1980s. Many positive blessings are foreseen because these baby boomers will be "in the prime of their lives, at the peak of their earning abilities, mature and affluent consumers." Changes in employment, birthrates, and households are also considered. Charts are used to graphically express various demographic statistics.

218. Wachter, Michael L. "The Labor Market and Illegal Immigration: The Outlook for the 1980s." *Industrial & Labor Relations Review* 33 (April 1980): 342–54.

Identifies a "forthcoming demographic twist" that will have a significant impact on the labor market in the 1980s. Specifically, there will be a "changeover in the younger age groups from the oversized baby boom cohort to the undersized baby bust cohort." Statistical analyses of labor supply and labor-demand projections are presented. The largest imbalance will pertain to middle managers, not unskilled labor. Notes that the larger baby-boom generation will be able to "outvote" the smaller baby-bust generation and may attempt political solutions to any perceived labor problems or inequities.

219. "Waking Up." *American Demographics* 1 (May 1979): 30–33, 47.

Discusses the section on demographics contained for the first time in the 1980s federal budget. This inclusion in the budget is considered significant because "it signals a new awareness by the government that federal programs, and the economy as a whole, are affected by changes in the demographic characteristics of the country's population." Notes that much of the analysis is devoted to the impact on the economy of the baby boom's aging. The complete text of the section in the budget dealing with demographics is reprinted at the end of the article.

220. Welch, Finis. "Effects of Cohort Size on Earnings: The Baby Boom Babies' Financial Bust." *Journal of Political Economy* 87 (October 1979): 565–97.

Analyzes the impact of the baby boomers' entrance into the work force, particularly the effect this cohort has on its own wage potential. Observes that wages of more educated baby boomers have declined relative to the earnings of less educated workers. Points out that there is direct evidence that "as work experience distributions shifted toward increased proportions of young workers, their relative wages fell." Notes, as well, that the wage-inhibiting effect of the baby-boom cohort subsides as careers continue. Predicts future reductions in cohort sizes and consequent increases in wages.

221. Wiegand, G.C. "Thirty Years of 'Full Employment' Policies and Growing Unemployment: Taxes, Inflation and Jobs." *Vital Speeches* 43 (June 1, 1977): 501–7.

Provides a historical overview and contemporary analysis of the concept of "full employment" in the United States. Places special emphasis on the 1930s and 1940s, when Keynes developed his full-employment theory. Points out that the theory is faulty for three basic reasons: (1) improper statistical analysis; (2) the mistaken belief that governments can create jobs; and (3) well-intentioned but unhealthy governmental measures affecting fiscal policy. Argues that the definition of full employment is not reliable and has been seriously distorted by two major forces: the large increase of women in the labor force, and the infusion of baby boomers into the work force. Notes that these changes have significantly affected work-force size.

222. Woodruff, Thomas. "Employee Pension Policy and Social Security." *National Underwriter: Life and Health Insurance Edition* 84 (September 27, 1980): 13.

Reviews the current activities and attitudes of the President's Commission on Pension Policy, with particular attention to the relationship between Social Security, employee pensions, and personal savings programs. Provides data on workers' attitudes toward and dependence on Social Security, and notes that the dependency ratio between active workers and retirees will slip substantially as the baby-boom population reaches retirement age. Considers the possibility of a "universal, minimum advance-funded employee pension system." Other possible methods for encouraging individual savings are briefly noted.

223. Young, Anne McDougall. "Educational Attainment of Workers, March 1981." *Monthly Labor Review* 105 (April 1982): 52–55.

Reports that as of March 1981, "there were almost as many workers age 25 to 64 who had completed a year or more of college as had ended their formal education with a high school diploma." Attributes this phenomenon to the coming of age of the baby-boom generation, which is comparatively highly educated. Educational opportunities in the sixties and seventies were expanded through increased facilities and more teachers. Predicts that the educational composition of the labor force will change as baby boomers age and move out of entry-level positions. Observes that those following the baby boomers are fewer in population and will have a less difficult time gaining entry-level positions.

224. Young, Anne McDougall. "Youth Labor Force Marked Turning Point in 1982." *Monthly Labor Review* 106 (August 1983): 29–32.

Emphasizes the significance of the graduation from high school of the last of the baby-boom generation in 1982. This will affect both unemployment and occupations in the 1980s. Notes that the "number of young people completing high school will probably decline through the 1980s, as smaller cohorts of youth pass through the conventional school age groups." Detailed statistical tables are presented to illustrate the labor force composition of youth.

225. Zech, Charles E. "The Post War Baby Boom and Inflation." *Review of Social Economy* 35 (October 1977): 200–204.

Presents a statistical analysis to determine the extent to which the baby-boom generation is responsible for current inflation. If structural inflation is partly caused by changes in demand, then the unusually large number of young marrieds in the early seventies could have increased the rate of inflation. Concludes that although "the economic power of the post war babies may not be the major source of current inflation, it is a phenomenon that is likely to be with us for some time after other current causes of inflation have subsided."

226. Zinkewicz, Phil. "Business Keeps Eye on Demographic Trends." *The Journal of Commerce* 349 (August 21, 1981): 1A, 7A.

Presents excerpts from a series of interviews with advertising, insurance, and employment executives discussing the importance of demographic trends. The maturation of the baby boom is seen as a significant development. The effects of both the baby boom and the baby-bust generations on the current and future American labor force are noted. Changes in media and print advertisements are required to market effectively to the aging baby boom. Stresses that "a proper evaluation of demographic data can enable one to forecast the next fad, predict what product will turn mediocre misanthropes into merry millionaires and for those in the political arena, prepare for the next revolution."

4
Marketing Articles

227. Andreason, Aaron. "Factors Influencing Changing Consumer Trends." *Montana Business Quarterly* 21 (Summer 1983): 16–18.

> Analyzes demographic, geographic, and socioeconomic conditions that have influenced American consumers' behavior. Notes that the maturing of the baby boom will be "the single most important economic stimulant of the 1980s." Baby boomers will dramatically affect major segments of the economy, such as housing, automobiles, and financial services. Companies are advised to adapt their business strategies to the changing demands of the aging baby boom.

228. "ARF's Object: Out to Improve Advertising's Image." *Broadcasting Magazine* (March 14, 1983): 158.

> Reports on the 29th annual conference of the Advertising Research Foundation. The need to consider demographic trends in television research is stressed, and the use of "psychographic segmentation techniques" is outlined. The importance of the "better educated workers of the baby boom generation" in the 1980s is emphasized. Consequently, advertisements must be believable and likeable.

229. "Baby Boom Generation: Work, Play and Shop Hard." *Supermarket Business* 38 (November 1983): 8.

> Highlights the conclusions of a study of the baby-boom generation conducted by the Monroe Mendelsohn Research Organization. Findings relevant to supermaket executives show that (1) male baby-boom shoppers are more experimental, more willing to spend money for quality, and less conscious of price; (2) baby boomers eat only 51 percent of their meals at home and are likely to skip a meal entirely; and (3) over one-third of the baby-boom generation admits to enjoying food shopping. Concludes that trends among this "work hard/play hard" generation are well worth following.

230. "The Baby Boom Giveth, the Baby Boom Taketh Away." *National Review*, August 21, 1981, p. 944.

> Observes that rock-and-roll music became successful through support of baby-boom teenagers, who were "mostly white, mostly suburban, numerous, cantankerous, and flush with money . . . " Asserts that the baby boomers have now aged and their music is toned down. Quotes Mick Jagger, who claims that rock-and-roll no longer outrages people and has no future.

231. "Baby Boom, 1-Stop Shopping Boost Baby-Need Depts." *Supermarket News* 33 (October 31, 1983): 15.

> Details the growth in the sale of baby products, especially high-margin baby accessories, in supermarkets and food stores. The baby boomlet, produced by the increased birthrate among baby-boom women, is responsible for these expanding sales. Supermarkets offer to working mothers the convenience of one-step shopping. Examples of products sold and of display techniques are presented. Nonfood baby items will be regarded as "a basic, not as a fringe category" in most supermarkets in the eighties.

232. "Baby Boomers: A Bountiful Bulge." *S&MM: Sales and Marketing Management* 127 (October 26, 1981): 39.

> Reviews briefly the future impact of the baby boomers on marketing. Reports that by 1980, there were almost 80 million baby boomers, or the equivalent of about one baby boomer out of every three consumers. Predicts that baby boomers will be the fastest growing market and will influence life-styles, households, and consumer trends. Includes graphs on marriage and divorce rates and on unmarried couples.

223. "Baby Boomers Prefer General Merchandise Stores." *Drug Topics* 126 (March 1, 1982): 1.

> Reports a recent study by Management Horizons, a market research firm, concerning the buying habits of the baby-boom generation. Differences between late baby boomers (currently aged twenty-seven to thirty-four) and early baby boomers (nineteen to twenty-five) are noted. The former prefer conventional department stores, while the latter shop at national mass-merchandise chains. All ages of baby boomers prefer discount department stores.

234. "Baby Boomers Shop DIY Stores for Lawn and Garden Items." *Lawn/Garden Marketing* 21 (March 1982): 63.

Summarizes a study conducted by Management Horizons to determine where baby boomers shop. Findings of special interest to the lawn and garden industry are the desires expressed for convenience, one-stop shopping, and value. Baby boomers are shown to shop heavily in do-it-yourself stores to purchase gardening, hardware, and automotive items.

235. Berry, Leonard L., and Ian H. Wilson. "Retailing: The Next Ten Years." *Journal of Retailing* 53 (Fall): 5–28.

Divides discussion into two areas of analysis: the current retailing environment, and the implications of retailing based on this environment. Provides detailed demographic reviews, with special attention to the baby-boom generation. As youngsters, this group affected suburbia schools and 'youth' markets, and as it ages, it will affect labor force competition, adult markets, and electoral results. Asserts that this group possesses new values with more emphasis on natural products, environmental concerns, simpler life-styles, and women's rights. Projects that there will be a movement toward (1) "waste-minimizing life styles"; (2) "stability-seeking life styles"; and (3) expectation of corporate responsibility.

236. Block, Susan. "Economics May Homogenize 'Alternatives.'" *Editor and Publisher*, June 5, 1982, p. 11.

Considers the issues and problems facing various "alternative newsweeklies." Problems inherent in national advertising, as well as means of attracting readers, were discussed at the fifth annual convention of the Association of Alternative Newsweeklies (AAN). Notes that "all AAN members claim that their most loyal readers are of the baby boom generation, the upwardly mobile, well-educated, professional 20-40 year olds." One publisher stated, "They're the only generation to demand their own newspapers."

237. Brennan, Denise M. "The Presidents' Forecast: 1984." *Restaurant Business Magazine* 82 (December 1, 1983): 131–42.

Reports the responses from a wide range of food-service executives to a Presidents' Forecast survey conducted by *Restaurant Business Magazine*. Four issues were raised: (1) impact of the baby boom; (2) labor force considerations; (3) competition; and (4) outlook for 1984. Virtually all types of restaurants reported benefits from the aging of the baby boom. Baby boomers are often affluent, are interested in nutritional foods, and are willing to pay for the quality they demand. The maturing of the baby boom is also beginning to affect the industry's work force. More older and experienced workers are being hired. Concludes that a "common thread of optimism connects these industry executives."

238. "Buying Power Survey Released." *Chilton's Automotive Marketing* 11 (January 1982): 9.

Reports a survey of buying power conducted by *S&MM: Sales and Marketing Management* magazine for its five-year forecast of market conditions. Baby boomers in the 1980s will be the "richest target" for manufacturers and will represent a "tidal wave of opportunities." Other rapidly expanding markets will be two-earner households, working women, and affluent black suburbanites.

239. "CFCF, in 65th Year, Centers on 'Baby Boom' in New Format." *Variety* 314 (April 18, 1984): 48, 64.

Describes how CFCF-AM, Canada's oldest radio station, has instituted a "complete image and format overhaul to capture the large 'baby boom' market now grown up." An "adult contemporary" format has been established to attract the large number of maturing baby boomers. In addition, magazine type and information slots have been included with a popular music play list, "all geared towards the 25–49 audience."

240. Ciccolella, Cathy. "Floor-Care: Eureka's 75th Year in Floor-Care Could Be the Industry's Biggest." *Mart* 30 (April 1984): 26.

Reports on the outlook for the floor-care industry and profiles the advertising campaign planned by Eureka to celebrate its seventy-fifth anniversary. Gil Dorsey, Eureka's marketing vice president, foresees a very good year in 1984: "It could be the biggest year ever for the industry, because of the optimistic retail atmosphere, all the baby boom generation in the market place (maybe buying their second or third vac), a gain in household formations, and the improved economy." Baby boomers are projected as potential buyers of Eureka's Mini Mite cordless rechargeable hand vacuum.

241. "Consumer: The Baby Boom Comes of Age." *Restaurant Hospitality* 65 (September 1981): 47–54.

Analyzes four segments of the population that will greatly affect the future of the commercial food-service industry: (1) working women; (2) singles; (3) senior citizens; and (4) baby-boom adults. Emphasizes that the baby-boom generation is "a group to watch, one ripe for new experiences." The high expectations of this group for quality of food and service are described. Notes that this generation is "attracted by affluent lifestyles, elegance, and an element of exclusivity." Restaurants can go far in meeting these demands.

242. Cox, William A. "Changing Consumption Patterns." *American Demographics* 3 (May 1981): 18–19.

Observes that marketers must keep an eye on the consumption patterns not only of baby boomers but also of the subsequent baby-bust generation. Predicts that (1) demand for apartments should decline sharply, but new single-family housing demand should be strong; (2) demand for appliances and other durable goods should decline in the 1980s and 1990s; (3) demand for electronics-industry products will remain strong; (4) the service sector will continue to grow; and (5) specialized cottage industries will be developed, as competition for jobs among baby boomers continues.

243. "Crayola Draws a New Image." *Marketing and Media Decisions* 16 (November 1981): 70.

Analyzes the current marketing strategies of Crayola, a division of Binney & Smith. Points out that Crayola established itself in the 1950s, taking advantage of the burgeoning market created by the postwar baby boom. Notes that the boom was followed by a baby bust that caused a diversification. Reviews the new products promoted by Crayola, and discusses the marketing approaches of the company's television advertising.

224. Dewel, B.F. "Birth-Rates Increase But No Baby Boom in Sight." *American Journal of Orthodontics* 73 (1978): 692.

Editorializes that in 1978 "nothing like a significant baby boom is anticipated, for all other signs point to a zero population rate—or even lower." Future birthrates will depend on childbearing decisions made by maturing baby-boom women in the early 1980s. General dentists can take solace in the large number of older patients as the baby boom matures, but orthodontists will face real problems if birthrates do not increase sharply.

245. Doyle, Mona Forman. "Baby Boom Consumers Sway FF Products, Packaging." *Quick Frozen Foods* 46 (April 1984): 28–30.

Provides a detailed analysis of the baby-boom consumers' impact on the frozen-food industry. Baby boomers are "directly responsible for the most significant thing about the new frozens—upgraded quality and price." In addition, this generation is shown to appreciate freshness, quality, muted colors in packaging, and fun-to-fix products. Concludes that frozen-food producers can "reach the boomers with many foods that are light and right as well as quick."

246. Dreyfack, Madeleine. "Why Advertisers Are Tuning-In Talk Radio." *Marketing and Media Decisions* 18 (February 1983): 60–61, 108.

Traces the rationale behind the switch to "talk radio" by many AM stations. Notes that as the "baby boom generation grows older, the target for advertising dollars is shifting from the 18-49 segment to the 25-54 year-old group." Since talk radio generally attracts an "upwardly mobile, sophisticated and well-educated, upscale audience," its increased popularity is directly related to the aging of the baby boom. Categories of advertisers are identified. Proprietary drugs are cited as a major advertiser to reach this expanding market of listeners.

247. "Drug Makers See Opportunity in Rise of Psychogeriatrics as Baby Boom Generation Ages." *Chemical Marketing Report* 225 (June 4, 1984): 4.

Discusses the future drug market for diseases related to aging, including dementia and cognitive loss. Reports that there are currently 30 million people over sixty-five and that this age group will increase significantly as the baby boom ages. Contends that this demographic phenomenon will turn the drug market for the aged into a "volatile growth area." Reports especially on the market for anti-depressants.

248. Dupont, Thomas D. "The New Breed of Travel Consumers," *Madison Avenue* 25 (June 1983): 28–34.

Describes a "New Breed" of leisure travelers that is "composed heavily of 'baby boomers.'" Demographic factors such as smaller families and two-income households are cited as reasons for this growth in leisure travel. Baby boomers "love to travel, can afford at least a moderate degree of luxury and are willing to spend for luxury if it fulfills their expectations." However, travelers of this New Breed differ dramatically from older travelers. They have more experience in traveling, seek adventures, and demand value.

249. Edwards, Joe. "Chain Restaurant Operators Target Strategies Toward 'Baby Boom' Generation." *Nation's Restaurant News* 18 (January 2, 1984): 6.

Reports the comments and predictions made by chain-restaurant executives at the Alex Brown Restaurant/Lodging Seminar in December

1983. Virtually all executives concluded that their "customers-of-choice for 1984 and beyond are the college-educated, weight-watching, upwardly mobile, fast food-weaned, health-conscious adults who were born in the boom years following World War II." New menu items, increased advertising, and redecorated restaurants are planned to attract the "New Adult Consumers." Notes that baby boomers want convenient but quality food. A summary of remarks made by chair executives at the seminar is included.

250. Edwards, Joe. "Marriott Targeting Expansion." *Nation's Restaurant News* 15 (July 6, 1981): 1, 109.

Discusses the expansion program planned by Marriott Corporation for its national chain of hotels and resorts. Notes that "Demographics for the 1980s generally favor the hotel industry." Specifically, the maturing baby boom will swell the twenty-two-to-forty-four age bracket, "traditionally the most frequent travelers." The median age for vacation travelers is forty, while for business travelers it is thirty-seven. Both of these figures "bode well for hotel companies with aggressive expansion and marketing strategies." An overview of Marriott's holdings and future plans is presented.

251. Eisenpreis, Alfred. "Reaching Undersold Markets." *American Demographics* 2 (January 1980): 20–23.

Claims that marketers have overemphasized market segmentation and that an opportunity exists in the 1980s to "rediscover and redevelop the undersold broad markets of this country, to bring a greater choice of products into the market place, and to market them aggressively within a broader price spectrum." Income is seen as a major market criterion. The maturing of the baby boom will provide large numbers of adults in all economic strata. A table lists the percentages of households that purchased one or more of a variety of items in 1977–78.

252. Fannin, Rebecca. "Comeback of the Culture Books," *Marketing & Media Decisions* 18 (July 1983): 40–41.

Discusses the successful comeback of magazines traditionally oriented to the sophisticated and cultured audience. Mentions the marketing strategies of such magazines as *Esquire, Vanity Fare, Harpers, Atlantic Monthly,* and *Connoisseur.* Points out that the baby-boom generation has aged into the thirty-year-olds and that this group is well educated and has sophisticated needs. Notes that this generation desires a full life with cultural enjoyments. Provides statistics on circulation growth for numerous magazines.

253. Feinberg, Samuel. "Baby Boom Generation: Profile of Lifestyles." *Womens Wear Daily* 143 (July 10, 1981): 16.

> Summarizes the findings of a Lou Harris poll commissioned by *House & Garden* on the baby-boom generation. Covers such subjects as goals, working, children, income, and life-styles. Cites among other results the following: (1) 72 percent of the women and 95 percent of the men were employed; (2) 72 percent have one or more children; (3) 39 percent feel both the man and woman are head of the household; (4) 72 percent are dissatisfied with the political leadership; (5) 3 percent are active in the community; and (6) 57 percent do not like the world in which their children will live. Notes as well that the baby boomers exhibit strong interest in housing matters.

254. Feinberg, Samuel. "Marketers Target Baby Boomers." *Womens Wear Daily* 142 (July 8, 1981): 6.

> Focuses on the baby boom's impact on retail marketing, particularly with respect to department store goods. Points out that as the baby boomers reach middle age, they become prime marketing targets. Many baby boomers come from dual-income families, and marketers are emphasizing ego-satisfaction products to attract the resulting affluence. Also notes that marketing is directed to the "solo" life-style that arises from baby-boomer divorces.

255. Finlay, Daniel. "Demographics for Fun and Games." *American Demographics* 3 (November 1981): 38–39.

> Discusses the use of demographics in the toy industry. Notes that the post-war baby boomers created a surge in the toy industry and that baby-boom women are now having children. Points out, however, that the outlook cannot be based on a simple analysis and that both good and bad times may be ahead. Observes that although baby boomers' families will be small, they will have two incomes because the wives work, resulting in significant discretionary income. Argues that their income, along with their spending less time with their children than in the past, will motivate parents, through guilt, to spend money on toys. Contends that this guilt is increased in families where divorce has occurred. Reviews the viewpoints of Milton Bradley and Coleco in particular.

256. "Firm Sees Opportunity in Failure of Census Bureau to Provide Reliable Forecasts of Demographic Shifts." *Marketing News* 17 (January 7, 1983): 8.

> Reports on the activities of Donaldson, Lufkin and Jenrette (DLJ) of New York and its efforts to provide accurate demographic data for marketers. Traditionally, business has relied on the U.S. Bureau of

the Census to provide demographic projections, but they have been unreliable. Argues that DLJ forecasts are superior. Predicts that "the 1980s will be the decade of the middle-aged as the baby boom generation matures. Persons age 35–54, having increased by only one-million in the '70s, will grow by 12.5 million and account for 75% of total growth." Makes several other demographic predictions, and concludes with a recognition of businesses' need for careful strategic planning based on sound demographic data.

257. Francis, David. "Playing the New Demographics." *Institutional Investor* 15 (November 1981): 79–86.

Discusses five demographic trends of importance to investors: (1) the baby boomlet; (2) the senior-citizen surge; (3) the aging of the baby-boom generation; (4) fewer new workers; and (5) a continued shift to the South and West. Recommendations from numerous portfolio managers and investment strategists are presented. While there are few "pure plays" for either the baby boomlet or the aging baby boomers, most analysts anticipate increased affluence for both parents and children in this generation. Consequently, investments are suggested in entertainment, financial services, quality apparel, home furnishings, and programmable appliances.

258. Fredrickson, C. "Changing Demographics Offer Opportunities." *Credit Union Executive* 22 (Summer 1982): 6–10.

Stresses that credit unions must adapt to changes in family attitude, size, and structure caused by the maturing of the baby boom. The family of the 1980s will be better educated, have fewer children, and will typically emphasize "self-gratification." In addition, many households will be headed by single parents or will be comprised of single individuals. Credit unions must expand their range of services to include access to Automated Teller Machines, and must be prepared to finance loans for single-family housing. Finally, a credit union must work to attract members of this generation as the baby boom represents a "fleeting opportunity to expand its membership base."

259. "From Hair-Care Mousses, A Boost for Chemicals." *Chemical Week* 134 (March 21, 1984): 71–72.

Predicts increased sales for chemical companies that make the various conditioning agents, surfactants, and aerosol propellants needed for new hair-styling products called "mousses." Mousses allow hair to be restyled and recombed without respraying, unlike conventional hair sprays. Predicts rapid entry of these products into the American market because the baby-boom generation "has retained its prejudices against the rigidly held look of hairsprays, yet welcomes products that condition and hold." Specific chemical companies that should benefit from mousse production are identified.

260. "Game Marketers in Pursuit of Trivia Fans." *Advertising Age* 55 (March 26, 1984): 52.

Identifies various trivia board games that are attempting to emulate the success of "Trivial Pursuit." Notes that a "Baby Boomer Edition" of "Trivial Pursuit" is being introduced and marketed to the members of that generation. Sales figures and projections are given. The sales of "Trivial Pursuit" and its competitors raised board-game sales to 10 percent of the toy industry in 1983.

261. Gardner, Fred. "Singles Boom Now . . . But Bust Later." *Marketing and and Media Decisions* 17 (December 1982): 70–72, 155.

Summarizes various research reports on the importance of singles to advertisers and marketers. Statistical breakdowns of the singles population are presented. One study notes that the increase of singles in the 1980s is a "demographic singularity spawned by the post-war baby boom." Most advertising-agency research directors foresee great opportunities in this expanding market. Notes that singles typically have more discretionary income, prefer print over electronic media, and are very mobile. Reasons for the growth in the singles population are briefly presented.

262. Garvin, Daniel F. "Forces at Work on the Future Tempo." *Public Utilities Fortnightly* 99 (April 14, 1977): 23–28.

Examines the future of energy production and consumption in the United States with special emphasis on electric utilities. Notes that numerous circumstances are affecting energy growth, including (1) longer life expectancy; (2) the aging of the population; (3) slackening birthrates; (4) the influence of the baby-boom cohort's energy costs; and (5) materials scarcity. The baby boomers caused serious teenage unemployment in the 1970s and are now trying as adults to participate actively in the labor force. Argues that unless energy policy promotes significant energy production, these baby boomers will not have jobs. Provides data on electric utility production, cost, plant construction, capacity, and revenue.

263. Giges, Nancy. "Study Follows Baby Boom Spenders." *Advertising Age* 52 (May 11, 1981): 45.

Notes that the baby-boom generation is entering the age categories when consumer spending is considerable. Summarizes a study conducted by Louis Harris and Associates for *House & Garden* on the lifestyle of this generation. They found that (1) 72 percent of those polled indicated they share the decision on how money is spent; (2) 82 percent felt home ownership is a major goal; (3) 69 percent reported both the male and female work full- or part-time; (4) 77 percent were married; (5) 72 percent had children; and (6) 50 percent had a man as head of household. Suggests to retailers that merchandising must appeal to both men and women.

264. "Good News for Diaper Manufacturers: Births Up." *Nonwovens Industry* 12 (October 1981): 24.

Notes that the nonwovens industry is "uniquely linked to the changes and trends of young American families." The disposable diaper segment of the industry is one example. The maturing baby boomers represent in the 1980s a "tremendous amount of young adults of marriageable age." Consequently, projections point to an overall increase in births and, of course, a concomitant increase in the sale of disposable diapers. Estimates of both marriages and births are briefly presented.

265. Gordon, Mitchell. "A Special Place: Fabri-Centers Sees Bright Future as Department Stores Leave the Fold." *Barron's*, April 18, 1983, p. 59.

Discusses in detail the financial and marketing prospects of Fabri-Centers of America, Inc. Indicates that the trend of general merchandisers to shut down their fabric departments should help sales. Notes that Fabri-Centers appeal primarily to those between the ages of thirty and fifty-four, and that these baby boomers give Fabri-Centers managers cause for considerable optimism.

266. Gray, Ralph. "Stroh Seeking to Untap New Products." *Advertising Age* 54 (December 5, 1983): 24, 28.

Profiles the marketing plans for the Stroh Brewery Company. John Bissell, marketing vice president, notes that the aging of the baby boom is "not working in our favor, and that's going to require a major push, or gaining business through market-share increases." New products, including low-alcohol and flavored beers, are planned to attract this growing market. Light beer is also appealing to older beer drinkers who are trying to control their weight.

267. Gregg, Gail. "Body and Sole: Gerber and Stride Rite to Cash in on Baby Boomlet." *Barrons*, February 14, 1983, p. 13.

Reviews the marketing strategies of Gerber and Stride Rite as they cope with changes in the U.S. birthrate since the 1950s. Observes that females born during the post-World War II baby boom are now deciding to have children, which has created a baby boomlet. Notes also that many of these females work, creating a strong demand for time-saving products such as disposable diapers and fast foods. Examines the diversification of both companies and the consequences for their economic stability. Includes tables on both companies that review their financial condition from 1978 to 1982.

268. Guzda, M.K. "Lifestyle Segmentation." *Editor and Publisher*, June 9, 1984, pp. 16–17.

Differentiates between various life-style groups, as delineated by Market Opinion Research. Advocates the use of "lifestyle segmentation" by newspapers to attract specific reader groups. Female life-style groups include (1) Vanguards, "the educated elite of the baby boom generation"; (2) In Office and Community College; (3) Young Busy Mothers; (4) Ms. Coping; (5) Mid-life Upscales; (6) Mrs. Traditionalist; (7) Nostalgics; and (8) Past Prime Passives. Male life-style groups include (1) New Breed Worker; (2) Young, Bored and Blue; (3) Ladder Climber, "upwardly mobile professionals"; (4) Agribusiness Actives; (5) Mr. Middle; (6) Upper Rungs; (7) Senior Solid Conservatives; and (8) Winter Affluents. Based on a talk presented by Barbara Everitt Bryant, senior vice president of Market Opinion Research, at the International Newspaper Promotion Association's 52nd Annual Convention.

269. Hammer, Frederick S. "Retail Banking: Formula for Survival." *Magazine of Bank Administration* 58 (November 1982): 25–28.

Reviews the future of the banking industry in the context of a rapidly changing social, economic, and technological climate. Discusses the impact of inflation, technological advances, greater competition, and changing demographic characteristics. The baby-boom generation is now reaching an age cohort that forms households and stimulates demand for credit. Warns that banks can no longer depend on regulatory strategies to respond to new trends. Possible changes include (1) market segmentation; (2) use of new technologies; (3) revision of pricing schedules; (4) branch reconfiguration; and (5) regulatory relief.

270. Harper, Sam. "Sporting Goods Sales Bit Flabby." *Advertising Age* 52 (July 6, 1981): 10.

Devoted mainly to a review of sales trends in the sporting goods industry. Notes that the recession has affected sales and that some interest in sports may have been diverted by home computers and video games. Reports that the market is soft in such divisions as racquetball, tennis, and recreational vehicles; and is strong in roller skates, softball, jogging equipment, basketball, and soccer. Points out that sales of sporting goods to consumers like schools and athletic leagues are down significantly because the baby boomers are aging and have left school behind.

271. Harris, Catherine. "The Baby Boomlet: Births Are Starting to Soar Again. Who'll Benefit?" *Financial World* 150 (July 1, 1981): 25–28.

Assesses opportunities for investors to benefit from what is perceived as a "baby boom echo" resulting from an increased birthrate among baby-boom women in the early eighties. Individual toy (e.g., Hasbro and Tonka), clothing (e.g., Stride Rite and Children's Place), baby food (e.g., Gerbers), and baby equipment (e.g., Kimberly-Clark and Children's Palace) companies are analyzed. The birthrate is expected to peak around 1985 and remain high through 1990. Concludes that "there will be an abundance of kids, and a healthy surge in business for companies that cater to them and their parents."

272. Harris, Diane. "USA Tomorrow: The Demographic Factor." *Financial World* 152 (September 15, 1983): 16.

Attempts to analyze the basic demographic factors that will shape our society. Identifies three major trends: (1) the rise of two-income families as more women enter the work force; (2) the formation of nontraditional households; and (3) the maturation of the baby-boom generation. Points out that there is a large surge upward in the number of persons between twenty-five and forty-four and that this has significant implications for industries serving this group. Cites among groups that will benefit from baby boomers the health-care industry, housing market, furniture, auto and household goods industries, and insurance. Notes that baby boomers are now having children, thereby opening up a growth market for the toy, child-care, and cereal companies. Provides the names of specific companies that may benefit. Includes tables on population projections and on age and work-force composition.

273. Harvey, Edward B. "Demographics and Future Marketing Implications in Canada." *Business Quarterly* 41 (Summer 1976): 61–65.

Uses demographic statistics to forecast future marketing trends in Canada. A graph illustrates "The Changing Age Composition of the Canadian Population" and points out the "travelling population bulge" of the baby boom. Future Canadian consumers are predicted to be better educated, wealthier, more choosy and demanding, and frequent complainers. Products that are dependable and convenient will do well. The possibility of a baby-boom echo is noted.

274. Hoke, Pete. "Mellow Mail Finds Niche in Baby Boom Market." *Direct Marketing* 46 (May 1983): 28–42, 85.

Presents an interview with Eric and Loraine Spector, president and vice president of Mellow Mail. Reviews the success of this catalog company, which started in 1977 by advertising smoking accessories and T-shirts in *Mother Earth News*. The baby-boom generation has been its sales target since that time. The company has evolved as its primary audience has changed from the twenty-five-to-thirty age bracket to those consumers between the ages of thirty and thirty-five. Buyers from the catalog are now "earning more and buying more things."

275. Hume, Scott. "Restaurants Pacing Their Aging Market." *Advertising Age* 55 (April 16, 1984): 37.

Reports on "The First Annual Thinking Person's Restaurant Conference," sponsored by Prudential-Bache Securities. Three socioeconomic trends in restaurant operations and marketing are identified: (1) maturing of the baby boom; (2) greater interest in nutrition; and (3) two-income families. Significantly, most restaurant executives "identified their target market as the fast-growing group between the ages of 25 and 49." The need for strong marketing programs is stressed.

276. "Imported Beer Expected to Increase Market Share." *Marketing and Media Decisions* 17 (February 1982): 28.

Lists reasons for the projected increase in the sale of imported beer within the United States. Cites a study of Find/SVP predicting that 10 percent of the beer purchased in 1990 will be imported. Five reasons are stated: (1) increased consumer awareness; (2) new geographic areas; (3) baby boom; (4) high profits; and (5) novelty appeal. Baby boomers are becoming old enough and affluent enough to influence significantly the market for imported beer. A graph shows the growth of imported beer's share of the market from 1970 to 1980 and offers projections for 1985 and 1990.

277. "Inflation and Interest Rates Will Dominate the '80s." *Credit Union Magazine* 47 (January 1981): 12–14.

> Concludes that the two most significant economic determinants in the 1980s will be inflation and interest. Credit unions will be in a position to assist members of the baby boom who will still be "in the stage of acquiring debt." Competition in the consumer-lending business will be high, and credit units must seek out alternative sources of income so they will have money to lend. However, "the demographics of the next decade ensure that the demand for credit will remain high."

278. Inhorn, Marcia C. "You've Come a Long Way, Baby!" *Drug Topics* 125 (March 6, 1981): 44–52.

> Outlines marketing techniques for baby departments in drugstores to profit from the "echo boom" as baby-boom women become mothers in the 1980s. Today's parents are shown to differ significantly from earlier generations. "Today's couples are marrying later, are better educated, are both working, are delaying having children, and once they do have them, are spending a lot." Consequently, drugstores should emphasize convenience and quality. Baby departments should be prominently located and designed to encourage impulse buying.

279. Jacobson, Sheila. "Cashing In on the Youth Market Boom." *Zip* 4 (April 1981): 28–32, 66–72.

> Provides a detailed study of the numerous direct-response marketers serving the youth market. Notes that the "most accessible, affluent and avidly sought youth market segment is the college crowd." Even though the youth market in the 1980s represents the end of the large baby-boom generation, the buying habits of this age group should help offset any decline in real numbers in the future. Companies offering direct-mail and other youth-oriented marketing techniques are profiled.

280. Jones, Landon Y. "The Baby-Boom Consumer." *American Demographics* 3 (February 1981): 28–35.

> Examines how the baby boom has transformed the marketplace and identifies key consumer products for baby boomers. Points out that baby boomers are well educated and are often part of two-income families with significant discretionary income. Asserts that as a group, baby boomers have consumer interests in (1) an extra car; (2) time-saving devices like frozen foods and a Cuisinart; (3) shoes, cosmetics, travel, theater, and liquor; and (4) participator sports such as tennis, racquetball, and jogging. Argues that the baby boomers will be the

dominant generation throughout their life. Based on the author's *Great Expectations: America and the Baby Boom* (See no. 30). One of a three-part series (see also nos. 103 and 192).

281. Joyce, Katherine. "Child's Play: How Three Stores Are Caring for and Feeding the New Baby Boom." *Stores Magazines* 65 (August 1983): 17–20.

Describes how three major department stores are marketing baby merchandise to meet the demand of the baby boomlet in the 1980s. Dayton's Department Store in Minneapolis and Boston's Jordan Marsh now have baby registries and regularly holds symposiums and seminars aimed at new parents. Strawbridge and Clothier stores also regularly hold "Big Saturday" events to attrack children and their parents. Retailers are advised to consider expanding their children's departments as they witness "the baby boom generation of 30 years ago burst forth with its own crop of new youngsters."

282. "Juvenile Business Thriving." *DM: Discount Merchandiser* 23 (September 1983): 68–70.

Surveys various discount chains and reports on the impact of the current baby boomlet. Discounters are found to be offering "new items, enlarged juvenile departments, and more brand name goods." Car seats and upgraded baby furniture items are good sellers. New floor plans are suggested. Specific manufacturers that cater to this expanding market are identified. Regional differences are also noted.

283. Laverty, Robert F. "OTC Mediations: Demographics Alter Field." *Drug Topics* 127 (December 12, 1983): 56–60.

Provides an overview of the over-the-counter drug market for 1984. Discusses such issues as the stabilization of the drug industry following the packaging-safety issues of 1983, and the influence of demographics on future OTC markets. Notes in particular the aging of the baby-boom generation, which affects the drug market in two ways: (1) as baby boomers move into middle age, demand will increase for analgesics, digestive aids, and vitamins; and (2) since baby boomers are having more children, demand will increase for drugs for infants and children.

284. Lawless, Mark J., and Christopher W. Hart. "Forces That Shape Restaurant Demand." *Cornell Hotel & Restaurant Adminstration Quarterly* 24 (November 1983): 6–17.

Notes that in order to plan for changes in the restaurant market, it is necessary to step back and examine changes in U.S. society. Discusses such issues as (1) competitive forces at work in a "commodity industry"; (2) effects of the proliferation of fast-food operations; (3) effects of increased numbers of restaurants; (4) greater sophistication in marketing techniques; and (5) changes in work-force composition, including more women and an aging labor force. Notes that the baby-boom population is "surging" through the country and "will continue to have a profound impact on the food-service industry."

285. Linden, Fabian. "Demographic Opportunities: Income by Degrees." *American Demographics* 5 (June 1983): 8.

Provides data showing the effects of higher educational levels on the marketplace. The baby boom has "boosted the college-trained population." Better-educated consumers are "more sophisticated, more knowledgeable, and more receptive to the new." Studies of household income by level of education and age of householder reveal that (1) incomes rise sharply with education; (2) households headed by high-school graduates show earnings 35 percent higher than those of high-school dropouts; (3) earnings of college graduates are 45 percent higher than those of high school graduates; (4) upward mobility is greatly affected by level of education; and (5) relative affluence of smaller, well-educated households is greater than average income figures state.

286. Lionel, Dan. "Senior Citizens' Sections Win Quick Support." *Editor and Publisher* 114 (December 5, 1981): 20.

Contrasts the "lackluster" potential of the young adult baby-boom market with the vast potential of the 55-plus market. These older citizens have double the discretionary income of those households headed by persons under thirty-four. The trend in newspapers to regularly run special sections aimed at senior citizens is explored. National advertisers like Amtrak, General Foods, and American Express have invested heavily in such marketing efforts. Concludes that "senior citizens' sections in the nation's newspapers may be just aborning."

287. "Liquor Marketing Demands Moderation, Segmentation, and Consolidation Tactics." *Marketing News* 17 (May 27, 1983): 10.

Reports on trends in marketing liquor according to John C. Holley, vice president of marketing for Austin, Nichols and Company of New York. Notes that there is a trend toward moderation and the consumption of lighter alcoholic beverages. The industry must adapt to consumer needs, and baby boomers form a "prime" group of consumers.

Observes that "these consumers, now moving into their 30s and 40s, are more concerned with health and physical fitness . . . when they do drink, the trend is toward moderation, with high quality and prestigious image always a factor."

288. Livingston, Peter. "Know Your ATM Program's Goals." *Credit Union Executive* 21 (Summer 1981): 7–11.

Reviews various national trends that will affect credit unions in the 1980s. Technological, economic, and political trends are considered briefly. Demographic characteristics of the baby boom are provided, and baby boomers are judged to be "financially sophisticated," "potentially new long-term members," and "interested in electronic and automated financial services." The advantages of using Automated Teller Machines to meet the "sophisticated demands" of this new generation are discussed in detail.

289. "Loans—Market to Different Groups." *Credit Union Magazine* 49 (May 1983): 12–16.

Contends that credit unions face a decline in loan activity as the baby boom matures. However, the immediate outlook is quite good since at present most baby boomers are "still in a high borrowing stage of life." Demographic trends affecting both current and future credit-union membership are analyzed. Stresses that each credit-union manager will have to "pay more attention to market segmentation so that you can better identify specific credit needs."

290. "Look for Growth of 10–12%." *Credit Union Magazine* 49 (July 1983): 42–46.

Reports on predictions made by the 1983 CUNA Environmental Scan concerning influences on the credit-union market. Identifies four major issues: (1) creation of financial networks; (2) uncertainties of economic recovery; (3) deregulation; and (4) the maturation of the baby boomers. Notes that as the baby boomers age they will form households, which will create a demand for mortgages. Points out that baby-boom families frequently have two incomes, which will stimulate credit-union services for demand accounts, line-of-credit loans, personal loans, and twenty-four-hour access to cash through machines. Contends there will also be demands for financial planning and investment services.

291. "Many Stores Must Attempt Vertical Format, Study Says." *Supermarket News* 33 (March 26, 1984): 14.

Reports the combined findings of forty-seven marketing studies made in the past two years by General Foods Corporation and Supermarket Insights. The "broad reach" supermarkets of the fifties and sixties, which attempted to market a wide range of products in different price categories, may be outmoded in the 1980s. A two-level market of major advertised brands and a lower-priced brand is predicted. Concludes that "consumer markets will become segmented as to age and ethnic groups."

292. Marion, Larry. "The State of the Street." *Financial World* 151 (January 15, 1982): 40–43.

Notes that Wall Street must be added to the "list of industries blessed by the baby boom." A large number of potential new shareholders will emerge in the eighties from the growing middle class of the aging baby boom. Brokers will compete fiercely for those investment dollars. Wall Street will also benefit from the new rules governing Individual Retirement Accounts (IRAs). Concludes that these demographic trends seem to ensure that "the brokers and their buyers can hardly miss."

293. "Market Research: Babies: Back in Style." *S&MM: Sales and Marketing Management* 120 (July 9, 1979): 16.

Reports on the current trend toward an increasing birthrate. Notes that the birthrate had dropped to one-half of what it was in the 1960s but is currently rising and may equal the baby-boom rate by 1985. Reasons cited for this increase are, first, that women who delayed having children are deciding to have them now; and, second, that the number of women reaching prime childbearing years is reaching its peak. Points out that families will still be smaller because (1) educational levels are higher: (2) birth-control techniques are more accessible; and (3) there are more women who pursue careers in addition to motherhood. Argues that the prediction of childbearing trends is critical for the marketer because trends affect consumer spending.

294. "Marketers Should Scrutinize Needs and Preferences of the Class of '74." *Marketing News* 17 (March 4, 1983): 3.

Reports on the observations of William D. Wells of Needham, Harper and Steers, Inc., of Chicago. Notes that the peak of the baby boom is currently between the ages of eighteen and twenty-eight. Marketers who understand the needs of this group can have a competitive advantage. Provides information on such items as (1) marital status of baby boomers; (2) number of children in baby-boom families; (3) educational level; (4) material wants; and (5) consumer products most desired. Indicates that baby boomers have special interests in sports apparel, music, cameras, digital watches, recordings, stereos, VCRs, and investment opportunities.

295. "Marketing on the Comeback Trail." *Marketing Communications* 9 (April 1984): 21–26.

Analyzes the recent rejuvenation of the American auto industry. Points out that the market is big not only for small cars but for larger sportier cars. Reports that marketing strategies are now being oriented to upscale baby boomers (young, upwardly mobile professionals (YUMPS) who are looking for quality. Observes that the baby-boom generation has values different from those of previous generations, that they are better educated, and are more sophisticated shoppers. Notes, for example, that baby boomers make an average of 6.2 trips to a showroom before selecting a car.

296. "Marketing Picks Up the Tempo for Musicians Going Solo." *Advertising Forum* 4 (November 1983): 46–47.

Reports on the marketing strategies of Tom Rush, folk guitarist, who was abandoned by the record companies when folk music fell out of favor. Notes that Rush's traditional market was the baby boomers, who then passed out of their teens. Points out that record companies are still teen-oriented. Discusses how Rush utilized various marketing strategies, with considerable success, to attract baby boomers. Employs statistics to reveal that the age structure of the recording industry is changing.

297. Markov, Nancy. "Major Appliances: Survivors of the '80s: Major Appliance Shipments Will Rise 2 to 4 percent in '81." *Merchandising* 6 (May 1981): 17.

Points out that in the recent past the appliance market has been poor. However, this trend is now changing. Reviews several possible reasons why sales are improving. The growth of single-person households and the increased numbers of working women have stimulated a need for time-saving appliances. Notes further that the 45 million children born in the baby-boom period have now reached the age group that purchases its first appliances.

298. Marney, Jo. "Four Key Changes That Will Shape the 80's." *Marketing* (July 26, 1982): 16.

Reports on the observations of Daniel Yankelovich concerning the future of marketing and research. Notes that the population is getting older and that this will have major social implications. The baby-boom generation set the tone of the country in the sixties and seventies, and this group is now competing for jobs and promotions. Contends that significant tension and dissatisfaction will result.

299. "Maternity Clothes Shop Banks on Baby Boom, Fashion Trend." *Marketing News* 15 (February 20, 1981): 3.

Discusses a new marketing plan developed by Motherhood Maternity Shops of Santa Monica, California, and the assumptions that underlie it. Notes that the birthrate has risen over the past decade and that the number of women in their prime childbearing years will continue to rise until the end of the decade. Many of these women have entered the work force, and their maternity clothes must reflect fashion. Observes that with the new baby boom there is greater emphasis on the home and that a housing boom will be created, as will a related demand for home-entertainment centers.

300. Mehlman, William. "Gerber Gearing for Predicted Surge in First Child Births." *Insider's Chronicle* 8 (January 31, 1983): 1.

Points out that recent demographic trends may create a strong general merchandising climate for the Gerber Products Co. Reviews the economic history of the company, including its growth during the post-World War II baby boom and the subsequent decline of the birthrate. Observes that a new spurt in the birthrate will create a good market for the baby products and that Gerber produces a substantial line of baby merchandise, including apparel, baby furniture, appliances, toys, nursery accessories, car seats, strollers, shampoos, and powders. Focuses on Gerber Childcare Centers. Places emphasis on factors in the company that affect its investment potential.

301. Meyers, Laura, and Earl Keleny. "Invest While the Iron is Hot: How to Make a Killing While the Market is Still Bull." *Los Angeles* 28 (September 1983): 240–44.

Discusses the current interest in the stock market as an investment opportunity. Contends that the surge of new money comes primarily from the baby-boom generation that was involved in social movements in the sixties and seventies but that is now concerned about finances. Argues that baby boomers are not interested in long-term prospects but in liquidity and flexibility. Notes that baby boomers frequently represent two-income, childless households with considerable income available for securities. Provides information on marketing strategies, especially in the area of mutual funds.

302. "The Middle-Aged: Living It Up." *S&MM: Sales and Marketing Management* 127 (October 12, 1981): 55.

> Points out that in the 1980s marketing will aim at selling to the middle-aged. This is the most affluent market, in which spending is for automobiles and goods and services, reflecting a life-style that results from the children's growing up and leaving home. Provides pie and bar charts on total income of householder, moving habits, and educational levels broken down by age categories. Observes that baby boomers have higher educational levels than the middle-aged.

303. Murphy, L. "The 'Birth-Dearth' will Hit Some Firms Hard." *Financial World* 142 (September 4, 1974): 22–24.

> Analyzes how various industries will adapt to the declining birthrate in the 1970s. Notes that "companies that have traditionally banked heavily on the infant market are now scrambling to broaden their bases, while firms selling primarily to the age two-to-ten group have begun some figurative thumbsucking of their own." Industries evaluated include baby care ("holding its own"), cereal ("cautiously broadening out"), soft-drink ("may have problems"), and toy ("seem concerned"). Concludes that analysts can "only guess at the real effects of the birth-dearth, since its full impact may not be felt for several years to come."

304. "Murray Ohio Who?" *Financial World* 151 (February 1, 1982): 44.

> Documents the growth of Murray Ohio Manufacturing Corporation, a leading bicycle maker and producer of lawn mowers. Demographics suggest two reasons for continued growth in the bicycle industry: first, baby boomers are increasingly fitness-conscious, and second, this same group is producing an expanding generation of new bicycle-riding children. In addition, new household formations by the aging baby boom in the 1980s should result in increased demand for lawn mowers.

305. "Mutual Fund Growth to Be Large, Products Varied." *American Banker* 147 (November 9, 1982): 5, 9.

> Reviews a study conducted by the Cambridge Research for the No Load Mutual Fund Association in 1982. Savings and investments are projected to increase dramatically in the eighties. Three contributory factors are cited: (1) new federal tax policies; (2) interest-rate deregulation; and (3) "growth in the number and affluence of saving households as the postwar baby boom reaches middle age." Mutual funds should

capture a significant portion of this new market. The do-it-yourself nature of mutual funds should appeal to baby boomers.

306. Nevans, Ronald. "The Distillers Swear Off Price Cutting." *Financial World* 148 (May 1, 1979): 12–14, 16.

Expresses the hope that the baby-boom generation will "give liquor sales a much-needed pick-me-up throughout the 1980s." Consequently, price cutting will be discontinued as a marketing strategy and new advertising will be aimed at selling premium-priced brands to the affluent members of the baby boom. A table provides investment figures for eleven major distillers. Three are singled out as those companies "best-positioned" to capitalize on the baby-boom market— Seagram, Brown-Forman, and Heublein.

307. "New Items Pour into Cereal Market." *Advertising Age* 55 (April 30, 1984): 3, 77.

Identifies the many new cereal products being introduced by the major cereal marketers. These new products are "aimed at the children of the baby boom generation, along with a few targeted at the baby boomers themselves." The latter products, e.g., Kellogg's Apple Raisin Crisp, are primarily healthful and nutritional. Children's cereals are increasingly based on licensed characters, e.g., General Mills's E.T. cereal.

308. "Newspapers Must Be Edited With Reader Interest in Mind." *Editor and Publisher* 115 (May 1, 1982): 11, 68.

Summarizes the comments of four speakers at the American Newspaper Publishers Association's 96th annual conference in 1982. One speaker, Ruth Clark, a senior vice president of Yankelovich, Skelly and White, Inc., stressed the need to edit newspapers to appeal to the "all important" twenty-five-to-thirty-nine-year-old market. The maturing of the baby boom means a "resultant older population, less optimism about the economy and new social values." The other speakers dealt with legal and ethical issues relating to newspaper publishing.

309. O'Brien, Donald. "Jordan Marsh: Metamorphosis of a Legend." *Retail Control* 52 (February 1984): 8–18.

Recounts the transformation of Jordan Marsh from a traditional, long-established department store to an upbeat, exciting merchandiser. Points out that a variety of demographic factors relating to the baby-boom generation affected marketing strategies significantly. Cites among these influences that (1) 72 million baby boomers were between sixteen to thirty-three years of age by 1980, with baby boomers between thirty and forty-nine leading in growth in the 1980s; (2) baby-boom families have two incomes that collectively are higher than the income of the traditional one-earner family; and (3) the maturing of the baby boomers significantly increased the numbers of "better customers." Discusses the changing values of this generation, including an emphasis on quality and convenience. Reveals in detail Jordan Marsh's marketing campaigns to attract this market.

310. O'Neal, Donna J. "Fragrances '80." *Military Market* 13 (September 1980): 29–60.

Provides a detailed analysis of the fragrance market. Individual fragrance marketers and specific fragrances and their advertising campaigns are discussed. The maturing of the baby boom is viewed with some alarm: "An increase in the 35–44 age group also foretells possible flat cosmetics industry growth, because these people—currently 24–35—already use more cosmetics than anyone else." The military market for fragrances is also briefly considered.

311. "Openers: An Unhealth Trend." *American Demographics* 5 (July 1983): 12.

Summarizes a report by the American Hospital Association that forecasts significant increases in in-patient days and hospital use in the 1980s. Notes that these increases "will continue as the baby boom generation reaches the older years starting about 2010." The larger number of older elderly, the seventy-five-to-eighty-four age group, will also affect in-patient hospital use in the coming decades.

312. "Openers: Follow the Crowd." *American Demographics* 4 (March 1982): 9.

Traces the evolution of the snow-ski industry as the baby boom matures. In the seventies ski manufacturers introduced short skis to attract baby boomers to skiing. Longer skis are being marketed in the 1980s to counteract traditional declines in skiing after the age of twenty-nine. Concludes that "following the baby boom means that the winter sports industry may eventually have to turn to promoting snowshoes to keep the baby boomers doddering across the slopes."

313. "Openers: Hospitality's Future." *American Demographics* 4 (April 1982): 10.

Analyzes the future of the hospitality industry. Contends that the industry's luxury market should "receive a boost as the baby boom generation enters its peak earning years." This generation's emphasis on natural foods and nutrition will also affect the operation of hotels in the 1980s. Increasing number of elderly travelers seeking inexpensive accommodations and of international tourists with unique ethnic demands will also impact on the hospitality industry.

314. "Openers: The Car Boom." *American Demographics* 1 (November/December 1979): 8.

Summarizes a report by Anthony Down, a senior fellow at the Brookings Institution, concerning new car sales. The attainment of legal driving age by virtually the entire baby boom, and the increase in the number of households, are considered directly responsible for the growth in car sales. In addition, multicar ownership is partially responsible. The gasoline crisis may affect growth, but "the desire for car ownership among Americans at each income level is still intensifying."

315. Osborn, John. "Does a 'Baby Boom' Loom on the Horizon for Cookie Bakers in the Mid-80s? Some Pros and Cons." *Bakery Production and Marketing* 16 (October 24, 1981): 19.

Summarizes a report on "The Cookie Market" prepared by Packaged Facts, a New York research service. Overall outlook for retail cookie volume is good, primarily because of the "coming of the long-awaited 'echo boom' or 'mini boom.' " These terms refer to children in the six-to-seven-year age bracket, "the prime cookie consumption years," who are the children of the original baby-boom generation.

316. Ostroff, Jim. "Perishables: Says Food Retailers Must Spot Trends, Restructure Operations." *Supermarket News* 33 (April 9, 1984): 36.

Records the comments made by E. Dean Werries, president of Fleming Companies, concerning demographic changes that will affect a supermarket's produce department. Emphasizes that "within a few short years our nation has turned from one that is youth-oriented to one in which the middle-age are setting the trends." Marketing opportunities are identified and other trends briefly noted. Concludes that "it is through produce that a company can achieve recognition as an upscale operation."

317. "Pay Attention to the Trends." *Credit Union Magazine* 47 (November 1981): 66–68.

Reports on presentations made at the Operations Conference, sponsored by the Credit Union Executives Society in October 1981. Major trends include (1) demographic changes caused by the baby boom; (2) concern by credit-union members for long-range financial security; (3) increased loan demand by baby boomers to buy houses; and (4) effects of banking deregulation on credit unions. Increased competition from savings and loan associations is predicted, and managers of credit unions are urged to "pay attention to the trends. Don't close your eyes to the constant changes in the marketplace."

318. Perdue, Lewis. "California's Boatbuilders Bounce Back." *California Business* 17 (September 1982): 76–79.

Profiles the California sailboat industry in the 1980s. Individual companies are briefly identified and their sales analyzed. Industry officials predict significant increases in sales because (1) fiberglass boats actually appreciate in value; (2) the baby boom is entering the thirty to forty-five age group ("the prime age for boat buying"); and (3) sailboats are not dependent on high-priced fuels.

319. Peterson, Robin T. "Viewpoint: Base Segmentation on Market Potential, Competition Analysis." *Marketing News* 16 (November 12, 1982): 4.

Analyzes the marketing tool of segmentation, especially in relation to potential shortcomings. Points out that the movie industry targets its films to teenagers, while the baby-boom generation is now in its third decade. Movie makers should be creating films for families and young children. Recommends that "segmentation decisions should be based on market potential and competition analysis. The number of consumers in each segment, their purchasing power, and their needs and desires should be considered in an attempt to estimate market potential."

320. "Population: Baby Boom Bulge Ages, Families Change." *Appliance Manufacturer* 30 (April 1982): 40.

Contends that the growing population base provided by the aging baby boom practically guarantees growth for the appliance industry, regardless of the economy or housing industry in the 1980s. However, changing household formations require changes in appliances. For example, microwave ovens and other convenience products can be readily marketed to singles and single parents. The baby boomers in the 1980s will be "the group to upgrade housing, making them prime targets for home comfort products."

321. "Postwar Baby Boom Boosts Carpet Sales." *Industry Week* 194 (September 12, 1977): 148.

Examines the impact of the aging baby boom on the carpet industry. Although substantially more households will be formed in the 1980s, this may not necessarily translate into increased sales. The most important consideration is the amount of disposable income available. Lack of competitiveness in the carpet industry is noted. Carpet sales are expected to increase if the economy improves because of "the number of family formations by the post World War II baby boom generation as consumers."

322. Prescott, Eileen. "Real Men Do Wear Aprons." *Across the Board* 20 (November 1983): 51–55.

Looks at the changing advertising and marketing techniques being directed at male consumers. Even though participation of men in traditionally female household chores is increasing, studies show that "most companies are slow to respond to this and other demographic changes." Studies investigating the characteristics of this new type of man are reported. Men are shown to value convenience, speed, efficiency, and gadgetry. The impact of the baby boom on this phenomenon is stressed: "Their values—incubated in the liberal 1960s—are inescapably present at many levels of American life, and the home is no exception." More and more household advertising will be directed at men in the future.

323. "Protein-based Creams Offer the Lure of Youth." *Chemical Week* 128 (April 8, 1981): 34.

Shows why three major cosmetics corporations, Avon, Revlon, and Estee Lauder, introduced new skin-care products containing collagen in early 1981. This natural protein substance is reputed to be a rejuvenating agent for dry and aging skin. The success of these products is the result of maturing baby boomer's "increasing interest in products to diminish signs of aging." Since most baby boomers have already been conditioned to shampoo every day, the hair-care market is "essentially saturated." However, the market for skin-care products should increase significantly in the 1980s.

324. "Radio Format Scramble." *Marketing and Media Decisions* 15 (February 1980): 68–69.

Reports on the changing radio listenership as the baby-boom generation matures. Discusses programming changes, particularly with respect to AM broadcasting, which is losing the youth market. Recognizes a trend toward talk radio and a transitional period for Top 40 stations, which may emphasize more adult selection. Predicts the youth market advertising dollar moving to FM.

325. Rentz, Joseph O.; Fred D. Reynolds; and Roy G. Stout. "Analyzing Changing Consumption Patterns with Cohort Analysis." *Journal of Marketing Research* 20 (February 1983): 12–20.

Accomplishes two tasks: one, provides an analysis of the effectiveness of cohort analysis in marketing; and two, assesses the market for soft-drink consumption as the population ages. Points out that baby boomers represent a major market and that strategies are designed to exploit this population. States that "the basic thesis of our article is that the response to the changing age distribution should be based on an understanding of the dynamics of aging, cohort succession, and environmental influences that produce consumers' responses to a given product or set of products, and not just the changing size of the age distribution." Concludes that contrary to what has been thought, soft-drink consumption should not decline as the population ages.

326. "Report Analyzes Toy/Game Industry." *Playthings* 81 (February 1983): 309.

Summarizes a report on the toy and game industry produced by Business Trend Analysts, a Long Island-based research company. Dollar sales of $5.5 billion were recorded for 1982. Adult-oriented products are cited as the main reason for increased sales. Notes that the "gradual aging of the post baby boom population has made the 25–35 age group the primary marketing target for new product developers."

327. Reysen, Frank, Jr. "Baby Boom Could Mean Blessed Event for Toy Firms." *Playthings* 79 (December 1981): 37.

Editorializes that rising birthrates should result in an "earnings bonanza" for many toy companies. This boomlet is the result of baby-boom couples' deciding to have children in the 1980s. Areas of great potential growth are identified and specific manufacturers noted. Companies that produce children's clothing, food, and toys will benefit from increasing birthrates. Concludes that "the spiraling birthrate will reward those manufacturers and retailers who help make it happen through carefully planned marketing programs and innovative merchandising concepts."

328. Rice, Dorothy P. "Long Life to You." *American Demographics* 1 (October 1979): 9–15.

Examines implications for medical care as the population ages. Changes in mortality and fertility rates are shown to have significant effects on the overall demographic composition of the population. Graphs illustrate percentage changes in death rates, projected number of residents in nursing homes, and percentage increase in population by age. Notes that the most rapidly growing age group is the oldest (persons over eighty-five) and that this will result in a "nursing home boom." Medical care requirements for the aging baby boom in the next century are extremely difficult to predict.

329. Roman, Monica. "Baby 'Boomlet' Boosts Maternity Wear Sales: Working Mothers Spending More." *WWD: Womens Wear Daily* 146 (October 6, 1983): 9.

Observes that the birthrate has increased significantly in the last few years, creating a "baby boomlet." States that this is part of the changing demographics in which women delay childbirth and continue working. Notes that this boomlet should be a boon to maternity-clothes distributors. Lady Madonna, Marshall Fields, Levi Strauss, and Saks are all mentioned as promoting this new market.

330. "Roman Meal Sets Olympics TV Spots." *Advertising Age* 54 (December 26, 1983): 1.

Announces a new $2 million television advertising campaign for Roman Meal bread to be introduced during the telecast of the Winter Olympic Games in February 1984. The campaign was designed to attract the "aging fitness-focused baby boomers, both men and women, age 25 to 49." This represents a change in market focus from the nutrition-conscious women over age fifty who have traditionally bought Roman Meal products.

331. Rosen, Marcella. "Putting the Cart Before the Horse: Do Media Beget Social Change or Does Social Change Alter Media?" *Advertising Age* 53 (September 27, 1982): M6.

Challenges the generally held view that media alter consumer behavior. Argues that much broader social forces are at work and that they alter the media. Identifies key social aspects, including (1) significant relocation of the population west and south; (2) breakdown of the family; (3) aging of the population; and (4) influence of the enormous baby-boom generation. Observes that the baby boomers are a central focus of marketers and that they constitute "the force" in the country. Notes that the baby boomers are now between the ages of twenty-five to thirty-four and are in their prime spending years.

332. Rosen, Marcella. "Social Evolution, Not Media Revolution." *Marketing and Media Decisions* 16 (December 1981): 66.

> Observes that some experts predict that advances in technology have significantly altered the number and types of media used by the public. Counters this assertion by arguing that it is the new demands of the public that stimulated the broadening of media alternatives such as cable TV, video games, and discs. Changes in the U.S. population that created this demand include (1) relocation of the population to the Sunbelt; (2) changes in family structure; (3) impact of the baby-boom generation; and (4) impact of the economy. Notes that the baby boomers grew up with TV and demanded more not only from television but also from newspapers and magazines. Predicts this will produce even more media segmentation.

333. Savage, Robert H. "The Real Marketing Revolution." *Zip* 6 (January 1983): 23, 38.

> Contends that a major marketing revolution has occurred which is not technological, but demographic. The baby-boom generation is revolutionary because it is a "totally unique generation." General characteristics of baby boomers are listed and members of this generation are considered "hedonistic, and narcissistic pleasure seekers." Consequently, traditional marketing techniques will not work. Concludes that to "match this sociological revolution, marketers of all sorts must respond with a *creative* revolution."

334. Shapiro, Leo J. "Consumers Primed to Increase Spending." *Advertising Age* 54 (August 29, 1983): 26, 30.

> Uses results from *Advertising Age*'s quarterly survey to predict significantly increased personal consumption in late 1983. The habits of baby-boom consumers cannot be predicted using "macro-economic patterns set by others decades ago." Respondents to the survey reported saving for a specific major purpose and, from those under forty, a desire for children. Notes that such savers are typically "sophisticated, relatively affluent, well-educated consumers, baby boomers in the middle of their family-forming, household-building years." The threat of increased inflation may also result in more immediate major purchases.

335. Shapiro, Leo J., and Dwight Bohmbach. "Consumer Poll Sees Surge of Optimism." 54 *Advertising Age* (April 25, 1983): 18.

> Reports the results of *Advertising Age*'s National Consumer Poll in March 1983. Among the results are the following: (1) 45 percent polled

felt that economic conditions were improving; (2) 44 percent felt now was a good time to make large purchases; (3) 36 percent feared that someone in their family would be unemployed or have their employment hours reduced; and (4) more than 33 percent of households were saving money for major purchases such as cars, houses, and vacations. Notes considerable consumer potential, particularly in the baby-boom generation, which is young, affluent, and better educated. Notes that 69 percent of Americans are under age forty-four, and 35 percent are between thirty and forty-four.

336. Sloan, Pat. "New Luster Seen for Hair Color Market." *Advertising Age* 54 (May 2, 1983): 10.

Reviews recent performance of the hair-color industry, with observations on future demands of the baby-boom generation. States that "if market researchers are on target the vanity of the baby boom generation, already pandered to by those who hawk fitness and skin-saving regimes, should sometime in the next five years make these consumers ravenous for products that conceal the toll that aging imposes on hair." Discusses the marketing of Clairol products such as Miss Clairol and Nice 'n Easy, and L'Oréal's Preference. Includes a brief discussion of Revlon.

337. Stern, Aimée. "Ageless Ad Appeal." *Marketing Communications* 8 (May 1983): 21–26.

Examines current marketing strategies of various cosmetic companies as they broaden their appeal to all ages rather than just the young. States three reasons for this strategy: (1) the country's concern with physical fitness; (2) the entrance of women into the labor market; and (3) the aging of the baby-boom population. Notes that by the 1980s, the baby boomers will be between thirty and fifty, which are prime years for consumer spending. Argues that if the baby boomers can be motivated to use cosmetics in this age bracket, they will continue to use them. Cites such companies as Elizabeth Arden, Avon, and Estee Lauder. Discusses also the use of older models to sell cosmetics.

338. Stevenson, Dick. "Liquor Industry Savors Taste of Success With New Liqueurs." *Advertising Forum* 4 (July 1983): 15–18.

Analyzes changes in advertising and sales in the liquor industry. Cordials and liqueurs have emerged as the most heavily advertised of distilled spirits. Demand for these sweetly flavored alcoholic beverages is from "the now-adult baby boom generation, brought up on junk food and soft drinks and now looking for alcoholic beverages that satisfy their penchant for sweets." Marketers view cordials and liqueurs as a means of attracting different drinkers and promoting new drinking occasions. The sales and marketing campaigns for specific brands are also presented.

339. "Study Cites Purchasing Trends." *Product Marketing and Cosmetic and Fragrance Retailing* 11 (March 1982): 4.

Summarizes the conclusions of a study released by Management Horizons on the purchase patterns of baby boomers. Discount department stores are shopped most frequently. A distinction is made between "late" baby boomers, who list conventional stores as their second choice, and "early" baby boomers, who lean toward mass-merchandise chains.

340. Sullivan, Michael P. "Developing Personal Financial Planning Programs for Banks." *American Banker* 149 (May 9, 1984): 4.

Reports on the growing market for personal financial planning, especially the new market of investors earning under $50,000 annually. Identifies a significant segment of new investors as the baby boomers, who are well educated and have matured into well-paid positions. Characterizes the baby-boom generation as "yuppies" (young urban professionals). Notes that the typical baby-boom investor is different from the traditional investor in that the baby boomer usually has two household incomes, few or no children, an advanced degree, and professional or executive status. Reviews the mix of services a bank can provide to different types of investors.

341. Tarter, Jeffrey. "Can He Keep His Customers Tuned In?" *Inc.* 2 (November 1980): 73–76.

Profiles Sandy Ruby, owner of the highly successful Tech Hi Fi chain. He founded the company in 1967 to "serve the needs of the free-spending baby boomers" by providing discount stereo components to college students in the Boston area. Tech Hi Fi strategists have conducted extensive market research so that they can adapt to changes in their market as the baby boom matures. Ruby complains that stereo manufacturers refuse to alter their overall strategy of marketing to college students because they've "ridden the baby boom all the way through high school, college, and graduate school, and all they understand is getting the easy sales." Tech Hi Fi is exploring the video disc market.

342. Taylor, Thayer C. "Markets That Marketers Pursue Are a Changin'." *S&MM: Sales and Marketing Management* 125 (July 28, 1980): A6–A19.

> Observes that the baby boom created a whole new set of marketing challenges. Notes that baby boomers as they moved through various age groups stimulated markets in children's goods, hi-fi's, and leisure-time products. Points out that the baby boomers are not a homogeneous group and that they require market segmentation. Identifies key demographic factors as (1) changing age mix; (2) population mobility; (3) fragmentation of household types; and (4) working women. Contends that a key marketing group, those aged thirty-five to fifty-four, will be the fastest growing age group. Also contends that the baby boomlet created by baby-boomer mothers will have powerful effects on markets. Analyzes several other areas, such as urban-suburban migration and regional migration.

343. Taylor, Thayer C. "Tomorrow's New Rich: Post War Babies Are Grown Up." *S&MM: Sales and Marketing Management* 127 (October 26, 1981): 7.

> Asserts that the baby-boom generation will have tremendous influence on marketing. Points out that some baby boomers will be reaching the thirty-five-to-forty-four age group, representing the peak buying years. Notes some disagreement about defining the chronological origin of the baby boom, depending on whether birthrates or number of births is used. Identifies key issues as (1) changing role of women; (2) nontraditional household formation; (3) regional migration; (4) income trends; and (5) fertility behavior. Predicts that income will grow generally and that the percentage of upper-income consumers will increase more rapidly than in the previous decade.

344. "10% Growth Predicted . . . On Both Sides of the Credit Union Balance Sheet." *Credit Union Magazine* 48 (June 1982): 10–11.

> Looks at four areas that will affect credit unions in the 1980s: (1) economics; (2) technology; (3) social and demographic changes; and (4) politics. Emphasis is placed on the impact of the baby boom because it "represents the last large group of people looking for their first financial institution." Effort must be made to attract and support these potential users of credit unions. Notes that baby boomers in the 1980s will be "net debtors, looking for entry-level housing."

345. "Those Doubts About McDonald's." *Financial World* 152 (June 15, 1983): 38–40.

Investigates the conflicting investment recommendations regarding McDonald's Corporation. Some analysts doubt whether the company's phenomenal growth rate can be sustained. The aging of the baby boom and the fragmentation of the fast-food market are cited as reasons for an inevitable decline in the company's profits. However, other analysts feel that McDonald's will adapt well to these changing market demands. Concludes that when "all the pluses and minuses are weighed, the balance still seems tipped in McDonald's direction."

346. "Togetherness Among the Baby Boomers." *S&MM: Sales and Marketing Management* 127 (July 6, 1981): 41.

Summarizes, primarily through bar and pie charts, the findings of a Louis Harris poll of baby boomers' attitudes toward shared decision-making. The poll, commissioned by *House & Garden* magazine, provided the following results: (1) 45 percent of persons polled have two or more wage earners working full-time; (2) 72 percent share buying decisions and household chores; and (3) 75 percent of the females hold jobs. Charts break down spending decisions by marital status and presence of children; household chores by type of chore; and household income by total joint income, from $20,000 to over $50,000.

347. Trager, Cara C. "Monitoring the Pulse of America." *Advertising Age* 55 (March 26, 1984): M48.

Examines the success of *American Health,* a health magazine that first appeared in March 1982. Publisher Owen Lipstein and editor T. George Harris are profiled. Lipstein explains his publication's success: "The magazine is out at a time when the baby boom is maturing, and the political movement of the '60s and '70s is translating into fitness." The format is strictly informational, but advertisers are attracted to its readers, "comprised mainly of upwardly mobile baby boomers." Notes specific advertisers and presents comments from advertising executives.

348. Trott, Donald I. "The Fast Food Future." *American Demographics* 1 (October 1979): 16–18.

Investigates the current status of the fast-food industry and analyzes potential future trends. Various demographic trends are shown to directly affect the growth of the industry. For example, teenagers, traditionally the business's best customers, are declining in numbers in the 1980s. If baby boomers in their thirties start families, this will decrease their discretionary income, which may lessen their expenditures for fast food. Concludes that, since 98 percent of Americans have ready access each day to a McDonald's, "Some claims for the growth of the industry as a whole in the 1980s are too optimistic."

349. "The True Look of the Discount Industry. Part 2: Merchandising—Girls' and Infants' Wear." *DM: Discount Merchandiser* 21 (June 1981): 54.

Anticipates a strong market for girls' and infants' departments as birthrates increase in the 1980s. This is attributed to a "strong fallout from the birth boom years of 1954–1964." Urges retailers to put more emphasis on these departments. Two distinct markets are identified and discussed: affluent parents with discretionary income, and thrifty-market families.

350. "The True Look of the Discount Industry. Part 2: Merchandising—Men's and Boys'." *DM: Discount Merchandiser* 21 (June 1981): 68.

Analyzes the impact of the aging baby boom on men's and boys' clothing departments in discount stores. Middle-aged Americans are in the most rapidly expanding age group and, consequently, clothing makers like Levi Strauss are marketing trousers with "action waists, knits, and more room." Diverse influences such as inflation and trendy name-brand items are analyzed.

351. Tyson, David O. "Any Full-Service Strategy Useless, Futurist Argues." *American Banker* 149 (March 6, 1984): 8.

Quotes Hank E. Koehn, vice president and director of Futures Research at the Security Pacific National Bank in Los Angeles, concerning the future of full-service banking. Banks are urged to market their services to very specialized consumer segments. Members of the baby-boom generation must be courted, but first it is necessary to identify their "changing preferences and new demands for the packaging of services." Banks must dramatically improve their marketing techniques to attract this new generation of customers.

352. Vineberg, Gary. "Baby Boomlet Bound to Bring Business Bounce." *Footwear News* 39 (March 28, 1983): 1, 8.

Describes the impact of increased fertility rates among baby-boom women on the children's shoe industry. Demographic data are presented to show that mothers in 1983 are older, college educated, involved in a career, and having smaller families. Since first births require more expenditures and the mature, working parent of the 1980s will theoretically spend more on each child, the increased birthrate "has had undeniable effects on the footwear industry." Stride Rite Corporation is identified as a major beneficiary of the baby boomlet.

353. Walker, Ruth. "The Baby-Boomer's Tastes Graduate to the Gourmet Hamburger." *Christian Science Monitor,* 21, June 1984, pp. 21–22.

   Reports on the introduction of an "upscale" hamburger restaurant trend. Identifies this phenomenon as "adult fast food" or "gourmet hamburger" establishment where the decor is nicer and the menu better than at McDonald's, Wendy's or Burger King. Discusses in particular T.J. Applebee's in Atlanta, Fuddruckers in San Antonio, and Chili's Inc. in Dallas. Contends that these restaurants cater to the maturing baby boomers, who have amassed considerable disposable income. Points out, however, that the three leading fast-food restaurants are doing well and that the gourmet hamburger restaurants are due for a shakeout.

354. Wallace, Anise. "Investment Management: Banks Advised to Work on Image." *American Banker* 149 (February 8, 1984): 3.

   Quotes Henry E. Koehn, futurist and vice president of Security Pacific National Bank, Los Angeles, on changes necessary if banks are to survive current developments in the financial services market. Stresses that "the baby boom generation, which is the driving force behind these changes, is entrepreneurial, demanding." Market segmentation is a necessity and banks must adopt new market images. Trust departments may not be fit into these market changes and may be eliminated.

355. Walsh, Doris. "The Grapes of Growth." *American Demographics* 5 (May 1983): 32–35.

   Studies wine-drinking demographics and notes that the wine industry must be concerned primarily with growth of its market. The maturing of the baby boom provides a large number of potential wine drinkers, but wine companies must actively target this market segment. Notes that several companies are marketing wine with less alcohol and fewer calories to "encourage their use by the health- and diet-conscious crowd." Regional consumption patterns are briefly noted. The overall market has great potential.

356. "Watch That Baby Boom." *Publishers Weekly* 222 (December 3, 1982): 24.

   Reports that demographers and marketers are following closely the baby boom population. Notes that this population is soon to enter the twenty-five-to-forty-four age group, which traditionally spends the most money. Predicts that as long as interest rates and mortgage rates come down, this group should have a dramatic effect on the economy. Points out that rising cultural and educational levels of Americans, coupled with the influx baby-boom spending, means the market for exploiting disposable income should be considerable as long as quality of goods is high. Identifies designer jeans, gourmet foods, and books as good markets.

357. Waters, Craig R. "Break Out the Cigars." *Inc.* (July 1983): 29–30.

Examines the potential market for cigars as baby boomers age. Focuses on the predictions of Alex Brainard, president of the Consolidated Cigar Corp. Points out that 76 million Americans of baby-boom age are approaching the thirty-five-year mark and that cigar smoking significantly increases in the over-thirty-five population. Predicts that this group will increase 50 percent by the year 2000. Discusses recent financial dealings of the company.

358. Willinger, Kurt. "The New Creativity: How to Put It to Work." *Broadcasting* 103 (November 22, 1982): 21.

Argues that a "new creativity" is needed in advertising to market to the baby boom, "the richest, best educated generation ever." Facts demonstrating the impact of the baby boom on marketing are presented. Music is seen as the key to effective advertising for this generation of Americans. Traditional forms of advertising must give way to an emphasis on "image and successfully creating a want rather than a need."

359. "Yesterday's Rebels Are Found to Have Positive Consumer Attitudes." *Marketing News* 17 (February 4, 1983): 6.

Summarizes the findings of a consumer survey published in *Chain Store Age Magazine.* Among the results are the following: (1) consumers born between 1946 and 1964 comprise one-third of the U.S. population and possess an income equal to 35 percent of the GNP; (2) baby boomers possess many of the same values as their parents; (3) 56 percent of those surveyed indicated they have reduced their standard of living; (4) one-third indicated that someone in their family has had employment problems; and (5) 38 percent expect to save money. Analyzes consumer trends and notes strong demands for such items as electronic equipment, video games, car sound systems, VCRs, cameras, barbecues, bicycles, cologne, exercise equipment, and strollers.

360. Yovovich, B.G. "Marketing to Affluents: Now, It's the Baby Boomers' Turn." *Advertising Age* 54 (April 4, 1983): M–11.

Probes the nature of the baby-boom generation, particularly its spending habits. Makes several key observations, including the following: (1) baby-boom families that are affluent are usually two-income families rather than one-income; (2) time constraints lead baby-boom families to seek time-saving items such as microwave ovens, quality frozen foods, and house-cleaning services; (3) baby-boom families have fewer children but give their children quality toys, such as computers or educational toys; and (4) baby-boom women participate and appear to remain in the labor force.

5
Marketing Articles: Automobiles, Housing, and Insurance

361. Ancipink, Patricia. "Changing Insurance Needs in a Changing Society." *Best's Review Insurance Edition* 82 (September 1981): 24.

> Analyzes the impact of the baby boom on the life insurance industry. The combination of a large aging population and significantly increasing life expectancies has profound implications for this industry. Lifestyle and attitudinal changes affecting the perceived need for insurance coverage are examined. Concludes that "in today's social environment the life insurance industry must learn how to deal with change and to think about the world in a different way."

362. "The Baby Boom Generation: Major Future Source for Agents According to LIMRA." *Life Association News* 76 (December 1981): 141–44.

> Reviews the results of a study conducted by the Life Insurance Marketing and Research Association (LIMRA) to determine future markets for life insurance. The baby-boom generation is judged to be "the hope of the industry's future, because it is a large percentage of the population while the young are just beginning to set up their families and future." However, baby boomers are difficult to sell insurance to because they dislike being approached by salesmen, have been hurt by inflation, and have generally been postponing major life events such as marriage, childbearing, and home buying. Insurance agents must develop new marketing techniques and products to meet the needs of these maturing baby boomers.

363. Brenner, Lynn. "How the New Demographics Is Shaking Up Insurers' Markets." *Institutional Investor* 16 (July 1982): 97–102.

> Argues that life insurance companies are living in the past and are unaware of the demographic trends represented by the baby-boom generation. Policies are still designed for "typical" families, which now represent a minority of American households. The ethnic and single-parent

markets for life insurance are virtually ignored. Significantly, studies show that "although they are now maturing, the baby boomers' attitudes toward life insurance continue to differ from those of the previous generation." Concludes that most insurance companies are exhibiting a "woeful blindness to demographic trends that are clearly eroding the market for traditional life and does not bode well for the future of the big insurers."

364. Cain, Thomas J., and Michael W. Scott. "Overconsumption and the 'Housing Crisis.'" *Real Estate Review* 11 (Summer 1981): 66–70.

Notes the generally held belief that housing costs have risen sharply in the last decade, putting serious financial strains not only on the poor but on the middle class. Counters this assumption by noting that (1) cost of home ownership has risen 4 percent annually between 1970 and 1980; (2) renters have declined 1 percent in the same peroid; and (3) supply of housing has increased 10 percent over demand. Notes that some have attributed rising housing demand to baby boomers entering the ages of primary housing consumption. The effects of higher incomes, costs of housing, and increased number of new housing units in the cities are also discussed.

365. Christian, James W. "A Housing Funds Shortage May Cut Off the Rainbow." *Savings & Loan News* 104 (June 1983): 46–52.

Contends that too little attention has been paid to the impact the maturing baby boom will have on savings. Although the demand for housing and durable consumer goods will increase, it is questionable whether enough credit will be available to finance these purchases. Notes that the "1980s will see the smallest number of Americans in the prime saving phase of the life cycle relative to those in the prime borrowing phase than at any time in the last half of the 20th century." Baby boomers may not have saved enough to allow them to borrow for major purchases as they enter middle age. Implications for savings associations are noted.

366. Collier, David C. "Looking Down the Road with the Auto Industry." *Business Horizons* (February 1981): 49–54.

Analyzes the American automobile industry and concludes it can return to a prolonged period of record sales if certain issues are addressed, (1) energy cost and supply; (2) government regulation; (3) economic and demographic trends; (4) product development; and (5) worldwide trends. The most direct and positive trend is the aging of those members of the baby boom who "are at a stage in the life cycle when spending on durable goods such as autos is comparatively high."

367. "Demographic Forecasts: Household Consumption." *American Demographics* 3 (August 1981): 46–47.

Emphasizes the impact of the baby boom on household consumption patterns in the 1980s. Baby boomers should have increased discretionary income that can be spent on home furnishings and services. Expenditures on such items should increase by 49 percent in the 1980s. Tables detail how money will be spent on household items and what percentage of household budgets this will constitute throughout the decade. The percent growth in household expenditures and the share of expenditures attributable both to families and individuals are graphically presented.

368. Donahue, Richard J. "Task for '80s: Living with Inflation." *National Underwriter: Life and Health Insurance Edition* 84 (January 19, 1980): 1.

Explores the many changes occurring in American society and their effects on the insurance industry. Identifies inflation as a primary concern for the industry and a key factor in influencing changes in the family structure. The aging of the baby-boom population will require new alterations in insurance programs, particularly in pensions and annuities. Discusses the increasing role of women and the effects of state and federal regulation.

369. Dunn, William. "Wheels for the Baby Boom: Detroit Discovers Demographics." *American Demographics* 6 (May 1984): 26–29.

Discusses how the Detroit auto companies have modified their ad campaigns and car designs to suit the desires and needs of the baby-boom generation. Notes that as a group, baby boomers are well-educated and skeptical consumers who want information before purchasing. Observes that baby boomers between twenty and thirty-seven constitute almost one-third of the U.S. population and, by 1995, will account for one-half the discretionary spending. Reviews the marketing strategies of Chrysler, General Motors, Ford, and American Motors, with particular emphasis on the Pontiac Fierro, AMC Jeep XJ, Chrysler T-115, and Cadillac Cimarron.

370. "Economic Researcher Predicting Less Inflation, More Production in 1980s." *American Banker* 144 (March 19, 1979): 4.

Excerpts comments made by James L. Essig, vice president of economic research for Prudential Life Insurance Company of America, at a panel discussion on business trends sponsored by the Iowa-Des Moines National Bank. Optimistic predictions of a sustained moderate economic growth in the 1980s are based on three factors: (1) a more experienced and productive work force; (2) support for tax reduction and savings; and (3) increased potential for foreign trade. The maturing of the baby boom and its assimilation into the labor force is seen as a major plus: "The labor force, at the same time, will be more experienced, better educated, more 'down-to-earth' in work attitudes." This will result in a "vast productivity payoff" for the entire country.

371. Findlay, Gordon S. "Canadian Comment: Baby Boom Comes of Age." *Best's Review: Life/Health Insurance Edition* 80 (June 1979): 48–50.

Reports on comments made by K.P. Kavanaugh, president of the Great-West Life Assurance Company. Notes that by 1985 the number of people between twenty-five and fifty-four (prime insurance-buying age) will increase by 24 percent in the United States. Argues that the number of purchasers will far exceed the number of agents and that insurance companies will have to analyze these new consumers and respond to their needs. Predicts tough competition and an inflationary force that will complicate the market.

372. Finlay, Daniel. "Using Demographics: Residential Real Estate." *American Demographics* 3 (February 1981): 42–44.

Considers how demographic information can aid the residential real estate industry. Emphasizes that "the crest of the baby boom wave will pass through the housing industry throughout the eighties." Three other conditions will increase the demand for housing: (1) regional shifts in population; (2) unstable economy; and (3) changes in household formations. Real estate companies are urged to make use of all available demographic and life-style data.

373. Freund, James L. "The Housing Market: Recent Developments and Underlying Trends." *Federal Reserve Bulletin* 69 (February 1983): 61–69.

Analyzes the prospects for the housing market in the years to come. Covers such areas as (1) the effect created by inflation; (2) costs of owning a home; (3) alternatives to single-family housing; and (4) the influence of demographic factors. Notes that the baby boomers have currently stimulated the housing market. Points out that a large number of baby boomers are reaching optimum age for household formation. Cautions, however, that the subsequent baby-bust generation will significantly slow the growth of the adult population. Predicts trend toward smaller, lower-cost units. Includes tables on private housing starts, inventories of unsold units, demographic factors, headship rates, construction costs, carrying costs, and residential mortgage assets.

374. Fulmer, Robert M., and Joan W. Edmondson. "Planning for Tomorrow's Business World." *Life Insurance Selling* 56 (May 1981): 58–64.

Identifies demographic trends that will affect the life insurance industry. Since the baby boom will clearly "continue to shape the character of this nation," life insurance agents are urged to become more aware of this phenomenon. Five specific trends are identified: (1) two-career families; (2) smaller families; (3) child care; (4) one-parent families; and (5) increase in number of singles. Major challenges affecting the entire country in the 1980s are also briefly discussed: (1) high political turbulence and uncertainty; (2) slow economic growth; (3) expensive capital and credit; (4) weakening support of the work ethic; (5) rising public demands; and (6) challenges to the private enterprise system.

375. Goetze, Rolf. "Urban Neighborhoods in Transition." *Social Policy* 10 (September-October 1979): 53–57.

Discusses the changing attitude toward urban living. Notes that housing demands have significantly increased as the post-war baby bulge increases competition for housing. Reviews trends in housing starts and asserts that more starts sometimes encourage young households to leave the city for newer subdivisions. Predicts that the baby bulge will force us to focus on housing issues in the 1980s. Several recommendations for public policy making are presented: (1) encourage housing demand in weaker neighborhoods to spread out the affluents; (2) encourage neighborhood confidence and positive attitudes in weaker neighborhoods; and (3) develop tax measures to equitably assess windfalls and encourage long-term residency.

376. Gray, Ralph. "Jeep Targets Baby Boomers." *Advertising Age* 54 (March 21, 1983): 56.

Discusses the marketing strategy of the American Motors Corporation, especially with respect to promotion of the Jeep. Points out that baby boomers are the primary target of Jeep promotions because AMC believes these consumers have aged to the extent that they are interested in adult recreation. Argues that baby boomers will be very active in the sports utility area, where the Jeep fits in. Reviews projected growth in the four-wheel drive market.

377. Harter, Thomas R. "Profitability Will Be Mediocre in '79 Despite Sales Activity." *Mortgage Banker* 39 (January 1979): 7.

> Discusses the future of the U.S. economy, especially the housing market. Since the 1974–75 recession, consumer spending has been considerable. Attributes this spending to anticipatory buying and the post-war baby boomers. Points out that the baby boomers have reached prime age for the consumption of items such as housing, automobiles, furniture, clothing, and appliances. The positive economic influence of the baby boomers is countered by tight money, government regulation, and inflation.

378. Harter, Thomas R., and Schuyler Schell. "Housing Demand Swells Due to 'Baby Boom.'" *Mortgage Banker* 39 (November 1978): 50.

> Attempts to predict the impact of the baby boom generation on the housing market. Notes that (1) post-war baby boomers will swell the ranks of first-time purchasers of housing, creating high demand; (2) a serious supply problem is indicated by comparing the number of first-time buyers with housing starts; (3) there is an increasing trend in household formation, based on singles population, lower birthrates, higher divorce rates, and tendency to delay marriage; (4) a trend toward higher incomes has materialized because of the increase in two-income families; and (5) baby boomers will ultimately create an additional market for more expensive housing. Includes tables on housing starts and housing prices.

379. Harter, Thomas R., and Schuyler Schell. "Mortgage Banking in the 1980s." *Mortgage Banker* 40 (April 1980): 29–42.

> Analyzes the future of mortgage banking with special emphasis on housing demand and income-producing properties. Notes that the baby-boom generation is reaching prime house-buying age and will account for significant housing demand. The baby boomers are also reaching prime childbearing age and may create a baby boom of their own, which will ensure housing demand in the long term. Argues that as the present baby boomers mature, they will also demand more expensive homes to satisfy their interest in "trading up." Points out that when population growth is compared to housing starts, a significant supply problem arises. The effects of inflation and government regulation are briefly discussed.

380. Hein, Scott E., and James C. Lamb, Jr. "Why the Median-Priced Home Costs So Much." *Federal Reserve Bank of St. Louis Review* 63 (June/July 1981): 11–19.

Explores why the cost of home ownership has risen so rapidly since 1965. Two separate influences are discussed: one, the overall increase in housing prices, and, two, the increase in mortgage rates and costs. House prices have risen because of significant demographic changes in the population. For example, "the post-World War II baby boom has moved into the homebuying age group." Other factors, such as inflation and the favorable tax treatment of home ownership, are also analyzed. Notes that conventional, fixed-rate mortgages are in fact detrimental to the home buyer because they result in substantial cash-flow problems.

381. "Housing: The New Demographics." *United States Banker* 90 (February 1979): 64–69.

Examines housing-market prospects for the future. Notes that the baby boomers will be reaching the thirty-year-old mark in the 1980s and that this extremely large cohort should mean a strong housing market. Cautions, however, that this market may not have traditional characteristics. Identifies the following as changes in the social, economic structure: (1) uncertainty as to the investment potential in housing; (2) prevalence of two-income families; (3) interest in short-term appreciation; (4) migratory patterns of the population; and (5) energy consciousness. Concludes that demand may be shaped by these nontraditional considerations.

382. "Inflation and the Insurance Industry." *Insurance Marketing* 80 (September 1979): 10–11.

Reports mixed feelings about the effect inflation will have on the insurance industry. Increased household income and a growth in the number of middle-aged Americans based on the maturing of the baby boom are considered positive indications that insurance sales should dramatically increase in the 1980s. Negative conditions to which inflation contributes include lack of capacity and lower margins of solvency.

383. Johnson, Michael S. "Gimme Shelter." *Cornell Executive* 9 (Fall 1982): 21–24.

Notes that Americans view home ownership as both an investment and a source of consumption. Inflation in the seventies stimulated housing, as did the baby-boom generation. Continued maturing of the baby boom in the eighties will influence both cost of buying and value of owning a house. The eventual entry of the baby-bust generation into the housing market may result in "house closings" if too many houses are produced in the seventies and eighties. Concludes that it is "time to reemphasize housing as a durable consumption good instead of as a financial cure-all of inflation."

384. Joseph, George G. "LIMRA's Joseph Sees Product and Agent as Still Growing." *National Underwriter: Life and Health Insurance Edition* 85 (November 7, 1981): 2.

Reports on the remarks of George G. Joseph, president of the Life Insurance Marketing and Research Association (LIMRA). Rebuts the charge that the life insurance industry is in decline. Notes that demographers are predicting that competition among baby boomers for entry-level management positions will create intense frustration for these individuals. Observes that a ready market of talented people will be available for recruitment by the industry. Demographers predict increased numbers of marriages, children, and home ownerships. Emphasizes that the marketing officer must pay attention to such factors as cost control, training, practical goal setting, and good market analysis.

385. Kettle, John. "Automobiles: Big Problems, Bigger Opportunities." *Executive* 22 (April 1980): 12–13.

Editorializes that the Canadian auto industry must adapt to changing needs created by the energy shortage and the baby boom. While baby boomers will initially buy old, energy-inefficient cars because these cars are affordable, eventually this large market will "likely move to slightly younger cars, and that should see not only an improvement in sales but a more dramatic improvement in average mileage." Auto manufacturers are also urged to begin producing a "world car," a vehicle that can be manufactured in various countries, using standardized components.

386. Koshn, Hank. "Changing Attitudes, Lifestyles, Reshaping Business, Society: Aging of the Baby Boom Generation Changing American Way-of-Life." *American Banker* 146 (August 21, 1981): 29.

Reviews consumer trends and behaviors that will affect the automobile leasing business. The maturing members of the baby boom are labeled the "pace setters" and are described as the group with the largest potential for auto leasing. The origin of the baby boom is briefly described, but emphasis is on why members of the baby boom will consider leasing cars. Financial considerations will be a major factor. Notes that "the parents of the baby boom failed to stress payment. Only entitlement was stressed, and entitlement became the ethic of this new generation." Convenience and amount of discretionary income will also influence car leasing patterns.

387. Kuklin, Anthony B. "The Housing Market: Bust or Boom?" *Real Estate Law Journal* 10 (Fall 1981): 154–61.

Discusses the arguments for and against an upcoming baby boom. Reviews history of the single-family residence and notes that it reached its full bloom following World War II. The effects of inflation both in stimulating housing purchases as a hedge and in deterring purchase on account of high cost are analyzed. Argues that housing will again increase as the baby-boom population enters prime home-buying age. Points out that in the 1980s the number of households will increase from 63 to 97 million.

388. Lareau, M. "Interiors That 'C'est Moi.' " *Madison Avenue* 25 (September 1983): 36–41.

Argues that both manufacturers and retailers of home furnishings will have to dramatically alter their marketing and merchandising approaches to meet the demands of the baby-boom generation. A portrait of baby boomers as serious consumers reveals them to be better educated, less traditional, more eclectic, more demanding of value and product quality, and individualistic. Suggestions for furniture manufacturers and retailers are listed. Concludes that "there's no doubt that marketers will have to be highly sensitive to the needs of baby boomers."

389. Lex, Richard A. "Charting the Future of Real Estate Prices: Pick a Theory." *Real Estate Review* 11 (Fall 1981): 116–18.

Contends that trying to predict real estate prices is an extremely difficult task. Reviews fourteen theories briefly, at times showing humorously how the same theory can be interpreted as either optimistic or pessimistic. Includes a baby-boom theory that predicts a strong real estate market as the baby boomers reach the age where housing demand peaks. Reviews other theories, taking into account such elements as purchasing power, foreign investment, location, inflation, and economic indicators.

390. Litchfield, Randall. "Tracking the Baby Bulge." *Canadian Business* 51 (November 1978): 123–30.

Examines the impact of the baby-boom population on the Canadian economy, especially on patterns of consumption. Observes that the baby-boom population is so large that it will always influence demand and social values. Notes that the housing and construction market will soften as baby boomers complete their purchases of first homes. Predicts good markets for smaller homes, multiples, and row houses. Argues that insurance will have a strong market. Predicts trouble ahead for pension systems as the ratio of pensioners to the working population increases.

391. Lurie, David M. "Flexible Financing, Baby Boom to Revitalise Housing Industry." *Air Conditioning, Heating and Refrigeration News* 153 (May 25, 1981): 8.

Summarizes presentations made at the Construction Marketing Seminar sponsored by the Construction Products Manufacturers Council. Speakers emphasized importance of new types of mortgages and role of the baby boom in recovery of the housing industry in the 1980s. "Pent-up demand" for houses is detected and, consequently, it is predicted that "forty percent of those born between 1954 and 1964 will purchase homes in the 1980s. This represents 30 million units."

392. McCormick, Jay. "Chevy Splits Citation Target Audience." *Advertising Age* 52 (November 9, 1981): 10.

Discusses Chevrolet's new promotion campaign for the Chevy X-car Citation. Observes that the new marketing strategy will target the baby boomers. Points out that this group, which is the biggest buying segment, has now progressed beyond the youth market to the working world and demands such items as cars. Describes the promotional themes of "Working Women" and "Family Man" that are intended to attract this market.

393. MacFarlane, William. "Seay Takes Optimistic View of the 1980s." *National Underwriter: Life and Health Insurance Edition* 83 (September 29, 1979): 2.

Recounts the comments of William H. Seay, chairman of Southwestern Life, at the American United Life underwriting workshop. Notes that the decade of the seventies was demanding and a time of tremendous growth. Predicts the future of life insurance, indicating negative aspects like inflation and positive aspects like a growing market. In the next decade the baby boomers will enter the age bracket of thirty to forty-five and will constitute a huge market of potential insureds. Concludes that Americans are increasing their reliance on insurance and prefer private insurance companies.

394. Marion, Larry. "Detroit's New Earnings Visibility." *Financial World* 151 (September 15, 1982): 16–24.

Offers an optimistic appraisal of the automobile industry in the 1980s. Demographics alone point to a significant increase in car sales. Notes that the "baby boom generation is now around 30 years old and hitting its stride in disposable income." Large reductions in the manufacturer's break-even point will contribute to increased profits. Outlooks for the major auto companies are briefly reviewed.

395. Martin, Thomas J. "Demographics Help Determine Demand." *National Real Estate Investor* 25 (May 1983): 28.

Reviews the various factors affecting real estate and housing demand. Cites (1) growth in households; (2) maturing baby-boom population; (3) declining mortality rates; and (4) declining population mobility. The baby-boom population is entering middle age and is swelling the ranks of individuals with a strong demand for housing. Asserts that the baby-boom cohort frequently is part of a two-income household with strong demand for consumer items like travel, recreation, and retail goods.

396. "Maturing Baby Boom to Need Two Million Homes Each Year." *Burroughs Clearing House* 64 (February 1980): 6.

Points out that by 1990, 23.6 percent of the population will be in the prime home-buying age group—between thirty and forty-four years old. This increase from 18.4 percent in 1978 is directly related to the aging of the baby boom. The Chicago Title Insurance Company estimates that 2 million new or rehabilitated housing units will be needed each year until 1990 to meet the needs of the maturing baby boom. Notes that baby boomers still retain the dream of owning a single-family home.

397. Mooney, Sean. "Surviving the 20th Century: A Strategic Planning Guide." *Journal of Insurance* 44 (September/October 1983): 2–7.

Speculates what the property/casualty insurance industry will be like in the year 2000. Facts and figures from Plan 2000, a study conducted by the Insurance Information Institute, are summarized. The greatest impact on the insurance industry overall will be the aging of the baby-boom generation. Baby boomers will need insurance as they progress from apartments to single-family homes to retirement condominiums. In addition, the maturing baby boom may reduce losses and even lower crime rates. The outlook for the future is "relatively optimistic." Includes number bar graphs and charts.

398. "New Roles for Insurance." *Trusts and Estates* 121 (July 1982): 7–8.

> Consists of an interview with James B. Goodson, chairman of the American Council of Life Insurance. Discusses dramatic changes occurring in the life insurance industry. Covers topics such as IRAs, changing demographics, government regulation, and the specialization and diversification of the industry. Argues that the baby-boom generation will significantly affect the marketplace by introducing one million adults per year to the thirty-five-to-forty-four-year-old age group through the 1980s. Predicts that, although the baby boomers have been slow to purchase insurance, this is only a delay, not a cancellation, of interest.

399. Newitt, Jane. "The Future of Home Sweet Home." *American Demographics* 2 (November/December 1980): 17–19.

> Examines the future of the housing market and asks the question, How much housing demand will the baby boom generation produce, and how long will it last? Reports that over 4 million Americans will attain home-buying age annually until 1995, although housing demand may be tempered by high energy costs and interest in condominiums. Predicts strong housing market dominated by first-time buyers. Contends that the baby boomers will migrate to the Sunbelt but will also become urban dwellers and participate in the gentrification of poorer urban neighborhoods. Predicts that the subsequent baby bust will produce an oversupply of single-family units thirty years from now.

400. Ortner, Robert. "Homebuilding Sets Vigorous Pace; Future Depends on Interest Rates." *Business America* 6 (July 25, 1983): 8–9.

> Attributes the recovery in new home construction to the combination of lower interest rates and increased demand from members of the baby boom. Notes that the baby boom "began to fuel new housing demand in the late 1960s, and the demand is continuing in the 1980s." The overall future of housing will depend, however, on financial conditions and mortgage rates. Graphs are used to illustrate private housing prices and new one-family house sales and stocks for the period 1977 through 1983.

401. Parliment, Thomas J. "Regional Migration Will Shape Future Housing Demand." *Savings and Loan News* 103 (April 1982): 22–23.

> Discusses factors that affect future housing demand, with special emphasis on regional migration. Notes that the baby-boom generation

is reaching the thirties age group and is making basic decisions that shape housing demand, such as family size, marriage, and single living. Argues that although the baby boomers will affect household formation and constitute significant pent-up demand, it is net migration that may have greater impact. Identifies the greatest beneficiaries of migration as the South Atlantic, West South Central, Pacific, and Mountain States.

402. Paskowski, Marianne. "Home Design: Furnishings Industry Looks Toward Recovery as Baby Boomers Trade Up." *Madison Avenue* 24 (September 1982): 72–75.

Discusses the prospects for the home furnishings industry, particularly the baby boomers' market. Points out that baby boomers are now maturing and reaching age brackets where home is taking precedence over travel. Reports on industry surveys indicating that baby boomers are "trading up" from starter furniture to quality furniture. Cites a new advertising campaign from Ethan Allen that emphasizes traditional values of family and home. Cautions that current home-furnishing market is not strong and notes countertrends that could affect the market.

403. Piontek, Stephen. "Pinpointing Our Pressure Points." *National Underwriter: Property and Casualty Edition* 86 (June 4, 1982): 82–83.

Reports on the comments of Henry W. Osowski, an insurance consultant, presented at the annual conference of the Insurance Accounting and Statistical Association. Reviews key areas that are influencing the financial service industries. Particularly influential is the emergence of the "baby boom affluent." Predicts there will be 40 million individuals in this generation with assets of $400,000 or more and that these individuals will require significant financial service.

404. Polzin, Paul E. "Population Age Structure: An Update." *Montana Business Quarterly* 18 (Summer 1980): 14–17.

Discusses the impact of the baby-boom generation on housing and employment, with explicit attention to its effects on the state of Montana. Points out the usefulness of age structure analysis and notes that soon the population bulge will move into the thirty-five- and fifty-four-year-old age bracket. Observes that baby boomers are likely to produce another more modest boom as baby-boom women decide to have children. Argues that "no growth" policies of some communities are inappropriate reactions to young adult baby boomers.

405. "Pru Economist: Enormous Market Is Waiting." *National Underwriter: Life and Health Insurance Edition* 84 (September 17, 1980): 4.

> Analyzes the future life insurance market, based on the remarks of J. Robert Ferrari from Prudential. Argues that the future is bright because the large post-war baby-boom generation is nearing middle-age, when demand for insurance is great. Life insurance must adapt to the changing life-styles of this generation by taking into account (1) single-person households; (2) two-wage-earner families; and (3) one-parent and female-headed families. Reviews aspects related to government regulation and inflation.

406. "Questions for the Working Wife." *Managers Magazine* 53 (September 1978): 15–16.

> Provides guidance to the insurance agent on dealing with two-income families in which the wife is permanently employed. Many two-income families are only temporarily so because the wife at some point has a child and leaves the work force. Contends, however, that the insurance agent should expect to see more women permanently employed in the future. Attributes this to the post-war baby-boom women, some of which are now approaching forty and reestablishing their careers. Points out that permanent two-income families demonstrate an interest in savings and are good prospects for whole life insurance and IRAs.

407. Riedy, Mark J. "Housing Prices Will Continue to Soar If Supply Fails to Meet Demand." *Mortgage Banker* 39 (March 1979): 4.

> Reproduces the testimony of Dr. Mark Riedy before the Committee on Banking, Housing and Urban Affairs of the U.S. Senate. Discusses the future of the housing market and identifies four key areas that influence this market: (1) economic and demographic trends; (2) legislative and regulatory actions; (3) the business and interest cycle; and (4) social forces. Asserts that the baby-boom generation has reached maturity and will create a major demand for housing. A need for at least 2 million new units per year for the next decade is predicted. Reviews the effects of inflationary expectations, environmental and zoning regulations, FHA/VA mortgages, rent control, and tax-exempt revenue bonds for housing.

408. Rufolo, Anthony M. "What's Ahead for Housing Prices?" *Business Review* (Federal Reserve Bank of Philadelphia) (July/August 1980): 9–15.

> Contends that rising housing prices are not as "socially undesirable" as many experts claim. In fact, although prices rose rapidly in the

seventies, "the current relation of housing prices to income does not seem to be terribly out of line with historic trends." Housing has developed a dual purpose in the United States: shelter and investment. Inflation and tax breaks have greatly benefited home owners by increasing the value of their investments. In addition, the quality of housing has significantly increased.

409. Russell, Cheryl. "The Condo Craze." *American Demographics* 3 (March 1981): 42–44.

Studies the trend to convert apartments to condominiums and the underlying demographic forces that promote this trend. Asserts that the post-war baby boomers have stimulated condominium growth because of their size and desire to purchase a home. Notes that (1) the number of individuals between the home-buying ages of twenty-five to forty will increase by 10 million in the 1980s; (2) condominiums are affordable in a period of serious housing inflation; (3) most condo owners perceive their units as temporary dwellings; (4) almost 50 percent of the owners of converted condos are under age thirty-five; (5) 57 percent of condo owners are single; (6) condo purchasers are young, white, and affluent; and (7) the baby-boom generation will sustain condo purchases for some time.

410. "Says Housing Starts to Increase." *National Underwriter: Property and Casualty Insurance Edition* 87 (September 9, 1983): 61.

Reports on a presentation by Sean Mooney, vice president/economist of the Insurance Information Institute and principal author of the institute's Plan 2000. Problems affecting the economy, e.g., inflation, federal deficits, and entry of the baby boom into the work force, are briefly reviewed, and the economy of the eighties is compared to that of the seventies. Contends that a strong economy and an increase in housing starts "will clearly be good for the insurance industry." Opportunities exist for innovation and experimentation in the entire industry.

411. Scarpa, Ralph J. "Changing Demographics Bring Investment Opportunities." *American Demographics* 4 (January 1982): 26–29.

Focuses on future investment opportunities, particularly on investments that will be strong because the post-war baby-boom generation is entering into the twenty-five-to-forty-four-year age group. Notes that this group fosters significant household formation, creates families, stimulates housing, and possesses discretionary income to purchase consumer goods. Makes numerous investment recommendations: (1) children's goods, including from such companies as Binney and Smith, Hasbro, Stride Rite, Gerber, and Eastman Kodak; (2) do-it-yourself firms such as Black and Decker, and Stanley Works; (3) construction firms such as the Ryland Group; and (4) furniture and appliance manufacturers such as Whirlpool, Sony, and Zenith.

412. Schell, Schuyler. "Baby Boom II." *Mortgage Banker* 39 (August 1979): 46–55.

Reports on likely trends in the housing market. Concentrates on the baby-boom population, which has now reached age levels at which housing demand is great. Points out that not only current but future demand will exist because the baby boomers will have children. Baby boomers are now in prime childbearing years and their children will create another peak demand for housing around the year 2020. Notes that population projections are hazardous and discusses the three different projections provided by the Census Bureau. Tables are presented on annual births, households, housing starts, and projections for birthrates and infant mortality rates.

413. Sirmans, C.F., and James R. Webb. "Housing Demand: The Demographic Future." *Appraisal Journal* 47 (October 1979): 556–60.

Argues that population characteristics strongly influence the housing market and must be studied closely to accurately predict future housing demand. Five factors are identified: (1) age profile; (2) household formation; (3) fertility rate; (4) mortality rate; and (5) migration. Dramatic changes in housing demands are predicted as the baby boom matures. Real estate appraisers must be aware of these demographic trends when they attempt to estimate the future value of houses.

414. Skinner, Steven J. "Staying Alive: The Life Insurance Industry." *American Demographics* 2 (March 1980): 11–13.

Emphasizes that demographic trends have an immediate impact on the life insurance industry. As baby boomers mature, their need for life insurance and their financial ability to pay for it both dramatically increase. However, members of this generation are better educated, and, consequently, demand quality products at a fair price from insurance salesmen. A particularly neglected area is insurance for women. Other new markets, such as divorced or young singles, are identified. Graphs report annual life insurance payments by age, education, and family income.

415. Stein, John. "Mitsubishi Enters the Auto Market with Cunningham and Walsh." *Madison Avenue* 25 (February 1983): 86–88.

> Discusses the new marketing campaign being developed by Cunningham and Walsh for Mitsubishi. Notes that the campaign focuses on the "top end" of the car market and stresses high-tech, performance, aesthetics, and comfort. Reports that the theme will be "Achieve Mitsubishi," which is oriented to the personal aspirations and life-styles of the post-war baby boomers. Points out that the target audience is young and educated, with two incomes totaling about $40,000.

416. Sternlieb, George, and James W. Hughes. "The Coming Housing Bust." *American Demographics* 4 (November 1982): 32–33.

> Contends that optimistic predictions for housing demand in the 1980s may be wrong. Inflation and changes in household formations may have permanently affected home-buying patterns. Charts show that almost twice as many housing units were added in the seventies as in the sixties and that Americans continued to buy houses in the seventies despite their greatly increased average price. Concludes that the "great housing expectations of the 1980s have not been beset by a temporary malaise, but rather must be recast to much more modest dimensions."

417. Sternlieb, George, and James W. Hughes. "The Housing Locomotive (and the Demographic Caboose)." *American Demographics* 6 (March 1984): 22–27.

> Questions whether housing demand will increase significantly in the 1980s simply because there are more people in traditional house-buying age brackets. As the last cohorts of the baby boom enter the housing market, they will be adversely affected by high interest rates and inflated housing prices. Changes in household formation patterns will also affect the demand for housing in the eighties. The baby boom itself is "segmented" between those who became home owners in the late seventies and those looking to buy their first home in the eighties. Stresses that "marketers must consider household and housing forecasts in greater detail today than they have in the last decade."

418. Sternlieb, George, and James W. Hughes. "Inflationary America: The Housing Dilemma." *American Demographics* 2 (June 1980): 21–23.

> Discusses the plight of the baby-boom generation in trying to locate affordable housing in inflationary times. Notes that half the popula-

tion of the United States was born after 1950 and that this post-Depression generation saves money not by putting savings in productive investments but rather by purchasing homes. Argues that as a consequence, capital investments have lagged and productivity has declined, fostering inflation. Predicts that ultimately baby boomers will face scarce housing with poor locations and high prices. Asserts that this will lead to serious political dissatisfaction and declining standards of living.

419. Sternlieb, George, and James W. Hughes. "The Post-Shelter Society." *Public Interest* 57 (Fall 1979): 39–47.

Discusses how the concept of housing has changed since the 1950s. Observes that the housing industry is skeptical about the future even though demographics would predict a housing boom. The post-World War II baby boomers are entering the twenty-five-to-forty-four-year-old bracket, and this group is a primary consumer of housing. Analyzes the sources of fear that preclude optimism about the housing market, including (1) pessimism about the future in general; (2) inflationary pressures; and (3) zoning and environmental constraints. Argues that housing is now viewed as an investment rather than as a protection against the elements.

420. Sternlieb, George, and James W. Hughes. "Who's Buying Homes?" *American Demographics* 4 (December 1982): 24–27.

Acknowledges that the housing industry has suffered severe declines since 1978, and offers no guarantees that this will change in the near future. Typical home buyers in 1981 were "well-off married couples of the baby boom generation." Demographics of first-time and repeat buyers and the types of houses purchased are presented in tables and analyzed. A side-bar article considers "The Vanishing Pool of Potential Homebuyers." Observes that given the "sheer scale of the maturing baby boom generation, more modest homes will dominate the housing future."

421. Sumichrast, Michael. "The Housing Outlook." *American Demographics* 4 (January 1982): 15–17.

Discusses the outlook for a variety of housing in the 1980s. Points out that the baby-boom generation is now reaching the "family-forming stage" and will keep the housing market strong. Notes that baby-boomer families will be smaller and less traditional in their household formation, which will create demands for condominiums and cooperatives. Contends, however, that costs of materials and labor will continue to increase and that rising prices will stimulate a mobile home market. Predicts strongest market growth in California, Texas, Florida, Oregon, Washington, Wyoming, Nevada, and the Carolinas.

422. Thygerson, Kenneth J., and Thomas J. Parliment. "Changes in Life Styles Boost Housing Demand." *Savings and Loan News* 99 (October 1978): 43.

Analyzes briefly the recent trend toward increased home buying. Notes that post-war baby boomers are now entering the twenty-five-to-thirty-four-year-old age cohort and that this bracket represents prime home-buying age. Not only is this group large in number, but it is also comprised of many nontraditional households, which increases housing demand. Describes nontraditional households as involving single, separated, and divorced individuals. Includes tables on population size, types of households, and home-owning households.

423. Thygerson, Kenneth J., and Thomas J. Parliment. "Home Buyers and Lenders Outbid Other Borrowers." *Savings and Loan News* 100 (September 1979): 40–41.

Reports that despite record-high interest rates for home mortgages, mortgage borrowing has not declined significantly. Attributes this in part to the large number of new households that are being created by the baby-boom generation. Boomers have entered the twenty-five-to-forty-year age bracket, which is a prime group for home buying. Also notes the effects of regional migration, increased rates of return, and the lifting of fixed usury restrictions.

424. Treadway, Peter. "Opinion and Comment: The Housing Scapegoat." *Journal of Housing* 38 (June 1981): 306–12.

Argues that an adequate supply of credit for housing must be maintained to avoid a resumption of debilitating national inflation. In the 1980s "an unprecedented and much heralded surge in potential housing demand—and hence, housing credit—will result from the coming of age of the baby boom generation and the continuing trend to smaller households." Although credit must be readily available, lenders should no longer offer long-term fixed-rate mortgages.

425. Treadway, Peter. "Outlook for Housing and Mortgages: They'll Come Back." *ABA Banking Journal* 74 (May 1982): 102–7.

Argues that despite a bad year in 1981, the outlook for housing activity in the rest of the decade is strong, though not quite at the levels of the more optimistic forecasts of the last few years. Four demographic trends support this prediction: (1) growth in the population; (2) the baby boom; (3) females in the labor force; and (4) growth of senior citizens. The baby boom will be establishing households in the eighties, and this normally translates into a housing unit. Notes that "separation from their parents' households and setting up a separate household still lies in the future for a significant portion of persons born during the baby boom." One major concern is the "affordability problem" caused by high interest rates and inflation.

426. "Whatever Happened to the Baby Boom?" *Housing* 61 (March 1982): 68–69.

Questions whether the maturing baby boom will have a significant impact on the housing industry in the eighties, as predicted by many experts. Affordability remains the key, and many baby boomers will simply be unable to afford the traditional single-family house. Older baby boomers who purchased houses in the late seventies will similarly not be able or anxious to become "move-up buyers." Builders are advised to "focus on less-expensive housing—primarily infill, high-density housing." Regional variations will also affect any eventual upturn in housing sales.

427. Wright, Richard A. "Closing in on Performance." *Advertising Age* 54 (June 6, 1983): M-9.

Reports on a current marketing trend among some auto makers to emphasize performance over fuel economy and efficiency. Notes that Ford Motor Co. is currently selling its "Boss Mustang," Dodge its "Driving Machine," and Buick its "T-Types" on performance claims. Asserts that this marketing approach is based on its appeal to members of the baby-boom generation between the ages of twenty-four to thirty-five. Observes that baby boomers are well educated and innovative and want to "blow the doors off" other cars. Mentions also the similar marketing strategies of Cadillac, Pontiac, AMC, and Volkswagen.

6
Management Articles

428. Bell, Chip R. "Training and Development in the 1980s." *Personnel Administrator* 25 (August 1980): 23.

> Analyzes potential changes in managerial training and development in the decade of the eighties. Points out that the baby-boom generation is now entering the "early" middle-aged category and that the average age of the worker will rise from twenty-eight to forty by 1990. Trainers will have to adapt to this maturing work force by placing emphasis on practical and immediate application. Stresses that this older work force places greater emphasis on leisure and that training will be done in conference centers where leisure activities are available. Examines the changing work attitudes of the labor force and notes that job satisfaction and enrichment will be a major concern. Managers will have to be regularly trained in "participative leadership, conflict resolution, interpersonal communications and matrix task force management." Explores also the growth of technology in training.

429. Califano, Joseph A., Jr. "Critical Pension Policy Issues." *Journal of Pension Planning and Compliance* 4 (September 1978): 409–15.

> Observes that with advances in medicine, the American population is aging and becoming a four-generation society. Analyzes the effect of the aging population on federal pension policy. Notes that there are four key trends: (1) life expectancy has increased; (2) people are retiring earlier; (3) the ratio of active to retired workers will continue to decline; and (4) the post-war baby-boom generation will become a "senior boom" by the year 2010. By 2030, 18 percent of the U.S. population will be 65 or older. Argues that because of the dramatic effect these trends will have on services to the elderly, the society must reconsider what is meant by "old age" and "retirement." Contends that a restructuring of Social Security is essential.

430. Chernoff, Joel. "Defined Benefit Plan Growth May Have Peaked." *Pensions and Investment Age* 10 (June 7, 1982): 50.

> Recounts the views of various speakers at a conference sponsored by the Employee Benefit Research Institute. Factors relating to the slowed growth in private defined-benefit plans are analyzed, but all agree that "rumors of the death of defined benefit pension plans are greatly exaggerated." Thomas H. Paine, a partner at Hewitt Associates, warns of the consequences of the inevitable retirement of the baby-boom generation in the twenty-first century. He concludes that the sooner planners "come to grips with the retirement crisis coming after 2010, the more likely that defined contribution plans will be encouraged."

431. "Climb Up the Corporate Ladder to Get Tougher." *Industry Week* 218 (October 4, 1982): 14.

> Reports the prediction of Paul Voss, demographer at the Applied Population Laboratory, University of Wisconsin, that competition for fewer management positions in the 1980s and 1990s will be extremely tough. The aging of the baby boom and the impact of significant numbers of women in the work force are noted as causes of this competition.

432. Dawson, Christopher M. "Will Career Plateauing Become a Bigger Problem?" *Personnel Journal* 62 (January 1983): 78–81.

> Observes that as the baby-boom workers enter the management structure, many will be plateaued earlier than in the past. Warns that this could lead to decreased morale, lower productivity, and high turnover. Distinguishes between plateauing of the job content and plateauing of the structural or organizational type. Notes that employees who grew up in the sixties and seventies have expectations that education and hard work will automatically lead to success. Recommends not only traditional responses to treat the symptoms, but also innovations in the hiring process so as to locate individuals who get satisfaction from things other than promotion. Recommends also organizational redesign, when appropriate, for handling structural plateauing.

433. Dunn, Brian D. "Baby-Boom Bankers Must be Nurtured." *ABA Banking Journal* 76 (June 1984): 71–72.

> Advocates the use of various career development programs and increased compensation to retain key middle-management executives in the banking industry. Notes that executives in the baby-boom generation are "traveling a congested—and therefore slow—route to senior management ranks." Career development alternatives discussed in-

clude (1) lateral training; (2) in-house education; (3) formal education; (4) team projects; (5) on-leave assignments; and (6) sabbaticals. Ways to overcome reluctance to participate in such programs are briefly noted.

434. Evans, Robert C. "The Vanishing Middle Manager." *Canadian Business* 54 (December 1981): 106–8.

Discusses the current lack of middle managers in Canadian businesses. A serious shortage of employees to promote to executive positions is documented. The solution lies in the maturing baby boom. Notes that the "baby boom generation is the talent pool for the future. If we understand it and use it well, we will survive and prosper." However, these new employees and potential middle managers will require different styles of recruitment and personnel management. Recommends that personnel executives be given more status in companies.

435. Feinberg, Samuel. "Baby Boom Bottleneck: Job Shortage." *Womens Wear Daily* 144 (July 21, 1982): 8.

Considers the current problems facing middle management as competition for these positions grows. Points out that the baby-boom generation produced 76 million people in a period of eighteen years and that these baby boomers are now reaching the ages when they expect to move into middle management. Argues that there will not be enough positions open, which will result in career frustration for many. Cites the views of J. Alan Ofner, who compares the traditional work environment to the highly competitive one about to emerge. Notes that employees may retire later or move to other positions. Concludes that human resources management will be essential.

436. Fombrun, Charles. "Environmental Trends Create New Pressures on Human Resources." *Journal of Business Strategy* 3 (Summer 1982): 61–69.

Describes how various environmental changes will dramatically affect corporate and personal success in the future. Four components of change are identified: (1) technological; (2) economic; (3) social; and (4) political. Both demographic and attitudinal changes among members of the baby boom as they enter the work force are especially significant. Notes that "understanding the characteristics of the baby boom can help predict the nature of the labor market through the 1980s." Three solutions are proposed to the human resource problems facing the country in the 1980s: (1) reindustrialization; (2) improved quality of work life; and (3) industrial democracy in action.

437. Friend, William. "Managing the Baby Boom Managers." *Association Management* 33 (August 1981): 58–62.

> Considers the impact of the "baby boom managers" in all types of organizations in the 1980s. Characteristics of this new breed of manager are described. Concludes that participatory management is "inevitable" and unionization of managers very likely. Professional associations will also be greatly affected by the maturing baby boom. Five suggestions are presented for association leaders: (1) reconsider training opportunities; (2) learn new management techniques; (3) evaluate promotion policies; (4) consider flexible work schedules; and (5) gives more responsibility to younger people.

438. Harvey, Edward B. "Managerial Manpower—Surpluses and Shortages." *Business Quarterly* 42 (Spring 1977): 52–58.

> Discusses the effects of the "travelling bulge" of the baby boom will have on supply and demand for middle managers in Canada. The baby boom caused educational expansion as it grew up, but, as it entered the labor force, it faced an abundance of young executives. Personnel officers must deal with the potential problems this shift from supply to demand will cause. Concludes that a "knowledge of demographic trends and their implications is indispensable to the modern business corporation."

439. Hayes, James L. "Management: Hiring Strategies for the 1980's." *Coal Mining and Processing* 19 (January 1982): 108.

> Addresses the problems involved in attracting, hiring, and retaining middle managers. Workers in the 1980s are better educated, less permanent, and skeptical about their ultimate future. In addition, the baby-bust generation has "cut the growth rate of this decade's work force in half." Employers are urged to consider internal promotions from the large number of baby-boom managers already with the company. Notes that these baby boomers are "people in their thirties and forties who have the experience, maturity, and desire to work hard at a challenging job, if it is offered to them. Employers are also advised to consider offering dual-career ladders, flex-time, and early retirement.

440. Henderson, Richard I. "Designing a Reward System for Today's Employee." *Business* 32 (July/September 1982): 2–12.

> Describes the variety of rewards organizations offer to employees. Two major classifications (compensation and noncompensation rewards) are analyzed in detail. Suggestions are given as to what "em-

ployers and reward system designers can do to 'turn on' their baby-boom employees." In terms of compensation, baby boomers are attracted to flexible benefits and financial counseling. Job redesign and participatory management can be significant noncompensation rewards.

441. Howard, Ann, and James A. Wilson. "Leadership in a Declining Work Ethic." *California Management Review* 24 (Summer 1982): 33–46.

Warns that baby boomers may be poorly suited to working as managers in large, traditional, hierarchical organizations. Data from longitudinal studies of managers by the American Telephone and Telegraph Company are studied and found to support the view that "a dispirited new generation of managers, unsure of future direction, wants primarily an interesting job and emotional sustenance from peers, with no heavy commitment to the organization." To adapt to this new generation of managers, companies may have to revise traditional reward methods, recruit differently, and offer a variety of early career experiences. Concludes that "the boom generation, in an existential crisis with no clear alternatives, is still plagued by uncertainty about what it should be or become."

442. Larack, Seymour. "Views." *Employee Benefit Plan Review* 35 (December 1980): 5–6.

Editorializes that the demographic shifts caused by the maturing of the baby boom "provide an opportunity to experiment with new forms of benefits." Benefit programs must become more flexible to accommodate the demands of this generation of workers. One complication is that the baby boom "will create three candidates—and women—for every top-level job being vacated. Second careers will be the choice of many of the disappointed aspirants."

443. LaViolette, Suzanne. "Hospitals Try to Relieve Frustration of Their Baby-Boom Era Managers." *Modern Health Care* 13 (February 1983): 70.

Reports on the problems of baby-boom managers in the health-care field as they seek promotions into middle management. Points out that the competition is so great that a manager may have to wait three to five years for an opportunity. Notes that the problematical job market leads to frustration and demoralization at work. Cites as a case study Intermountain Health Care, Inc., in Salt Lake City. Argues that managers may have to take specialist positions in finance, marketing, or planning. Contends that more strategic planning will probably result as employers try to find challenges for trapped managers.

444. Lee, Chris. "Identifying and Developing the Next Generation of Managers." *Training* 18 (October 1981): 36–39.

Observes that until recently individuals looking for high-level promotions were in short supply because of the low birthrates of the thirties, forties, and fifties. Argues that the baby boom has reversed this condition and produced a large group of people competing for relatively few promotions. This has placed a special burden on management to provide management development programs for its employees. Reviews the key elements in such a program and cites approaches used by General Electric, General Motors, Martin Marietta, and Schering-Plough Corporation.

445. LeRoux, Margaret. "Companies Trying to Head Off Pension Problems Down Road." *Business Insurance* 16 (June 7, 1982): 22.

Points out that many companies are already attempting to deal with pension problems that will intensify still more when the baby boom reaches retirement age. Examples are given of companies that have taken steps to ensure adequate benefits for current and retired employees. Eastman Kodak is cited as an example of companies that offer a salary reduction, or 401(k) Plan. The importance of IRAs is also noted. Stresses that "as the baby-boom generation grows older, both government and industry pension responsibilities are likely to increase."

446. Long, Jeffrey E. "The Office of 1990: Management." *Management World* 11 (January 1982): 2–8.

Observes that as our society enters the "Information Age," the work place, particularly the office, will undergo a significant transformation. Argues that two major forces are at work: automation and changes in labor force composition. Notes that the baby boomers will be entering the thirty-to-forty-year-old age bracket by 1990 and will create tremendous competition for management positions. Contends that at the same time a constant influx of women into the labor force will exert pressure to change the office environment. Predicts that emphasis on clerical workers in offices will encourage unionization as well.

447. McCroskey, Jacquelyn. "Work and Families: What Is the Employer's Responsibility?" *Personnel Journal* 61 (January 1982): 30–38.

Examines corporate responses to employee demands for family-oriented services and benefits. Observes that the American family has changed significantly in the following ways: (1) a smaller number of extended families; (2) increase in single-parent families; and (3) more women working outside the home. The baby-boom generation in the labor force also has greater expectations for its work and a stronger inclination to "balance" work and the needs of the family. Discusses the steps toward developing a family-oriented program and specifically reviews such areas as referral programs, flexible schedules, child care, flexible benefits, and employee assistance programs. Mentions programs at TRW in California and First Interstate Bank in Los Angeles.

448. Magnus, Margaret. "Trends and Issues in Personnel Managemen: Demographic Changes." *Personnel Journal* 62 (March 1983): 238.

Recounts the content of a speech by Dr. Peter Morrison of the Rand Corporation on demographic factors affecting personnel practices. Notes that there will be significant variation in the age profiles and participation in the work force primarily due to the baby boom and subsequent baby bust. The baby bust will produce a decline in entry-level workers, while the baby boom will produce congestion at middle-management levels.

449. Mauro, Tony. "Age Bias Charges: Increasing Problem." *Nation's Business*, April 1983, pp. 44–46.

Reports on the increasing number of age-bias suits being filed under the Age Discrimination in Employment Act of 1967. Points out the likelihood of more such suits as the baby-boom generation ages and expects to receive middle-management promotions. Makes numerous recommendations to protect against age-discrimination suits, including programs that would prepare for the baby-boom pressures soon to come, such as "phased retirement, part-time work, early retirement plans, retraining opportunities and preretirement planning programs."

450. Metz, Edmund J. "Job Security: The Quality of Worklife Issue." *Managerial Planning* 31 (October 1982): 4–9.

Considers attempts by industries to respond to workers' concern for their quality of work life (QWL). Notes that attitudes of the American worker have changed significantly in the past decade. Some areas receiving attention are (1) the need for more leisure activity; (2) greater demand for freedom of choice in careers; (3) more hostility to business and industry; and (4) greater need to plan one's own future and to be treated with dignity. Businessmen have not recognized the effects of the post-war baby boom and its subsequent baby bust on organizations. Recommends that businesses look into "alternative work options" such as restrictive emloyment contracts, part-time work schedules, and flex-time. Proposes that such options may be more effective than casual layoffs that threaten job security.

451. Metz, Edmund J. "The Missing 'H' in Strategic Planning." *Managerial Planning* 32 (May/June 1984): 19–23.

Contends that many organizations neglect the human resources dimension as they engage in corporate strategic planning. Identifies long-term issues that will affect personnel planning within a company. Cites the aging of the baby boom as a key issue for the following reasons: (1) baby boomers are healthier and live longer, which will affect both retirement programs and the ability of younger workers to get promotions; (2) baby boomers have different expectations of the work place and demand more flexible work policies, along with participation in decision-making; (3) baby boomers were followed by a baby bust, which will shrink entry-level positions and increase salary costs; and (4) in the rapidly changing work environment, companies will be forced to develop retraining programs to keep the baby boomers up-to-date. Emphasizes that companies will need to adopt the concept of "Life Long Learning" for their personnel.

452. Mobley, William H. "Some Unanswered Questions in Turnover and Withdrawal Research." *Academy of Management Review* 7 (January 1982): 111–16.

Reviews earlier research in employee turnover and outlines possible negative and positive consequences of such turnover. The relationship between "withdrawal" work behavior and eventual turnover is also analyzed. Research in all aspects of the turnover process is urgently required because of the entry of the baby boom into the work force. Concludes that "with the expansion of mandatory retirement, longer life expectancies, and the aging of the baby boom cohort, promotional and career advancement opportunities may be limited for this age group."

453. Murray, Thomas J. "The Coming Glut in Executives." *Dun's Review* 109 109 (May 1977): 64–65.

Warns that the maturing of the baby boom will cause a "glut of corporate executives." This situation is labeled "potentially explosive" because severe morale problems may result among the unpromoted middle managers. The entry of women and minority individuals into the pool of potential managers complicates this problem. Management experts urge immediate action to create new jobs that will absorb the educated middle managers of the baby-boom generation.

454. Niehouse, Oliver L. "Breaking the Promotion Barrier with Flexible Leadership." *Business* 32 (October/November/December 1982): 22–26.

Advises middle managers to develop a style of "flexible leadership" to ensure their advancement to top management positions. Delayed retirements and the entry of the baby-boom generation into middle-management levels will make promotion very difficult in the future. Characteristics of flexible leadership are discussed in detail and typical examples are used as illustrations.

455. Nkomo, Stella M. "Stage Three in Personnel Administration: Strategic Human Resources Management." *Personnel* 57 (July/August 1980): 69–77.

Reviews the evolution of the personnel function in business and industry. Notes that there have been three stages: (1) defensive stage, in which personnel was a minor function concerned with record-keeping and organizational maintenance; (2) derived-demand stage, in which the purpose of personnel was to predict manpower needs and control labor costs; and (3) strategic model, in which personnel is involved in strategic planning to ensure that "decisions regarding the use of people contribute to the achievement of organizational objectives." Argues that this last stage is necessary because of factors such as governmental regulations, stagnating productivity, and social and demographic trends. Points out that the post-World War II baby-boom generation has produced highly educated men and women who are competing for a small number of supervisory positions. The baby boomers will force personnel departments to consider such issues as career pathing, job design, performance evaluation, and retirement counseling, as well as participative management and job enrichment.

456. Patton, Arch. "The Coming Promotion Slowdown." *Harvard Business Review* 59 (March/April 1981): 46–52.

Warns that inflation and the aging of the baby boom in the 1980s will cause extremely serious personnel problems. Continued inflation will slow early retirement and lower the executive promotion rate at the same time that larger numbers of baby boomers begin competing for middle-management positions. How companies respond to these changes in advancement opportunities will greatly affect their overall success. Notes that the "arithmetic of inflation plus demography has been given far less attention than it deserves."

457. Polczynski, James J. "Building a Foundation of Power." *Supervisory Management* 27 (October 1982): 36–39.

Points out that the 1980s will be a particularly challenging period for front-line managers. This is true because the full impact of the baby boomers will enter the labor market and will compete for jobs. Asserts that these baby boomers will be better educated and fiercely competitive. Advises front-line managers to (1) be very observant in work environment, especially regarding loyalties; (2) maintain quality control; (3) avoid paperwork controlled by middle management; (4) permit others to share manager's power, and (5) behave like a middle manager.

458. Rodriguez, Robert A. "How to Judge Your Day Care Options." *Personnel Administrator* 28 (August 1983): 41–44.

Compares the advantages and disadvantages of employer-assisted child care. Demand for daytime care for children will increase dramatically as the children of the baby-boom generation begin "to have their own babies, which will greatly increase the number of preschool children over the next 10 years." Three other "seemingly inexorable forces" are involved: (1) inflation; (2) divorce; and (3) the women's movement. Personnel directors are urged to consider the following alternative ways to support child care: (1) information option; (2) referral option; (3) reduced rate; (4) company subsidy; (5) voucher system; and (6) on-site facility.

459. Rosow, Jerome M. "The Coming Management Population Explosion." *Advanced Management Journal* 44 (Fall 1979): 4–16.

Asserts that by the mid-1980s the baby-boom generation will have transformed itself from "an educational bottleneck to a middle-management and professional-personnel bottleneck." Factors that will create this "middle-age bulge" include (1) national and organizational demographics; (2) increased life expectancy and the extension of working life; (3) career span; (4) early retirement trends; (5) the Equal Employment Opportunity agenda; and (6) increased educational qualifications and occupational expectations. Companies can lessen the impact of this managerial bottleneck by instituting responsive programs such as educational sabbaticals, retraining, job redesign, and new incentive systems.

460. Saikowski, Charlotte. "Reagan Aims to Win Over 'Baby Boomers.'" *Christian Science Monitor*, 8 June 1984, p. 1.

Reports on the Republican strategies being designed to attract baby boomers to Ronald Reagan. Points out that 100 million baby boomers between eighteen and thirty-nine are eligible to vote. Notes also that the campaign strategists have determined that the baby boomers who voted for Gary Hart may not vote for Mondale. Cautions that baby boomers are not yet dependable voters but in general are economically conservative and socially liberal. Asserts that the Reagan campaign will therefore emphasize his economic record and play down social issues.

461. Shapiro, Kenneth P. "Age Discrimination—Final Regulations." *Journal of Pension Planning and Compliance* 5 (July 1979): 350–53.

Focuses on the amendments to the Age Discrimination in Employment Act passed in 1978 and the final regulations issued by the U.S. Department of Labor based on these amendments. Discusses such issues as benefit accrual and benefit calculation for individuals working beyond the normal retirement age; regulations for supplemental and nonsupplemental plans; and special exceptions for executives. Many factors will affect future enforcement and interpretation, including the aging of the baby-boom population, which will eventually become a "retirement boom" and create a shift from early to late retirement due to lack of replacement workers.

462. Shapiro, Kenneth P. "Baby Boom to Cause 'Promotion Squeeze.'" *Business Insurance* 16 (March 8, 1982): 32.

Suggests that the maturing of the baby boom will cause a "promotion squeeze." The number of workers in the twenty-five-to-forty-four age group will increase by one-third in the 1980s. This group of baby boomers "not only will slow the upward management flow, but potentially disrupt it as well." Three solutions to this promotion squeeze are briefly discussed: (1) total remuneration; (2) motivation; and (3) planning.

463. Shapiro, Kenneth P. "Managing the Impending Promotion Squeeze." *Personnel Journal* 60 (October 1981): 800–804.

Reviews the impact of the baby-boom generation on competition for management positions. Points out that although the total labor force will shrink, baby boomers between the ages of twenty-five and forty-four will increase by 33 percent. As competition for promotions increases, so does the potential for "burn-out" and frustration. Argues that a wide-ranging approach is required, encompassing such issues as remuneration, motivation, planning, training and retraining, and accurate selection and assessment. Recommends merit raises, long-term incentives, flexible benefits, mentoring, job enlargement, and nonlinear work patterns.

464. "Trainers Told to Placate Baby Boomers and Stir Excitement." *Savings Institutions* 104 (November 1983): 128–29.

Reports on the remarks made by Cecelia Burokas, senior vice president at Talman Home Federal, Chicago, as she spoke to the Institute of Financial Education Human Resources Development Conference. Argues that trainers face new challenges in dealing with the baby-boom generation as it moves into middle-management age groups. Points out that by 1990, the number of people between thirty-five and forty-four will increase by 42 percent, but middle management positions will increase by only 19 percent. Asserts that the short supply of positions should lead organizations to develop innovative programs, including participative management, team building, quality circles, bonuses, and stock options.

465. "Training Evolves to Meet the Needs of Organizational America." *Training* 19 (October 1982): 56.

Discusses how training in various industries has evolved. Points out that the baby boom/bust cycle has significantly affected manpower supply, which in turn has had a serious impact on organizational training. Makes numerous observations on the impact of demographic factors, such as: (1) individuals under age thirty-five comprise almost one-half of the U.S. labor market; (2) previous U.S. Bureau of Labor Statistics forecasts were inaccurate and underestimated the impact of the baby boom; (3) the baby bust of the sixties will create better opportunities for those born in this period; (4) baby boomers will experience crowding for promotions along with low relative income; and (5) participation by women in the work force will continue to increase. Reviews also the effect of government regulations and new technologies on training.

466. Tyler, Richard F. "Motivate the Older Employee." *Personnel Journal* 63 (February 1984): 60–61.

Enumerates various "motivational prescriptions" a young manager can use to direct the activities of older subordinates. This is a major problem and will become even more serious because the American work force is dramatically aging. This new phenomenon is attributed to "the end of the baby boom, extensions of the mandatory retirement age, and increases in life expectancy."

467. Waddell, William C. "Management Viewpoint: Organization for the Eighties." *Business Forum* 4 (Spring 1976): 26.

Asserts that all companies in the 1980s must develop new methods to improve "productivity as well as the quality of working life." Baby boomers will paradoxically fuel demands for goods and services as they mature, while becoming increasingly dissatisfied workers. New management techniques, such as task teams, quality circles, and matrix organizations, are briefly explained.

468. Waddell, William C. "Organization for the Eighties." *Los Angeles Business and Economics* 4 (Spring 1979): 26.

Warns that all companies and organizations must adopt radically new ways of organizing work and workers. The inability of the traditional work force to absorb the large number of impatient, highly educated baby-boom workers may lead to "massive apathy and tumult in the eighties." Companies must take steps to increase participation of all workers in decision-making. Japan's use of quality circles is cited as a possible approach. Concludes that "any company that is not now looking at new ways of organizing work and people can expect a deterioration of morale and slow or no growth in productivity."

469. Walker, Alfred J. "Management Selection Systems That Meet the Challenges of the '80s." *Personnel Journal* 60 (October 1981): 775–80.

Asserts that Human Resource Inventories (HRI) are making a comeback in determining the skills of managers. Contends that this is partly the result of improved technology. The baby boom will increase the number of people between twenty-five and forty-four by one-third, and this is a primary age group for management jobs and promotions. Argues that HRIs will be useful not only for job-matching but for career counseling and human resource planning.

470. Wallace, Anise. "Why the New Demographics Will Raise Pension Costs." *Institutional Investor* 16 (July 1982): 105–10.

Warns that "there's bad news for pension officers in the latest demographic trend." The aging of the work force will impact significantly on employee benefit plans. Early retirement plans may be used at the beginning of the 1980s to create middle-management positions for the larger baby-boom generation. More significantly, long-range planning must be done to ensure the economic viability of benefit plans when the baby boomers begin to reach retirement age in the next century. The desire for "cafeteria" benefit plans by many workers and the effect of increased numbers of women in the work force are also analyzed.

471. Weiner, Edith, and Arnold Brown. "1950s Baby Boom Echoes in the 1980s." *Association Management* 35 (May 1983): 171.

Depicts impact of the baby boomlet of births by baby-boom women on associations that deal with child-care products and services. This boomlet is judged to be a "low order" boom and, consequently, will have the largest impact on family spending. Although benefits to certain industries are obvious, potentially negative aspects of this increase in fertility are briefly noted.

472. Wilcox, John L. "Employee Attitudes in the Eighties." *Journal of Retail Banking* 2 (December 1980): 1–9.

Analyzes the impact of the baby-boom generation, with emphasis on management of baby-boom employees. Notes that two basic problems arose as the baby boom aged: massive spending in education in the 1950s and 1960s, and high unemployment as the baby boomers entered the work force. Predicts two future problems: a 35 percent increase in the labor market by 1990, and severe strain on pension plans and the Social Security system as baby boomers reach retirement age. Baby boomers have different values, having grown up in unbroken prosperity, and their expectations for advancement are high. Notes, however, that the flooded labor market works against baby boomers. Identifies three key aspects of baby-boomer values: (1) social concern; (2) social disintegration; and (3) self-orientation, and applies them to management strategies for the eighties. Argues that "participative" management, "effective leadership," and "meaningful work" will be essential.

473. Wolf, James F. "Career Plateauing in the Public Service: Baby Boom and Employment Bust." *Public Administration Review* 43 (March/April 1983): 160–65.

Examines some of the impacts on public employment as the baby-boom generation takes entry-level or middle-management positions in public services. Notes that between 1955 and 1980, government jobs expanded significantly and increased in status. This created high expectations in baby boomers just as government jobs began to shrink in the 1980s. As increased numbers of workers compete for smaller numbers of jobs, there will be career plateauing. Argues that organizations must plan for the plateauing phenomenon. Points out that this can be handled in three ways: (1) expand promotional opportunities; (2) assist employees in leaving the organization; and (3) provide for personal growth within the organization by nonpromotional means.

474. Yovovich, B.G. "Job Hunting: Baby Boomers Battle Mid-Level Bulge." *Advertising Age* 53 (January 4, 1982): S-1.

Discusses the competition for middle-level positions among the baby boomers. Notes that by 1990 the labor force may shrink by as much as

10 percent, but that the population between the ages of twenty-five and forty-four will increase by one-third. Predicts significant modifications to a company's fringe benefits, personnel policies, and organizational structures. Projects changes that include (1) increased disenchantment as promotions slow; (2) increased lateral movement to varying responsibilities; (3) increased potential for burnout; (4) placement of overeducated people in inappropriate jobs; and (5) proliferation of small businesses, especially in computer software industries. Concludes that the future is unpredictable. Includes charts contrasting the baby-boom and Depression cohorts by age.

475. Zemke, Ron. "To Train Baby Boom Managers, Learn What Makes Them Tick." *Training* 17 (December 1980): 36–40.

Warns management that members of the baby-boom generation are now entering the labor market and seeking upward movement in their organizations. Makes the observations that by 1990 (1) there will be twice as many managers as organizations will need; (2) people between the ages of twenty and thirty-four will hold 88 percent of the management positions; (3) young managers will have high expectations; (4) frustration of being unable to rise further will lead middle managers to build "mid-level power principalities and fiefdoms"; and (5) managerial unions will develop to protect older managers from competition of young aspirants for management positions.

7
Education, Psychology, and Sociology Articles

476. Adams, Melissa M.; Godfrey P. Oakley, Jr.; and James S. Marks. "Maternal Age and Births in the 1980s." *Journal of the American Medical Association* 247 (January 22–29, 1982): 493–94.

Cites U.S. Census Bureau projections that analyze how changes in the maternal age distribution of births will affect pregnancy-related problems. A substantial increase in prenatal chromosomal diagnosis (amniocentesis) is predicted, based on the expected 37 percent increase in births to women over twenty-five years old between 1980 and 1990. Tables include (1) Projections of Maternal Age-Specific Fertility Rates and Total Fertility Rates, United States, 1980–1990, and (2) Estimated Births by Maternal Age and Total Births, United States, 1980–1990. A decreased demand for prenatal care for teenagers is also projected. A graph showing total fertility rates for American women is used to demonstrate the effect of the baby-boom generation.

477. Anderson, Polly. "College Enrollment Decline." *Illinois Issues* 4 (February 1978): 15–17.

Details effect of decline in number of eighteen-to-twenty-one-year-olds on higher education in Illinois. The end of the baby boom will significantly alter enrollment figures in the 1980s. Factors other than demographics that also influence enrollment levels are summarized. However, the conclusion is inescapable: "The end of the baby boom in the early 1960s means a drop in the college-age population in the 1980s." Three solutions to the enrollment problem are analyzed: (1) increase the number of nontraditional students; (2) use the decline to improve the overall quality of education; and (3) allow weak programs to be eliminated. Concludes that the best solution will offer a compromise among these three alternatives.

478. Bakan, David. "Youth, the Future and Liberal Education." *Liberal Education* 58 (March 1972): 189–98.

> Recognizes the paradoxes involved in recommending a liberal arts education, which is frequently regarded both as nonvocational and as appropriate preparation for many professions. In addition, a liberal education often produces critics of society and contemporary institutions. These factors in the 1960s were dramatically affected by "a huge growth of young adults in the population, bringing with it both a huge enlargement of needs and an unusually well-educated adult labor supply. Simultaneously there has been a flagging of corporate performance." Asserts that attempts to minimize the value of a liberal arts education must be fought.

479. "Blame Baby Boom for Drop in School Aptitude Scores." *Family Planning Perspectives* 8 (July/August 1976): 181–83.

> Reports the conclusions of R.B. Zajonc, a University of Michigan psychologist (see no. 555), that the baby boom is directly responsible for decline in scores on a variety of standardized scholastic aptitude and intelligence tests. Specifically, he claims "the root of the problem is the runaway birthrate of the 1950s, during which time too many children born too close together diluted the beneficent effect of adults and older siblings, cheating those in the higher birth orders of their time in the sun of adult intelligence." Test results from other countries are used to test the validity of the theory. A table presents mean scores of the National Merit Scholarship Qualification Test, by family size and birth order, for 1965.

480. Blumenstein, Alfred C.; Jacqueline Cohen; and Harold D. Miller. "Crime, Punishment, and Demographics." *American Demographics* 2 (October 1980): 32–37.

> Studies ways in which demographic character of U.S. population influences prison population. Notes that baby boomers reached peak age for criminal activity in the 1960s and 1970s, and that predictions indicate crime should decrease in the 1980s. Points out, however, that the age bracket in which criminals are sent to prison is later than the age for most criminal activity. Concludes that the size of prison population and current overcrowding will continue for some time. Makes predictions concerning various aspects of the criminal justice system, including number of arrests, racial makeup of future prison populations, and number of commitments to prison.

481. Bouvier, Leon Francis. "America's Baby Boom Generation: The Fateful Bulge." *Population Bulletin* 35 (April 1980): 3–35.

Provides an in-depth discussion of the baby-boom generation and its effects on society. Covers such topics as (1) what the baby boom was and when it occurred; (2) reason for the baby boom; (3) demographic effects; (4) impact of the baby boomers on themselves; (5) social problems created by the boom; and (6) future prospects. Includes discussions of the baby boomers' effects on education, household formation, labor force, political institutions, and Social Security. Tables and charts on fertility rates, baby-boom cohort as it moves through the population by age and sex, school-age population projections, households, and voting-age population are included, as is an extensive bibliography.

482. Brown, Barbara I. "Baby Boom Generation Now Mirrors the Values and Attitudes of Its Elders." *Marketing News* 18 (April 13, 1984): 9.

Reports on a survey conducted by Monroe Mendelsohn for *People* magazine on the values of the baby-boom generation. Findings demonstrate that (1) family relationships play a strong role in baby-boomer values; (2) the work ethic is stronger in baby boomers than in previous generations; (3) baby boomers feel there is too much governmental regulation and that people have lost faith in their government; and (4) baby boomers feel there is too much emphasis on sex and on sexual issues. Concludes that overall the basic values of the baby boomers are the same as those of their parents.

483. Brown, Barbara I. "How The Baby Boom Lives." *American Demographics* 6 (May 1984): 34–37.

Reports on findings of a survey conducted by Monroe Mendelsohn Research for *People* magazine on the leisure-time activities of baby boomers, including the following: (1) major physical activities of baby boomers are swimming, dancing, camping, baseball and softball, jogging, bicycling, and calisthenics; (2) the more the individual takes part in physical activity, the less likely it is that he or she is married; (3) 66 percent of baby boomers go to movies; and (4) 91 percent go to parties or social gatherings. Observes that baby boomers partake of leisure activies significantly more than other generations. Also examines the listening and viewing habits of baby boomers. Includes tables on leisure activities.

484. "A Busted Baby Boom Teaches School Builders New Tricks." *Building Design and Construction* 14 (September 1973): 46–48.

Acknowledges that demand for new school buildings is down dramatically, but contends that architects and builders who specialize in conversions, renovations, and flexible designs will readily find work.

Examples are given of school building projects that emphasize "maximum flexibility." School buildings must be designed so that they can easily be rearranged for outside organizations or other levels of education. Schools that can also serve as "human resource centers" will be required as the baby boom gradually ages and retires.

485. Butler, Robert N. "A Generation at Risk: When the Baby Boomers Reach Golden Pond." *Across the Board* 20 (July/August 1983): 37–45.

Labels baby boomers a "generation at risk" because of the problems that will be caused by their retirement and aging in the early decades of the next century. Expanded average life expectancy will combine with the aging of the baby boom to significantly "stress our institutions." It may be necessary to extend the adult work span. Further research in geriatrics is urgently needed. A brief description is given of the first medical-school department of geriatrics established in 1982 at the Mount Sinai Medical Center.

× 486. Caffarella, Edward P. "How Will the Baby Boomette Affect School Enrollments?" *Schools Business Affairs* 50 (January 1984): 14.

Differentiates between the baby boom and a current "baby boomette" that started with increased births in 1973. This baby boomlet is being "caused largely by the baby boom children who are now adults of prime childbearing age." Urges school officials to begin planning for increased enrollments at all levels during the 1990s. Enrollment projections by individual grades for each school year in the 1980s are presented in a table.

488. Califano, Joseph A., Jr. "The Aging of America." *Vital Speeches* 44 (May 15, 1978): 450–54.

Discusses four basic social issues that confront America as the U.S. population ages: (1) increasing life expectancy; (2) evolution of the "baby boom" into a "senior boom"; (3) increasing early retirements; and (4) changing ratios of active workers to retired citizens. Points out that in 1940, 7 percent of the population was sixty-five or over, whereas by 2030 18 percent of the population will be sixty-five or over. Notes that 45 percent of the elderly will be seventy-five or older by 2030. Sketches out key concerns of the aging population, including (1) the meaning of the term "old age"; (2) the need to restructure income security; (3) the delivery of services to the elderly; and (4) the role of families in caring for the elderly.

487. Califano, Joseph A., Jr. "The Aging of America: Questions of the Four-Generation Society." *Annals of the American Academy of Political and Social Science* 438 (July 1978): 96–107.

> Points out that "the American nation is about to become a four-generation society." The baby boom will be transformed in the early years of the next century into the "senior boom." The consequences for budgets and employer pension funds are emphasized. It may be necessary to redefine "old age," reconsider early retirement policies, and revise current systems of caring for the elderly.

489. Carlson, Allan C. "Families, Sex, and the Liberal Agenda." *Public Interest* 58 (Winter 1980): 62–79.

> Begins with a review of liberal perspectives that advocate a "family policy" for the United States. Identifies key issues in the policy such as (1) income security; (2) full employment; (3) affirmative action; (4) health care; (5) social services; (6) day care; (7) liberal sex education and contraception laws; (8) liberal family and work laws; and (9) more government intervention. Argues that the liberal view is faulty, and attributes problems in the American family to demographic, psychological, and ideological causes. Notes that the baby-boom generation passed through its adolescent years in the sixties, causing tremendous turmoil socially and within the family.

490. Carlson, Elwood D. "Divorce Rate Fluctuation as a Cohort Phenomenon." *Population Studies* 33 (November 1979): 523–36.

> Attempts to explain changes in the divorce rates, especially the significant rise in divorces in the past two decades. Argues that the primary cause of increased divorces stems from the manner in which the baby-boom generation was raised. The baby-boom population was so large that its socialization was effected not by the family, but by larger institutions such as schools. Contends that schools by their nature segregated baby boomers from adults and that the marriage expectations of baby boomers were thus inadequately shaped outside the family structure. Suggests that resulting ideas about marriage were unrealistic and led to high divorce rates. Includes numerous tables on divorces.

✗ 491. Carlucci, Carl. "Higher Education: After the Baby Boom." *New York Affairs* 5 (1978): 179–89.

> Focuses on the higher-education system in New York State. Begins with a discussion of the enrollment trends in the sixties and seventies,

particularly the institutional responses and expansions of the educational system. As the baby-boom generation passed through college, severe problems developed. Attributes declining enrollments to three factors: (1) decline in birthrate; (2) out-migration of students; and (3) declining confidence in the B.A. degree. Reviews alternatives for financial support of ailing institutions and emphasizes the need for governmental cooperation.

492. Chiang, Cheng-Hung, and Richard Kolhauser. "The 'Baby Boom' Generation." *Illinois Business Review* 38 (July 1981): 3–5.

Presents an overview of baby boom's demographic characteristics and then focuses on its impact on Illinois state government. Six areas of demographic change are considered: (1) education; (2) labor force; (3) prison inmate population; (4) general welfare assistance; (5) aid to families with dependent children; and (6) health care and retirement. Notes that in 1981 baby boomers constituted almost one-third of the Illinois population.

493. Corman, Louise, and Judith B. Schaefer. "Population Growth and Family Planning." *Journal of Marriage and Family* 35 (February 1973): 89–92.

Gives the results of a study conducted to determine attitudes of young people toward family size and planning. A questionnaire was distributed in 1971 to 313 college students enrolled at three institutions in the Boston area. Respondents expressed concern about overpopulation, but anticipated having an average of 3.02 children. This lends credence to the conclusion drawn by the Commission on Population Growth and the American Future that "another baby boom is likely in the immediate future." Most respondents considered abortion acceptable and almost one-third viewed sterilization as a possible means of birth control.

494. "Courting the Elderly." *American Demographics* 6 (January 1984): 15–16.

Notes that politicians should be as concerned about the generation gap as they are about the gender gap. Since older people are statistically more likely to vote and their numbers are increasingly rapidly, politicians should start aiming significant portions of their campaigns at the elderly. Census Bureau statistics demonstrate predicted effects of the aging baby boom on national demographics. Concludes that "no society has ever had such a large group of aged in its midst, and it is hard to predict what these people will want—let alone plan how to give it to them or what to promise them. But you can count on the politicians to try."

495. Cunningham, Danny. "Population Shifts Demand Library Response: Are We Ready for the Middle-Age and Tiny-Tot Booms?" *American Libraries* 13 (September 1982): 505.

> Discusses the impact of the baby boomers on library collections and services. Notes that the number of people between ages thirty-five and forty-four will increase by 42 percent in the next decade and that the fifteen-to-twenty-four-year-old group will decline in relation to the total population. Argues that services for the thirty-five-to-forty-four group must be increased, including in areas such as "self-education, travel and hobbies, career change, financial investment, planning for retirement and health care." Contends that since baby boomers are now having children, demand for services to children should consequently increase.

496. Cutler, Neal E. "Demographic, Social-Psychological and Political Factors in the Politics of Aging: A Foundation for Research in 'Political Gerontology.' " *American Political Science Review* 71 (September 1977): 1011–25.

> Examines current and predicted demographic statistics concerning the older population, and then considers how the large "gerontology boom" will affect the United States in the next century. Questions whether elderly members of the baby boom will exhibit traditional behaviors of increased conservatism and withdrawal from the political process. Concludes that this will not be the case because "tomorrow's older population will reflect the education, political experience, and activist life-styles which characterize the younger adults of the 'sixties' and 'seventies.' "

✗ 497. Dodd, John. "The Youth Unemployment Dilemma." *Personnel Journal* 60 (May 1981): 362–67.

> Reviews the overall problem of youth unemployment in the United States, with special emphasis on programs that train young people. Points out that youth programs benefit employers by (1) reducing training costs; (2) increasing productivity; (3) reducing taxes; (4) reducing the overall cost of social programs; and (5) reducing crime. Reviews several programs, including the National Fair Break Program from Control Data; Smokey House Project of Danby, Vermont; Job Search Workshops, Inc., of San Mateo County, California; and Inner City, Inc., from Polaroid Corporation. Notes that the youth unemployment problem is exacerbated by the population of baby-boom teenagers, which doubled the number of youths in the work force from 2 to 4 million.

498. Donnelly, Harrison. "Percentage of Aged to Grow Sharply . . . As Baby Boom Generation Turns Gray." *Congressional Quarterly Weekly Report* 39 (November 28, 1981): 2330–31.

> Predicts an enormous increase in the number of elderly in the next century as baby boom ages. Statistics are presented for those over sixty-five in 1981. While life expectancy and fertility rate are not expected to change dramatically in the future, immigration represents a "wild card" in population projections. The "dependency ratio" is defined and its impact on the ability of society to care for the elderly considered. Concludes that the aging baby boom, "which first asserted itself during the protests of the 1960s, could once again become a militant force pressing its demands on the government."

499. Elder, Glen H., Jr. "Scarcity and Prosperity in Post War Childbearing: Explorations from a Life Course Perspective." *Journal of Family History* 6 (Winter 1981): 410–33.

> Provides a detailed examination of the "conceptual task of linking depression experiences with adult status and childbearing in the postwar era." An empirical test of such linkages is attempted. Three conclusions are presented: (1) the relative income thesis is best supported by adults from lower-income families who entered the upper middle class; (2) a "depressant" effect of low fertility from economic pressure is evident mostly in deprived adults from lower-income families; and (3) the low fertility of middle-status adults is appropriate in groups with higher material standards but limited resources. Results seem to "reinforce the critical importance of life-path specifications in modeling the relation between economic change and demographic behavior."

500. "End of Baby Boom May Mean Less Crime." *Christian Science Monitor,* 2 February 1979, p. 8.

> Quotes Connecticut Corrections Commissioner John Manson, who claims that aging of the baby boom will virtually eliminate the growing crime problem and lessen the need for additional prisons. He states, "Politicians, judges, law enforcement officers, social scientists, and corrections commissioners can do what they want, but the only thing around the corner that's going to deter crime is that 'baby boom.' "

501. Glenny, Lyman A. "Demographic and Related Issues for Higher Education in the 1980s." *Journal of Higher Education* 51 (July/August 1980): 363–80.

Analyzes how fertility and birthrates have affected the number of potential students in higher education and notes that this number will decline in the 1980s and early 1990s. The growing diversity of post-high school education is discussed and probable trends in enrollment distribution are identified. The theory that enrollment of adults will compensate for loss of younger students is rejected.

502. Glick, Paul C. "Remarriage: Some Recent Changes and Variations." *Journal of Family Issues* 1 (December 1980): 455–78.

Analyzes various demographic factors affecting remarriage. Statistics and interpretive comments are presented for (1) marriages by previous marital status; (2) age at first marriage; (3) lifetime marriage patterns; (4) living arrangements of the currently remarried; (5) fertility of the remarried; (6) education of the remarried; and (7) employment and income of the remarried. More current marriages are remarriages because of the increased divorce rate. The extent to which young adults of the baby boom postpone marriage has changed the entire pattern of lifetime marriage and remarriage patterns. Extensive bibliography is included.

503. Gordon, Margaret S. "The Labor Market and Student Interests." *Liberal Education* 61 (May 1975): 149–60.

Notes that a crisis has arisen for college graduates in the job market because of a significant rise in the proportion of workers with high levels of education. Observes that in the fifties and sixties three conditions were at work: (1) increases in expenditures for research and development; (2) growth of aerospace industries; and (3) the high birthrate after World War II, which produced a strong demand for teachers. Argues that these factors are no longer significant in the seventies, and that the birthrate has dropped below the replacement rate. Demand will vary by occupation chosen. Counseling in college is critical to give students a realistic view of job opportunities.

✕ 504. Greenough, William C., and Francis P. King. "Is Normal Retirement at Age 65 Obsolete?" *Pension World* 13 (June 1977): 35–36.

Raises a variety of issues concerning the advisability of a set retirement age and its effects on future retirement systems. Reviews the history of pension plans and discusses in particular the Social Security system. The long-range financial problems of Social Security will be severe owing to the post-war baby boom population, which will swell the ranks of retirees by the year 2030. Observes that at present there are ten workers for every three retirees, but by 2030 there will be only two workers for each retiree. Predicts that Social Security taxes will have to rise dramatically unless the system is significantly modified. Supports a reexamination of our whole concept of retirement.

505. Hagstrom, Jerry. "Baby Boom Generation May Have to Wait a While to Show Its Political Clout." *National Journal* 16 (April 28, 1984): 804–10.

Studies the potential impact of the baby-boom generation as it participates in the electoral process. Notes that Gary Hart's campaign may have been premature and that greater effects will be felt in the 1988 presidential elections. Reviews the historical events that shaped the baby-boom generation, including (1) economic prosperity; (2) the Civil Rights movement; (3) the Vietnam War; (4) the influence of Eugene McCarthy; (5) the draft; and (6) rock music. Analyzes the political views of baby boomers and compares them with those of the public at large. Identifies this group as a "prize" to be won by either political party. Included are tables of voter turnout from 1972–1984. Gallup Opinion Poll on baby boomers' political attitudes, and state-by-state breakdowns of the baby-boom population distribution by age.

506. Hartley, Shirley Foster. "Our Growing Problem: Population." *Social Problems* 21 (Fall 1973): 190–206.

Argues that recent declines in the U.S. birthrate have led to complacency on the part of social scientists toward the problems of population growth. Observes that "the purpose here is to remind problem oriented social scientists of the many ways in which population influences other social factors." Discusses the effects of family size on such factors as housing density, food, health, intelligence, education, and power. Points out that even though the birthrate has dropped, the number of women entering childbearing age has greatly increased. These baby-boom women may create a "second wave" of children. Includes an international analysis of population growth and advocates population stability if the quality of human life is to be improved. A bibliography is appended.

507. Hauser, Philip M. "Our Anguished Youth: Baby Boom Under Stress." *Adolescent Psychiatry* 8 (1980): 270–80.

Argues that the baby-boom generation has been placed under stress much greater than that of the Depression cohort that preceded it. Notes that educational quality was sacrificed when baby boomers flooded the school systems. Baby boomers could not find jobs in the labor force, had unhappy marriages and more divorces, and lived through environmental degradation, social upheaval, and domestic violence. Contends that the high delinquency and suicide rates of this generation attest to its degree of anguish. Notes that this generation may now, however, be more responsive to change and more insistent that our governmental, social, and economic institutions be improved.

508. "History Repeats Itself." *American School and University* 55 (April 1983): 10–13.

Presents the comments of five educational-facility planners on the need for expanded building facilities as the first members of the 1980s baby boomlet enters kindergarten. The problem of increased primary-school enrollment is exacerbated by the decline in other levels of school attendance. These experts favor facility revitalization, environmental improvements, and flexibility in building design. Observations made by Edna Manning, Tuloso Independent School District in Corpus Christi; Alan C. Gree, Educational Facilities Labs; John Andrisek, Boca City Schools (Ohio); C. William Day, Indiana University; and Stanton Leggett, school consultant.

⋆509. Hodgkinson, Harold L. "Guess Who's Coming to College: A Demographic Portrait of Students in the 1990s." *Academe* 69 (March/April 1983): 13–20.

Provides a detailed analysis of the demographic forces that will affect educational institutions, especially colleges and universities, in the next decade. Traces historical factors, including the post-war baby boom, subsequent baby bust and baby boomlet, noting the effect of each on education and the work force. Observes that the baby bust occurred primarily in the white middle class and that minority population trends remained high, which increased their percentages in schools. Notes baby boomers' habit of returning to some type of school for further training, but points out that this training is not necessarily through colleges and universities but through government, private industry, community colleges, and voluntary agencies.

510. Kern, Richard. "Demographics in Action: Gray Matters." *S&MM: Sales and Marketing Management* 133 (May 14, 1984): 20.

Previews the effects that the aging of the baby boom in the next century will have on all aspects of society. Both new products and new problems will appear. Notes that pension plans, Social Security, and care for the elderly will be dramatically affected by the retirement of the baby-boom generation. Current changes in food (e.g., salt-free), banking (e.g., Individual Retirement Plans), and travel (e.g., increase in leisure expenditures) are only "rumblings" of significant transformations that will occur in the coming decades as a result of the "graying of America."

511. Klerman, Gerald L. "Age and Clinical Depression: Today's Youth in the Twenty-first Century." *Journal of Gerontology* 31 (May 1976): 318–23.

Considers why clinical depression has increased significantly among teenagers since World War II and suggests that this occurrence may lead to more cases of depression in adulthood and old age. The possibility that the baby-boom generation and its emphasis on adolescence may have unduly stressed a great number of individuals is hypothesized. Concludes that if optimistic expectations of young adults are frustrated by the economy or other social factors, there will be increased "symptoms of depression in the latter decades of the 20th century and well into the 21st century."

512. Krajick, Kevin. "Annual Prison Population Survey—The Boom Resumes." *Corrections Magazine* 7 (April 1981): 16–20.

Reports that in 1980, the prison population increased faster than at any time in the past three years. Attributes this to (1) the passage of mandatory minimum sentencing laws; (2) the passage of determinate sentencing laws; and (3) the post-war baby boom population, which has reached the age of peak criminal activity (sixteen to twenty-five). Observes that although criminal activity should peak and decline as baby boomers age, the prison population should continue to grow because the average age of persons commited to prison is higher than that of those engaging in criminal activity. Includes table on inmates in federal and state prisons.

513. Kuhn, James W. "Immense Generation: What Consequences of the Baby Boom?" *Current* 156 (November 1973): 46–53.

Traces the history of the baby-boom generation and its effects on American society. Notes that as they aged, baby boomers have "inundated successive institutions, battering and transforming them as they went." Effects on schools, crime, church attendance, suburbia, and the economy are listed. Baby boomers are also expected to become politically conservative as they grow older.

✗514. Jacobs, Frederick. "Educating the Boom Generation." *American Demographics* 1 (June 1979): 18–19.

> Suggests that colleges and universities must face the demographic fact that they need to actively recruit and serve adult learners to make up for the declining enrollment of young people. Frequent career changes and technological advances will require continuous and ongoing education in the future. Institutions should adopt a fluid curriculum and flexible academic calendar. Concludes that "adult learners are becoming an increasingly large and vocal component of the educational system, and we need to learn to serve them well."

515. Jencks, Christopher. "Declining Test Scores: An Assessment of Six Alternative Explanations." *Sociological Spectrum* 1 (December 1980): 1–15.

> Reports on decline in Scholastic Aptitude Test (SAT) scores over the last fifteen years. States that the purpose of the article is to examine six explanations: "the postwar baby boom, the declining economic value of the B.A., the spread of television viewing, changes in family structure, increasing parental permissiveness, and changes in the schools." Points out that baby-boom families have more children spaced closer together and notes theory that these factors generally affect scores. Contends, however, that the theory is seriously flawed. Recommends focusing on complex measures to determine the effects of parental permissiveness and changes in the schools.

516. Jencks, Christopher. "What's Behind the Drop in Test Scores?" *Working Papers for a New Society* 6 (July/August 1978): 29–41.

> Probes why recent scores on standardized tests have declined significantly. Presents lengthy analysis of what the tests really measure and how useful they are. Three reasons for the declining scores are considered: (1) family and demographic factors; (2) television and parental permissiveness; and (3) changes in the schools. Speculation that scores were unduly influenced by changes in family size during the baby boom are shown to be incorrect. Other factors are similarly dismissed. Concludes that "the problem is not so much declining test performance as the fact that millions of students are serving time in secondary schools without learning anything of importance."

✗517. Johnston, Denis F. "Sixty Million Strong: Their Challenges to Education." *Liberal Education* 62 (May 1976): 177–84.

> Observes that between 1947 and 1961 almost 60 million people were born in the United States. Notes that the earliest effects of this in-

crease were felt by the nation's school system. Attempt to predict impact of this population as it moves into the 1980s, particularly with respect to the labor force. As the baby boomers age and progress beyond entry-level positions, there will be increased demand for housing and other consumer items. Contends that there will be greater demand for adult education in an effort to expand career options. Includes tables on projections for the population to 2035.

518. Lague, Louise. "Another Way of Living." *Institutional Investor* 16 (December 1982): 131–32.

Analyzes the influence of baby boomers on personal relationships and family structure in the coming decades. Notes that by the "start of the next century, baby boomers will range in age from 36 to 54, and the fallout from their mid-life crisis will decide the tenor and shape of society." Trends forecast include later marriages, acceptability of cohabitation, easy divorce, corporate child-care benefits, and baby boomers as active grandparents. Concludes that "the family, in its broadest sense, isn't dying; it's diversifying."

519. Leggett, Stanton. "Echoes of the Baby Boom." *Independent School* 37 (February 1978): 25–28.

Notes that independent or private schools will have to dramatically increase their share of the market to maintain present enrollment as the baby boom "becomes a tiny cry in the night." The reluctance of baby-boom women to have children will result in a substantial decline in the number of school-age children in the future. Independent schools are urged to offer extended day-educational programs for young children to attract more students. Concludes that "the independent school will serve a clientele in which the career woman–mother will be a dominant pattern."

X 520. Lind, Matthew M. "Economic Policy in an Aging Society: Report of the Technical Committee on the Economy of the 1981 White House Conference on Aging." *Employee Benefits Journal* 6 (December 1981): 2–6.

Reports on the conclusions of the committee. Contends that the aging of the U.S. population will have profound consequences on our social, political, and economic life. Argues that the population is aging for three reasons: declining mortality, declining birthrates, and the "graying" of the baby-boom population. Recommends four courses of action: (1) increased employment opportunities for the elderly; (2) increased incentives for personal savings; (3) increased domestic private investment to improve the economy; and (4) increased income transfers to the elderly needy.

521. Long, Sandra M. "An American Profile: Trends and Issues in the 80's."
     Educational Leadership 39 (March 1982): 460–64.

> Analyzes various demographic trends to determine their impact on the
> entire educational process in the 1980s. Census figures are provided to
> detail population shifts that must be considered by educators in making
> both immediate and long-range plans. The aging of the baby boom will
> have wide-ranging impacts, from the need to portray the elderly dif-
> ferently in textbooks to a potential lessening of public support for public
> education. Other trends considered include single-parent families,
> regional migrations, and movement from urban areas to the country.

522. Marchant, Janet. "Endangered Species." *Canadian Business* 54 (October
     1981): 152–58.

> Warns that professionals in many fields are "endangered species."
> Predicts the ability of future generations of computers to perform
> many tasks currently requiring professionals. Demographics will also
> play an important role in the decline of professionals: "Seven million
> ambitious Baby Boomers will intensify past all imagining the competi-
> tion for top jobs, and working women will make the race even
> fiercer." Notes that baby boomers have many attitudes toward work
> and professionals that are "directly antagonistic to professionalism's
> sense of noblesse oblige." Two new professional types, "superspecial-
> ists" and "supergeneralists," are foreseen.

523. Mare, Robert D. "Trends in Schooling: Demography, Performance, and
     Organization." *Annals of the American Academy of Political and Social
     Science* 453 (January 1981): 96–122.

> Observes that the level of formal educational attainment has risen
> throughout the century, particularly in primary and secondary schools.
> Attributes this in part to (1) improvements in familial attitudes; (2) leg-
> islation promoting attendance; (3) economic incentives; and (4) changes
> in school organization. Observes that school enrollment levels have been
> significantly affected by the post-war baby boom. Discusses differences
> of educational attainment by race, analyzes standardized test-score
> trends, and reviews growth trends for primary and secondary schools.

524. Masnick, George S., and Joseph A. McFalls, Jr. "A New Perspective on the
     Twentieth-Century American Fertility Swing." *Journal of Family
     History* 1 (1976): 217–44.

> Attempts to provide a new theoretical basis for understanding the
> "causes of variation in child bearing behavior." Notes that the twenti-
> eth-century U.S. population experienced a pattern of declining fertility

in the first third of the decade, disrupted by the post-war baby boom and followed by a new birthrate decline. Analyzes in detail three traditional explanations for birthrate trends that are identified as "Demographic Transition," "New Household Economic," and the "VD Hypothesis," and notes their inadequacies. Proposes a new model focusing on the process of reproduction—spacing of children and when reproduction ends. Emphasis is placed on contraceptive practices. Employs data obtained in a study of 718 black women in Philadelphia to support the new perspective.

525. Mattessich, Paul W. "Childlessness and Its Correlates in Historical Perspective: A Research Note." *Journal of Family History* 4 (Fall 1979): 299–307.

Presents a historical overview of the extent of childlessness in the United States. Four social correlates of childlessness are considered in detail: (1) age at marriage; (2) education; (3) income; and (4) labor force participation. Shortcomings in recent attempts to analyze the causes and consequences of increases in childlessness are also identified. Current fertility rates are seen as nothing more than a "swing back from abnormal rates of childlessness which occurred within an extraordinarily pronatalist historical context." In addition, motherhood is found to be compatible with nonfamily activities such as work.

526. Metzger, Walter P. "The American Academic Profession in 'Hard Times.'" *Daedalus* 104 (Winter 1975): 25–44.

Considers the role and future of the academic profession. Professors enjoy a wide range of benefits, but some retrenchment is possible as institutions of higher education enter a period of "financial crisis." However, the "hard times" theory of inevitable decline in enrollments because of the end of the baby boom is emphatically rejected. Notes that "the demand for academic services is a function not of the rate of fertility but of the rate of participation, which can be raised by reducing attrition, lowering the barriers to college-going, and enticing men and women in the older age range, into places heretofore reserved for the high school's latest crop."

527. Morrison, Peter A. "How Demographics Can Help Legislators." *Policy Analysis* 6 (Winter 1980): 85–96.

Contends that demographic patterns have significant effects on legislation and public policy. States that "this article describes the major shifts that have occurred in long-term patterns of fertility and migration

during the past two decades . . ." Observes that the baby-boom generation has already had an impact on schools and universities and is now affecting the job and housing markets. Predicts further adverse impact as
baby boomers reach Social Security age, particularly since the baby
boom was followed by a baby bust that increased the elderly dependency ratio. Concludes that program planning and budgets must reflect
future demographic projections.

528. Newton, Blake T. "A Forward Look: The Economy in '78." *Insurance Marketing* 79 (February 1978): 24.

Reviews important issues facing the country, e.g., Social Security legislation, tax reform, and energy policy, and concludes that "the life insurance business will continue to achieve high levels of growth in
terms of premiums, benefits, assets and life insurance in force." This
growth will be made possible by the entry of the baby boom into the
work force and by the increased family formations of this maturing
generation. Stresses the importance of the life insurance business to
the overall American economy.

529. Nordstrom, Carl. "The Long Shadow of the Baby Boom." *Optical Spectra*
15 (October 1981): 14.

Provides an overview of baby-boom birthrates and the subsequent
baby bust. Points out that many baby boomers "dropped out" in college or failed to complete scientific or technical training. Asserts that
the baby bust will not produce enough qualified technical workers,
which will lead to a shortage of labor for the optics industry. Argues
that optics manufacturers must find ways to encourage members of
the current labor pool to seek higher levels of skill that will enable
them to work in the optics industry.

530. "Openers: My Daughter, the Lawyer." *American Demographics* 4 (April
1982): 9.

Considers the impact of the baby-boom generation on the legal profession. Figures from the 1981 *Lawyers and Statistical Report* indicate
that 40 percent of all lawyers are between twenty-nine and thirty-five
years old and that in 1980 there was one lawyer for every 410 Americans. The most noticeable change caused by the baby boom is the
number of women lawyers. Notes that the "younger your lawyer, the
more likely he is to be a she."

531. Ornstein, Allan C. "Baby Boom: Bad News for City Schools." *Principal*
62 (November 1982): 9–13.

Analyzes current projections of educators that indicate an increase in primary-school enrollments in the near future. Challenges the optimism felt by some administrators that systems will revert to the healthy conditions experienced when the post-war baby boomers entered schools in the 1950s. A detailed analysis of the composition of the new urban baby boomlet is provided. Points out that current urban dwellers come from five areas: (1) rich and unmarried middle class; (2) ethnics; (3) economically trapped; (4) immigrants; and (5) the structurally poor. Concludes that schools will have to respond to the economically disadvantaged.

532. O'Toole, James. "Education Is Education and Work Is Work—Shall Ever the Twain Meet?" *Teachers College Record* 81 (Fall 1979): 5–21.

Provides a philosophical analysis of the higher education system, particularly its attempts to adapt to the demands of the work place. Argues that colleges have responded by increasing specialization, rather than training individuals to deal with the complex human problems that the work place creates. Notes that the baby-boom generation created a huge cohort, which resulted in rising unemployment and a subsequent infusion of workers into the labor force. Contends that this demographic phenomenon has had a significant impact on higher education and that baby boomers have a unique set of work expectations.

533. Pebley, Anne R., and David E. Bloom. "Childless Americans." *American Demographics* 4 (January 1982): 18–21.

Attempts to examine the phenomenon of childlessness in U.S. society. Notes that childlessness can be separated into four groups: (1) the physically unable; (2) those who choose childlessness; (3) those whose circumstances force them to be childless; and (4) those who are uncertain whether to have children. Questions the ability to predict childlessness merely by studying women's birth expectations and points out that as much as 30 percent of the current childbearing population may remain childless. Points out that the number of childless women will grow significantly as baby-boom women enter childbearing years, but also notes that because of the size of this baby-boom generation, the number of children born will continue to rise.

534. Peterson, William. "Population Policy and Age Structure." *Policy Studies Journal* 6 (Winter 1977): 146.

Discusses the political and economic implications of zero population growth (ZPG). Argues that the proponents of ZPG have provided no basis for controlling the U.S. population. Observes that ZPG developed as an outgrowth of the baby-boom population, which suffered from overcrowded schools and intense competition for jobs. These negative factors prompted baby boomers to support ecological reforms, most notably a stationary population. Asserts that a reduced youth population will significantly affect the age composition of the population, changing the political climate in negative ways.

535. Pifer, Alan. "Don't Forget the Children." *American Demographics* 1 (September 1979): 32–37.

Notes that America has become "an aging society, with relatively few children, a plethora of young adults, and mounting numbers of elderly." The significance of this situation is analyzed in detail. An increase in fertility among baby-boom women is labeled "highly improbable." Therefore, children will be viewed as a very valuable asset in the future. These children will also be responsible for the support of the aged baby boom in the next century.

536. Price, Barbara A. "What the Baby Boom Believes." *American Demographics* 6 (May 1984): 30–33.

Reports on a study conducted by the *American Council of Life Insurance* on the attitudes of baby boomers. Notes among the findings that baby boomers (1) have traditional values regarding hard work, family and religious ties, and respect for authority; (2) are more liberal on sexual mores and desire less materialism; (3) marry later and expect to have fewer children; (4) see marriage as an equal partnership in which the woman is likely to work outside the family; (5) are optimistic about their own future but not their children's future; and (6) feel they have at least some responsibility for taking care of elderly parents. Includes tables on baby-boom attitudes and life-styles.

537. Rao, S.L.N. "A Comparative Study of Childlessness and Never-Pregnant Status." *Journal of Marriage and the Family* 36 (February 1974): 149–57.

Analyzes data compiled by the Rhode Island Health Study. Studies sociological characteristics of families that are childless and "never pregnant" families (childless by choice). Examines three birth cohorts: (1) Depression families; (2) baby-boom mothers; and (3) individuals under thirty years old. Concludes that "there is an indication as judged from the 30–49 group, that the educational differentials in permanent childlessness have disappeared for those with more than 8 years of schooling . . . Again the 30 to 49 group points to a decline in the con-

ventional white collar–blue collar differential in permanent childlessness." Also notes that involuntary childlessness occurs at around 4
percent.

538. Raoul-Duval, Michael. "The New Middle Class: International Realities."
    Vital Speeches 48 (April 1, 1982): 360–63.

    Attempts to identify key forces that will shape the political, social, and
    economic environment in the next decades. Enumerates three: (1) do-
    mestic and international economics, particularly inflation; (2) inter-
    national interdependence; and (3) the rise of the baby-boom genera-
    tion as an active political and economic force. Points out that baby
    boomers have strong activist roots from the sixties and that their
    values are economically conservative but socially liberal. Predicts that
    as the baby boomers age, they are concerned with traditional issues of
    housing and family and will develop concerns for taxation, inflation,
    quality of life, and environmental conditions.

539. Reinhardt, Hazel H. "The Ups and Downs of Education." *American Demo-
    graphics* 1 (June 1979): 9–11.

    Examines demographic and educational trends. For better or worse,
    "school enrollments will continue to fluctuate." Regional differences are
    analyzed and graphs are used to depict the impact of migration on educa-
    tion. School-age population, based on the number of annual births, is
    projected to decline until 1985 and then gradually increase. Implications
    for school funding and teacher education are briefly explored.

540. Reynolds, Reid T. "The Demographics of Energy." *American Demographics*
    2 (June 1980): 25–31.

    Offers a hypothetical newspaper headline to highlight the relationship
    between demographics and energy consumption: "Work-age Boom
    Spells Energy Doom." The need to consider not only energy supply,
    but also energy demand, is emphasized. Energy demand will be affected
    by population growth, but the real impact will come from the maturing
    of the baby-boom generation. Baby boomers will increase energy con-
    sumption by establishing households and entering the work force. Con-
    cludes that "as the population grows, as people strive for a higher stan-
    dard of living, and as a less dense settlement pattern emerges, the goals
    of conservation will become more difficult to achieve."

541. Riche, Martha Farnsworth. "The Fall and Rise of Religion." *American
    Demographics* 4 (May 1982): 14–19.

Contends that the baby boom "may be responsible for the decline in religious involvement that has plagued churches for nearly two decades." Detailed justifications for this conclusion are presented. Geographic, economic, and age differences in religious activity are analyzed. Recent increases in church membership are hypothesized to be the result of the aging of the baby boom. Concludes that church planners must study the members of this generation: "If they were responsible for a religious decline in the past, will they now lead the ascendancy? God knows."

542. Roberts, Mary Lou; Laurence J. Kirshbaum; and Linda R. Cooper. "Profile: Two-Income Shoppers." *American Demographics* 6 (March 1984): 38–41.

Studies the "lifestyles and shopping habits of the affluent upper two-thirds of dual-income households." Based on a survey of 639 households conducted by Conde Nast Publications and the Allen Lewis Organization. The growth in the number of dual-income families is demonstrated and responses to the survey analyzed. Husbands and wives are shown to have similar attitudes about shopping for food, but differences in actual shopping behavior are noted. With the aging of the baby boom, as many as 33 million households may have two incomes by 1990.

543. Robey, Bryant. "On Demographics: In Old America." *American Demographics* 3 (June 1981): 2.

Reviews briefly the issues surrounding the aging of the U.S. population. Observes that by the year 2000, 32 million people will be over sixty-five and that the over-eighty-five age group is the fastest growing cohort. Focuses particularly on the Social Security system and notes that as the baby boomers reach retirement age, the ratio of workers to nonworkers will decrease. Contends that retiring baby boomers will have greater responsibility to support themselves. Predicts political tensions as politicians try to respond to a powerful elderly population and resentful young workers burdened with supporting the pension system.

544. Robey, Bryant. "On Demographics: Turning One Hundred or So." *American Demographics* 6 (March 1984): 11.

Raises the issue of the aging of American society. By the year 2000, over 100,000 Americans will be over 100 years old. The inexorable aging of the baby boom means that the elderly will be the fastest growing part of the population. In addition, the "oldest of the old," those 85 and older, are increasing even faster. Their needs for medical services and nursing home care are emphasized. A chart projects the growth of the "very old" from 1982 to 2080.

545. Robey, Bryant, and Mary John. "The Political Future." *American Demographics* 2 (October 1980): 15–21.

Studies the impact of demographics on voting behavior. Points out that the baby-boom generation is now reaching the ages where voting occurs and that these baby boomers have concerns similar to those of other voters, i.e., housing costs, welfare roles, and deficit spending. Notes that as the baby boomers age, the median voting age will increase and that the voting public will be better educated, increasingly female, and have a larger proportion of blacks and Hispanics. Discusses also the impact of geographic regions and decreasing party identification on voter habits.

546. Schonbak, Judith. "Changing Demographics: The Effect on Pensions." *Pension World* 16 (March 1980): 54–56.

Explores the future of retirement systems, particularly with regard to the changing age composition of the U.S. population. Notes that by 2000 to 2010, the baby-boom generation will be reaching traditional retirement age, which will place a severe burden on pension systems. The problem is heightened by the baby bust that followed the baby boom, significantly increasing the retirement dependency ratio. Identifies possible alternatives to alleviate the problem, including a later retirement age and changes in the Social Security system. Concludes that a major alteration in the pension structure is required.

547. Shapiro, Kenneth P. "The Reversing Early Retirement Trend." *Personnel Administrator* 25 (April 1980): 77–79.

Predicts that the trend toward early retirement will soon be reversed and analyzes the conditions underlying this prediction. Notes that the post-war baby boom was followed by a baby bust and that consequently the support of a large retirement-age population of baby boomers will depend on a relatively small workforce. As the baby boomers age, there will be less pressure from the younger workers for their jobs, and retirement will not be emphasized by the employer. Cites additional reasons for the projected decline in early retirement, including (1) age discrimination laws; (2) increased life expectancy; and (3) problems with Social Security.

548. Sjogren, Cliff. "The Changing College Admissions Scene." *NASSP Bulletin* 67 (February 1983): 5–18.

> Discusses how the criteria for college admissions have changed over the years. Identifies four basic periods since the 1950s: (1) Sputnik Era (1957–1960); (2) Post Baby Boom Era (1964–1967); (3) "New Groups" Era (1971–1974); and (4) Stable Enrollment Era (1957–1960). In the baby-boom era, numerous changes occurred including the following: (1) the number of enrollments increased dramatically; (2) college and universities underwent significant, often unplanned, expansion; (3) hundreds of new institutions were formed, including community colleges; (4) admissions requirements were stiffened; and (5) college students were deferred from the draft, which created a pool of students enrolled for noneducational reasons. Recommends for the future more colleges with tougher admission requirements.

549. Steglich, W. "Sociology Faces No-Growth and Decline in Enrollments." *Free Inquiry* 5 (November 1977): 41–47.

> Discusses the impact of the baby boom and subsequent baby bust on the job market for sociologists and on the education systems that teach sociology. Points out that sociology departments expanded rapidly as the baby boomers entered college, which produced a high number of tenured faculty during the same time that the birthrate has markedly declined. Notes that today faculty positions are few and college enrollments are declining. Predicts a poor job market for sociologists and recommends that sociology curricula adapt to the needs of the marketplace by emphasizing a "problem-focus" rather than a theoretical or statistical one.

550. Sternlieb, George. "The Small City: Vanguard or Remnant?" *Wisconsin Sociologist* 15 (Fall 1978): 131–36.

> Decries the decline of small communities in the United States. Without a viable downtown area, small towns become nothing more than "a fairly massive mixed up, muddled, built-over subdivision." The remnants of the baby boom, and the baby bust caused by decline in fertility rate among baby-boom women, are cited as underlying population factors that contribute toward the trend away from "localism." Other elements of the problem include employment, the elderly, and the decline in family capitalism.

551. Stewart, Ian R., and Donald G. Dickason. "Hard Times Ahead." *American Demographics* 1 (June 1979): 12–23.

Emphasizes the precarious shape many colleges and universities are in as the peak of the baby-boom generation graduates in 1979. With a declining pool of potential students, schools have only two options: get or retain more students, or broaden the base of potential applicants. Many state systems that expanded rapidly to accommodate the large generation of baby boomers may now have to constrict just as rapidly. Efforts to attract older or nontraditional students are encouraged, but will be met with competition from less expensive community colleges. Characteristics of colleges that may even close in the 1980s are briefly identified. Concludes that the "coming demographic decline heralds a buyer's market in higher education."

552. Wilson, Ian H. "The Blooming Baby Boom." *Planning Review* 7 (September 1979): 3–8.

Proposes that the next decade is one requiring adaptability and assimilation of the social and political transformations of the past decade. Notes that the "pre-eminent" force in the future is the post-World War II baby boomers. By 1990, this generation will constitute almost one-third of the U.S. population. Points out that baby boomers have already influenced the growth of suburbia, colleges and universities, and teenage markets. Predicts that this generation will have significant impact on politics, public policy, unions, consumer markets, and the work force as its members age. Asserts that values are being altered by baby boomers, e.g., shifts from quantity to quality, independence to interdependence, authoritarianism to participation, and centralization to decentralization. Discusses the impact of the baby boomers on corporate and strategic planning.

553. Winter, Bill. " 'Baby Boom' Backlash to Hit Law Schools Next." *ABA Journal* 66 (February 1980): 134.

Emphasizes that enrollment in law schools and the need for faculty will both decline in the 1980s as "the baby boom era fades from college campuses." The impact of fewer potential students may mean schools will become less selective. Prospects for law school professors appear "ominous," but women and minority applicants for faculty positions will have a substantial advantage.

554. Wolfgang, Marvin E. "Real and Perceived Changes of Crime and Punishment." *Daedalus* 107 (Winter 1978): 144–57.

Describes the impact of the baby boom on changing crime rates and then debates the rationale behind various forms of punishment. The large increase in fifteen-to-twenty-four-year-olds in the 1960s and

1970s contributed significantly to the rise in violent crimes during these years. This age group is generally considered to be the most "crimogenic." Theorizes that all the expensive efforts to control or reduce crime were necessarily doomed to failure. Notes that "no matter what social interventions may have been made to control, prevent, or deter crime, the changing age composition of the population has been importantly responsible for the increase in crimes of violence."

555. Zajonc, R.B. "Family Configuration and Intelligence." *Science* 192 (April 16, 1976): 227–36.

Analyzes reasons for the steady decline in the average Scholastic Aptitude Test (SAT) scores of high school seniors since 1964. Presents a theoretical basis for the effect of family configuration on aggregate intelligence. Birth order, spacing of siblings, and parental absence are factors considered. Previous studies and statistical analyses are presented to support the conclusion that demographic factors inherent in the baby-boom generation "are deeply implicated in the declining SAT scores as a special case of a general phenomenon that manifests itself also in a variety of national, ethnic, regional, racial, and sex differences in intellectual test performance."

8
Popular Articles

556. Abrams, Bill. "More Affluence . . . When Was Baby Boom? . . . Sponsor Recall." *Wall Street Journal*, 24 March 1983, p. 35.

   Argues that the traditional assignation of the baby-boom years between the end of World War II and the late 1950s is incorrect. Notes that the largest number of births occurred between 1954 and 1964, when births topped 4 million annually. Points out that the real baby boomers are between nineteen and twenty-nine years old and constitute 30 percent of adult population.

557. Alsop, Ronald. "Liquor Concerns Are Creating Fresh Ads for Baby-Boomers." *Wall Street Journal*, 21 June 1984, p. 31.

   Reports on the efforts of the hard liquor industry to attract baby boomers into its market. Notes that the market has steadily declined and some attempts have been made to improve conditions by selling sweet creamy drinks that are low in alcohol content. Discusses the efforts of Benedictine Marketing Service in promoting to twenty- to thirty-year-olds. Also notes the efforts of Canadian Club to sell its product as if it were a fashion item or an image product. Points out that attempts are being made to appeal to the young professional, with emphasis on status and sophistication.

558. "Americans Change: How Drastic Shifts in Demographics Affect the Economy." *Business Week*, February 20, 1978, pp. 64–69.

   Attempts to predict social changes that will occur as the baby-boom population passes through the 1980s. Points out that there have been three major demographic shifts: (1) the "birth dearth" during the Depression; (2) the post-World War II baby boom; and (3) the baby bust that followed the baby boom. Indicates that the immediate problem is the absorption of the baby boomers into the labor force. Makes numerous predictions for the future, including that (1) unemployment will drop in this decade; (2) federal expenditures on education and crime will drop; (3) migration to the Sunbelt will slow down; and (4) consumer spending will increase.

559. "An Appliance Boom That May Not Last." *Business Week*, March 10, 1980, pp. 79–87.

Analyzes the current appliance market. The market should be beneficially affected because young adults born in the baby-boom years are entering the consumer market. Reviews the progress of leading appliance manufacturers such as Magic Chef, Whirlpool, White Consolidated, Norge, Amana, and others. Includes tables on appliance shipments and sales. Covers primarily refrigerators, washers, microwaves, electric ranges, and dishwashers. Concludes that competition will be stiff and caution is necessary.

560. Arenseon, Karen W. "The Elusive Boom in Productivity." *New York Times*, 8 April 1984, p. 1F.

Analyzes the current trend toward increased productivity and prospects for consistent growth. Argues that it is too early to be confident in sustained growth because the recent growth has been largely due to cyclical and recessionary factors. Notes that part of the productivity increase can be accounted for by the 20 million baby boomers who entered the work force as inexperienced laborers and are now maturing into productive workers. Predicts that demographic considerations will not affect productivity in the near future.

561. "As U.S. Baby Boom Comes to an End." *U.S. News and World Report*, March 13, 1967, p. 20.

Reports on statistics on births provided by the National Center for Health Services in 1966. Asserts that number of births in that year was the lowest since 1950, even though the number of marriages increased. Suggests that the birth rate decline may reflect the trend among married couples to limit family size. Speculates that as the baby-boom generation reaches marriage age, the number of births may again rise.

562. "A Baby Bonanza." *Forbes*, October 12, 1981, p. 8.

Reports on what appears to be a new baby boom in the 1980s. Notes that the Census Bureau is projecting an increase in the under-five population to 19 percent by 1990. Observes that the current baby boom stems from post-World War II baby boomers, who are now having children. Indicates that the infant market should be strong, and mentions specifically Crayola and Gerber. Asserts also that with the increase in working mothers should come demand for appliances and other "home-chore machines."

563. "The 'Baby Boom' Grows Up." *Prevention*, March 1981, p. 176.

   Reviews briefly the report of a Congressional Joint Economic Committee concerning future population composition. Observes that (1) there will be an abundance of adults and a dearth of children in the next fifty years; (2) colleges will experience smaller enrollments; (3) number of prospects for home buying will double; (4) competition in the job market will be intense; and (5) strains in the Social Security system will grow as the baby-boom population ages.

564. Baby Boom Moves from U.S. to Europe." *U.S. News and World Report*, March 30, 1964, p. 67.

   Contrasts U.S. baby boom of the fifties to the concomitant baby-boom in Europe in the sixties. Discusses population increases in Britain, France, Italy, Switzerland, West Germany, Norway, Denmark, and Finland. Explains that reasons for the boom vary, including earlier marriage, government promotion of family bearing, and heavy immigration.

565. "Baby Boom Slows: What Will It Mean?" *U.S. News and World Report*, January 7, 1963, p. 54.

   Reports on the significance of the declining birthrate following the baby boom, with special emphasis on marketing. Predicts that (1) there will be a shrinking market for baby products; (2) pressure on elementary schools will diminish; (3) market will be strong for young adults and will include autos, clothing, TVs, records, and phonographs; and (4) the labor force will increase dramatically as baby-boom babies become workers. Includes a chart on the birthrate from 1919 to 1962.

566. "Baby Boom Starts Slowing." *Business Week*, November 17, 1962, p. 64.

   Observes that there has been a trend toward decreasing births and smaller families in recent years. Reflects that the post-war baby boom is now over. Quotes Pascal K. Whelpton, a leading demographer and director of the Scripps Foundation for Research in Population Problems. Notes that in Whelpton's surveys, young women said they would have smaller families than their older sisters. Reviews some implications for marketers, including a strong market for durable goods like stoves, refrigerators, and cars, but possibility of smaller houses, with fewer baths and bedrooms.

567. " 'Baby-Boomers' Expand Middle-Aged Population." *Wall Street Journal*, 25 May 1984, p. 30.

   Reports on the demographic composition of the U.S. population as the baby-boom generation ages. Cites these facts among the data: (1) population between thirty-five and forty-four grew by almost 15 percent in the last three years; (2) population of those under age five is the largest in fifteen years; and (3) number of teenagers between fourteen and seventeen dropped by nearly 10 percent. Attributes rise in the under-five category to baby-boom mothers, who are now in their prime childbearing years.

568. "Baby Boomers Push for Power." *Business Week*, July 2, 1984, pp. 52–59.

Discusses the impact of the baby-boom generation on business and politics. Analyzes three major areas: (1) job market for baby boomers; (2) consumer needs of baby boomers; and (3) political power of baby boomers. Points out that the large number of baby boomers in the labor force has created numerous problems, particularly for employees seeking middle-management positions. Cites several companies attempting to deal with this problem, including Burger King, AT&T, Honeywell, Citicorp, and Westinghouse. Notes that baby boomers are often two-income families and that the working woman has stimulated significant demand for specialized services, premium-quality products, and household services, premium-quality products, and household services. Describes the efforts of Republicans and Democrats to attract the baby-boomer vote, which will transform American politics.

569. Baker, Russell. "Baby Boomers." *New York Times Magazine*, April 1, 1984, p. 15.

Presents a humorous perspective on what it is like to be supervised by a baby boomer. Points out the contrasting influences of childhood on the baby boom and previous generation, with special attention to media influences.

570. "The Battle Over Repairing Social Security." *Business Week*, September 28, 1981, p. 116.

Reviews the current political crisis over efforts to stabilize the Social Security system. Points out that there are short-, medium-, and long-term problems. Identifies the long-term problem as the maturation of the post-war baby boomers. Notes that at present there are 31 beneficiaries for every 100 workers, but by 2000 there will be 70 beneficiaries per 100 workers. Projects a possible 40 percent increase over current rates. Explores several alternatives presented by political leaders, including interfund borrowing, reduction in benefits, and inflation adjustments.

571. Beck, Melinda; Deborah Witherspoon; Donna Foote; Jody Brott; Jerry Buckley; Kim Rogal; and Joe Contreras. "The Baby Boomers Come of Age." *Newsweek*, March 30, 1981, pp. 34–37.

Provides an overview of the problems baby boomers are experiencing as they enter the job market. Notes that baby boomers are facing intense job competition, and that many are overeducated and underpaid. Presents statistics to indicate that a baby bust will follow, creating a serious imbalance in the labor markets. A smaller group will be burdened with supporting the baby boomers as they reach retirement age. Predicts federal policy will eventually respond to these demographics, leading to decreases in aid to education, more day-care centers, increased mortgage assistance, and a modified Social Security system.

572. "A Bit of the '60s Live on at Lotus." *Business Week*, July 2, 1984, p. 59.

Provides a case study of baby boomer, Mitchell D. Kapor, and his company, Lotus Development Corp. Describes how Kapor inculcated the values of the sixties into his organization, emphasizing teamwork, equality, and respect for individuals. Notes that women and minorities are part of upper-level management and that staff meetings are held weekly. Cautions that some of the company's informality will probably change in the face of a rapidly growing staff.

573. Bleakley, Fred R. "Playing the Demographics." *New York Times*, 4 December 1983, pp. 12F–13F.

Reports on the current trend toward using demographic analysis for marketing and investment purposes. Cites an example of an individual who invested in day care and children's shoe industries because he anticipated the baby boomlet. Points out that he accurately predicted that baby-boom women would now be having children, thus creating rising demand for child-care products. Reviews the growth of *American Demographics* magazine and examines how demographics are useful in determining what market segments are most promising.

574. "Blue-Collar Boomers: The Most Frustrated of All." *Business Week*, July 2, 1984, p. 58.

Analyzes the problems of the blue-collar baby boomer. Notes that labor-market frustrations that characterize the baby-boom generation began on the blue-collar level, as job layoffs reduced employment chances and unions attempted to protect the jobs of older workers. Discusses the work attitudes of baby boomers and identifies specifically the efforts of District 925 of the Service Employees International Union to unionize clerical workers who are frustrated in jobs with few promotional prospects. Predicts that frustrated baby boomers are likely to form the vanguard of union efforts.

575. Blyskal, Jeff. "Gray Gold." *Forbes*, November 23, 1981, p. 80.

Discusses the future of the nursing home industry. Observes that the American population is getting older and that the baby boomlet of

the Depression and post-World War II baby boom will produce a sig-
nificnt rise in the over-sixty-five population. Reviews the impact of
the Medicaid program on the financial status of nursing homes. Includes a table on the ten largest nursing-home chains and the number
of beds available.

576. Blyskal, Jeff. "A Mercedes in Every Nursery." *Forbes*, December 6, 1982,
pp. 65–66.

Reports on the baby stroller industry, with special attention to the
Italian producer, Giuseppe Perego. Notes that the baby stroller industry is now a $75 million sales enterprise. Points out that Perego
preserved the "foldability" of the umbrella stroller but added a padded
rather than a canvas seat. Asserts that the demographics for the stroller
industry are very good and that a baby boomlet is occurring, with 43
percent of the births being first births. Reviews several of Perego's
competitors, including Hedstrom, Kassai Inc., and Bilt-Rite.

577. Brackman, Jacob. "Shock Waves from the Baby Boom." *Esquire*, June 1983,
p. 197.

Reprinted from *Esquire* in October 1968, provides a personal reflec-
tion of the writer growing up in the sixties. Observes that it was a
period of great turmoil and that new definitions of maturity and pleasure were required. Notes the political turmoil created by the Civil
Rights movement and Vietnam and the consequent social unrest.
Asserts that the struggle was against the diminution of the human per-
sonality.

578. Breckenfeld, Gurney. "Is the One-Family House Becoming a Fossil: Far
From It." *Fortune*, April 1976, pp. 84–89.

Discusses the future of the housing market, particularly the demand
for single-family homes. Notes some reason for optimism from a demographic perspective due to the housing demand that is expected from
the post-war baby boomers. Points out that the number of households
will rise 31 percent by 1990. Contends that the apartment market is
not bright because members of the baby-boom population, who created a rapid expansion of the apartment market as they passed through
their early twenties, have now matured beyond this market. Also reviews the market for mobile homes, and studies the effects of inflation,
regional migration, local government policies, and energy issues.

579. Briggs, Jean A., and James Cook. "Help Wanted." *Forbes*, April 25, 1983,
pp. 58–60.

Interviews labor economist Lawrence Olsen of Sage Associates concerning the possibility of a labor shortage in the near future. Despite current high levels of unemployment, a severe labor shortage will inevitably occur in the future if American businesses invest in new technologies and compete effectively in the world market. The baby boom has been absorbed into the work force and, consequently, "we're moving from a labor-surplus but not challenged economy into an internationally challenged labor-short economy." Companies must adapt if the United States is to avoid following the British "into genteel poverty."

580. "The Brighter Side." *Forbes*, May 24, 1982, p. 8.

Reviews briefly the current labor market composition, particularly unemployment and management opportunities. Notes that as the economy creates new jobs, the impact on the unemployment rate in the eighties should be much greater than in the seventies because far fewer people are entering the labor force. Points out that as Depression-born workers retire, greater management opportunities will arise for baby boomers.

581. Brown, Paul B. "Beverages." *Forbes*, January 4, 1982, pp. 210–11.

Discusses current marketing trends in the beverage industry. Notes that the "Pepsi Generation" of soft-drink users is now aging and getting overweight. Identifies this generation as the post-World War II baby boomers and points out that beverage producers are orienting their marketing strategies toward diet drinks. Asserts that diet drinks are improving as they improve the aftertaste problem of saccharine. Also reviews the approach of the light beer market and the new marketing of light wine by Paul Masson and Taylor. Includes table on the management performance of the beverage industry.

582. Brown, Paul B. "36th Annual Report on American Industry: Household Goods." *Forbes*, January 2, 1984, pp. 204–5.

Projects a very good year for household goods in 1984. Both marriage and divorce rates are projected to increase and, since both statistics mean new household formations, "these are good times for the companies that make washing machines and stoves, bleaches and scouring powder." In addition, the oldest members of the baby boom, who purchased their appliances between 1969 and 1973, should have to replace them very soon. New housing starts and lower interest rates are labeled "other bright spots."

583. Bulkeley, William M. "Raising the Roof: Baby Boom of 1947–57." *Wall Street Journal*, 27 July 1978, p. 1.

Examines the potential for a housing boom in the 1980s. Attributes this new demand to the aging of the post-war baby-boom generation. Notes that in the eighties, 42 million people will reach the age of thirty and that this age group is involved in household formation. Baby boomers also stay single, marry later, and divorce more often, thus creating a significant number of nontraditional households. Points out that families frequently have two incomes, making houses more affordable. Reviews the prospects for urban redevelopment, given this pent-up demand.

584. "The Burgeoning Benefits of a Lower Birth Rate." *Business Week*, December 15, 1973, pp. 41–42.

Attempts to understand the impact of changing demographic trends on the society and economy. Notes that because of the post-war baby boom, the median age of the U.S. population will rise to thirty-four by 2000. Predicts the following trends due to aging of the baby boomers: (1) increase in the savings rate; (2) increase in productivity as greater numbers of workers gain maturity and experience; (3) increased standard of living due to smaller families; (4) shifts in resources as money is channeled from schools where enrollment is low to environmental, recreational, and security matters; (5) changes in marketing trends to appeal to older consumers; and (6) greater demand for major consumer items such as refrigerators, autos, and furniture.

585. "Business Week Harris Poll: Yes, They Are Different." *Business Week*, July 2, 1984, pp. 56–57.

Reviews results of a Harris poll on the attitudes of baby boomers. Thirty-four percent of those polled affiliate themselves with Democrats, 26 percent with Republicans, and 32 percent are independent. Findings also show that baby boomers (1) favor stricter environmental controls but want to reduce government regulation; (2) support abortion, reductions in defense spending, and a nuclear freeze; (3) are frustrated by the political system and feel they are excluded from real political power; and (4) believe they face more competition in the job market. Concludes that baby-boomer attitudes overall are different from their elders'. Includes chart on differences in attitudes.

586. Byrne, John A., and Paul B. Brown. "Those Unpredictable Babies." *Forbes*, November 22, 1982, p. 203.

Observes recent increase in births attributed largely to women born during the baby boom who are now in childbearing years. Notes that this increase is not comparable to the 1957 peak and that the Census

Bureau believes this upsurge should hit a high point in five years. Reviews the performance of a variety of companies, including Gerbers, Proctor & Gamble, Johnson & Johnson, Beech-Nut, Nestlé, Fisher-Price, and Kinder-Care. Discusses the marketing of such products as disposable diapers, formula, toys, car seats, and baby food. Indicates management will be the key to this competitive market.

587. Carlson, Eugene. "Americans Don't Seem to Be Moving as Much These Days." *Wall Street Journal,* 9 February 1982, p. 33.

Discusses briefly the current view on migration in the United States. Notes that almost 18 percent of the population changes its residence each year. However, migration may be slowing. Cites as part of the reason the aging of the baby-boom population into a segment that is more stable. The prevalence of two-income families and desire of people to find a quality community in which to settle permanently are also noted. Challenges the belief that recession increases migration.

588. Coates, Joseph F. "Population and Education: How Demographic Trends Will Shape the U.S." *Futurist,* February 1978, pp. 35–42.

Identifies a large number of demographic and social trends that affect education. These include (1) the changing family; (2) immigration and non-English speaking students; (3) local mobility and internal migration; (4) teenage childbearing; and (5) decline in enrollments. Suggests solutions to problems in schools caused by replacement of the baby-boom with the baby-bust generation. Concludes that the "need for demographic research relevant to plans concerning adult education, day care, nursery care, and after-school services is increasing along with the increased demand for such services."

589. Collins, Glenn. "The Goods News About 1984." *Psychology Today,* January 1979, pp. 34–48.

Summarizes the controversy created by recent predictions of the theorist Richard A. Easterlin. Provides an overview of the Easterlin theory and age-structure analysis, explaining his beliefs that (1) the baby-boom cohort has depressed relative incomes and inhibited the establishment of families; (2) as the baby boomers enter the job market, the unemployment rate will drop; and (3) SAT scores will rise again as baby boomers pass out of college and high-order births enter college. Numerous critics of Easterlin are cited. Includes tables on birth trends, fertility and cohort size, children and divorce rates, homicides and youth, and SAT scores and family size.

590. "Construction." *Forbes*, January 8, 1979, p. 62.

> Analyzes the prospects for construction in 1979. Discusses in detail the effects of tight money, inflation, and debt. Predicts a slowdown, but notes that some demographic factors should improve house sales. Points out that baby boomers are now having their own families. Observes also that they are entering the twenty-five-to-thirty-four age group, which uses its disposable income for big-ticket items. Contends that this age category is growing at triple the rate of the general population.

591. "Consumer Wariness on Credit May Not Go Away." *Business Week*, July 21, 1980, pp. 158–62.

> Attempts to predict the willingness of consumers to buy on credit as the Federal Reserve begins to loosen its tight monetary policies. Cautions not to expect a strong expansion in credit buying. Identifies such reasons as the decline in real income since 1979, current debt responsibilities, and the aging of the baby boomers. Argues that as the baby boomers reach their mid-thirties, they are passing out of their prime consumer years and entering a period when security and savings become more important.

592. Conte, Christopher. "Administration Looks for New Way to Lure Pension Funds to Mortgages." *Wall Street Journal*, 20 September 1982, p. 33.

> Reports on governmental attempts to attract pension funds into the mortgage market. Observes that the present interest rates are so high that mortgage demand is low. Predicts that when the rates fall, a strong pent-up demand will be released. Identifies the source as postwar baby boomers, who may manifest a demand worth $200 billion a year. Pension managers are reluctant to enter mortgage markets because they are less familar with them than they are with stocks and bonds. Discusses the attractiveness of the resale mortgage market and other administrative strategies to bring pension managers into the mortgage area.

593. Cook, David T. "Levi's (And Others) Apply the Stitch-In-Time Theorem: Business Scene." *Christian Science Monitor*, 19 January 1982, p. 11.

> Considers the impact of the aging baby boom on both manufacturers and advertisers. Levi Straus and Co. is profiled as a company with a great interest in retaining baby-boom customers. Consequently, not only has it changed its advertisement strategies, but its jeans have been

made roomier and looser. Other examples (Skippy Peanut Butter and and vitamin-supplement ads) are cited to show how companies are marketing to this aging segment of the population.

594. Cook, James. "The Molting of America." *Forbes*, November 22, 1982, pp. 161–67.

Considers the significance of the collapse or severe contraction of basic industries in the United States. Discusses how industries are "downsizing" to respond to international competition and reduction in demand. Analyzes specifically autos, energy, metals, farming, and rails. Argues that "reindustrialization" proposed by some politicians is naive. Points out that there are some expansion industries, especially in electronics, but generally the labor market will be small. Notes that the harmful effects of such a labor market will be softened by the baby bust, which will shrink the available number of workers. Includes chart of labor force composition by age groups from 1950 to 2000.

595. Curley, John. "Some Think a 'Baby Boom' Spending Spree Could Lead to Strong Economic Recovery." *Wall Street Journal*, 24 January 1983, p. 27.

Explores the possibility that the baby-boom generation may be ready to spend substantial money on basic consumer items such as appliances, cars, housing, and furniture. Baby boomers are now reaching the twenty-to-thirty-four age range, in which basic decisions such as child raising and marriage become dominant. Examines the saving and indebtedness habits of the baby boomers and expresses the possibility of a rapid recovery from the recession if baby boomers decide to have children. Includes table on population of the baby boomers from age fourteen to thirty-four.

596. Curtis, Carol E. "Household Goods." *Forbes*, January 5, 1981, p. 86.

Assesses the market prospects for household goods, particularly the appliance market. Points out that a major market, the post-World War II baby boomers, has advanced beyond the prime buying ages for such things as refrigerators, washers, and dryers and, consequently, buying will slow. Points out, however, that the number of households, particularly single-person households, is growing, and that these nontraditional households represent a strong market for convenience appliances. Notes a market for microwave ovens. Includes a table on the management performance of numerous appliance, houseware, furnishing, and housekeeping companies.

597. "Demographic Disadventure." *Scientific American*, July 1981, p. 76.

> Asks the question, "What price will the children of the baby boom pay for having been born into an exceptionally large cohort?" Predicts that the most disadvantaged group, those graduating from school in 1977, will have the "lowest life-time earnings of any group from 1940–1990." Summarizes an article by James Smith and Finis Welch concerning cohort size and wages. Discusses the degree of competition that will occur at the entry level of employment and contrasts this with opportunities on higher management levels. Concludes that salaries of baby boomers will improve on senior levels.

598. DeMott, John S. "Going After the Mightiest Market." *Time*, September 14, 1981, p. 56.

> Observes that the marketing strategies of Madison Avenue have been adapted to reflect the changing attitudes of the post-war baby boomers as they age. In the 1970s the baby boomers had few responsibilities, but in the 1980s they look for stability. Points out that the mean income of baby boomers has almost doubled in ten years and that the present baby-boom age bracket (twenty-five-to-thirty-four) spends its money on large consumer items such as applicances, furniture, curtains, rugs, housewares, and electronic equipment. Discusses specifically the marketing strategies of such businesses as Johnson & Johnson, Kraft, Levi Strauss, L.L. Bean, General Motors, and Microwave manufacturers.

599. Diggs, J. Frank. "Baby Boomlet: Its Impact on the '80s." *U.S. News and World Report*, June 15, 1981, pp. 51–52.

> Reports on the current increase in U.S. birthrate and its possible impact. Attributes the increase to (1) a decision by young women over thirty to have children; (2) mothers in their twenties choosing both career and family; and (3) the post-World War II baby boomers' having reached childbearing age. Notes that demographers predict that births in the 1980s may approach the 1957 peak of 4.3 million births. Discusses the positive business effects that baby boomlet will have on the toy industry and disposable diaper producers. The potential impact on schools, colleges, and labor market is also noted. Asserts that the 1986 birthrate is crucial because in that year the maximum number of women will be in their childbearing years. Includes tables on birthrates since 1920, and U.S. birth cycles.

600. Dougherty, Philip H. "Baby Boom and *People* Magazine." *New York Times*, 19 April 1984, p. 23D.

Reports on a marketing campaign soon to be launched by *People* magazine to attract baby boomers and advertisers who market to baby boomers. Attributes the inspiration of this campaign to S. Christopher Meigher 3d, the thirty-seven-year-old publisher of the magazine. Notes that the campaign will cost $3 million and will advertise in the *New York Times,* the *Chicago Tribune, Advertising Age,* and *Adweek.* Notes also it will include radio ads in New York City featuring Bert Berdis. Discusses the actual content of some of the magazine ads.

601. Dougherty, Philip H. "Filling a Niche with Beer." *New York Times,* 13 July 1981, p. 7D.

Reports on the marketing of Private Reserve beer created by Neal W. Kaye. Observes that Mr. Kaye believes the baby-boom generation is looking for more than light beer; that baby boomers are looking for a quality full-bodied brew. Reviews Kaye's attempt to find a brewery and to market his product in Europe.

602. Dullea, Georgia. "Baby Boom Generation Turning 30." *New York Times,* 7 May 1984, p. 7B.

Discusses a broad range of concerns held by members of the baby-boom generation as they mature into their thirties. Among these concerns are the following: (1) many baby-boom women need to make decisions about their careers or raising children; (2) success has not come easily, contrary to their belief that if they followed the rules everything would fall into place; (3) financial security is elusive and the need for financial planning evident; and (4) baby boomers have a preoccupation with career, relationship, and life extension. Notes that 4 million baby boomers will enter their thirties this year.

603. Edgerton, Jerry. "Can the Real Estate Boom Last?" *Money,* March 1979, pp. 44–48.

Reports on the financial advantages and disadvantages in buying real estate. Notes that in the 1970s, many people bought homes to protect against inflation but that leveling prices may make house-buying less attractive. The inflation of the seventies was caused in part by the baby-boom population as it reached house-buying age. Contends that outcomes in the real estate market depend on whether baby boomers invest in single-family homes or in alternatives such as condominiums or rentals. Warns that the real estate market may also be affected by overspeculation, energy costs, economic downturns, and tax policy changes.

604. Edgerton, Jerry. "A Home of Their Own." *Money*, March 1983, p. 86.

Observes that the American dream of a nice home may not come to fruition for the baby-boom generation. Buying a house can be financially dangerous and lead to overextension. Reports on a variety of living arrangements and financing techniques, including (1) parental assistance; (2) trading up; (3) renting; (4) refurbishing an older home; (5) purchasing a mobile home; and (6) moving to the country. Concludes that tight housing may change living arrangements even to the point that unhappy couples may stay together in order to hold on to the house.

605. Ehrbar, A.F. "Heading for the Wrong Solution." *Fortune*, December 13, 1982, pp. 113–20.

Analyzes the viability of the Social Security system, particularly its ability to accommodate the baby-boom generation at retirement age. Reviews the efforts of Congress to keep Social Security solvent. Discusses some of the recommendations of the National Commission on Social Security Reform. Indicates that by 2015 the problem will become severe and a payroll tax of 40 percent may be required. Recommends increasing the retirement age to sixty-eight. Expresses concern that current policy is fostering an illusion of security that will create political strife if benefits are altered just before the baby boom retires.

606. Ehrbar, A.F. "How to Save Social Security," *Fortune*, August 25, 1980, pp. 34–39.

Analyzes the Social Security system, particularly its future stability. Notes that current strains on the retirement system are small compared to the period around 2010 when the baby boomers will reach retirement age. Asserts that size of laboring class supporting the baby boomers will be small and that payroll taxes could rise to 36 percent. Proposes two solutions: one, raise the retirement age, and two, adjust the benefit formula, indexing benefits to prices rather than wages. Also recommends that the earnings test be eliminated and that benefits be taxed rather than payroll. Argues that Congress must act soon.

607. Eisenberg, Richard. "Do-It-Yourself Retirement." *Money*, March 1983, pp. 99–106.

Deals with the issue of planning for retirement among the baby-boom population. Many baby boomers have little confidence in Social Security and seek alternative methods for securing their future. Discusses a variety of security techniques, such as tax-deferred corporate pensions and savings plans, IRAs, Keogh plans, small-saver bank CDs, and zero coupon bonds. The advantages and disadvantges of employer savings programs are reviewed. Recommends that baby boomers take into account both growth and tax savings when planning for retirement. Contends that mutual funds may be best for upper-income baby boomers.

608. "End of the Baby Boom?" *Newsweek*, June 15, 1964, p. 94.

Speculates briefly on the reason for the declining birthrate. Among the reasons cited are the introduction of the birth control pill, wider choice of family planning techniques, and trends to delay children and to have fewer children. Indicates that the declining rate is more surprising given the rising marriage rate and an increase in the number of women of childbearing age.

609. "End of the Baby Boom in America." *U.S. News and World Report*, June 14, 1965, p. 67.

Notes the trend of declining birthrates since 1957, the peak of the baby boom. Attributes this decline to several factors, including (1) the view that raising a family is costly, especially in the areas of housing, clothing, and schooling; (2) the increasing use of birth control pills; and (3) a decrease in marriages at a young age. Asserts that a continued birthrate decline will seriously affect the markets for housing, schools, and business.

610. "End of the 'Baby Boom': What It Means to the Country." *U.S. News and World Report*, May 29, 1972, pp. 51–53.

Discusses the impact of a declining birthrate following the baby-boom period. Observes that theoretically there should be increasing births as baby-boom mothers reach childbearing age. Argues that the primary reasons for the baby bust are bad economic times, contraception and abortion, and concern with overpopulation. Reviews the effects of the declining birthrate on institutions such as hospitals, baby products (especially Gerber), cereal makers (such as Kellogg), toy makers (such as Mattel and Fisher-Price), and clothiers (such as Levi Strauss). Problems due to declining enrollments in the school systems are also considered. Includes several tables on enrollment problems in primary and secondary schools.

611. "End to the Baby Boom." *U.S. News and World Report*, March 2, 1964, pp. 83–84.

Notes a seven-year trend toward declining birthrates and focuses on the reasons for the decline. Asserts that the cost of raising, educating, feeding, and clothing a family has been a significant factor in limiting family size. Also points out that the birth control pill has had a similar effect. Reviews possible effects of a declining birthrate. Predicts a slower market for items such as baby clothes, infant food and toys, and a larger market for apartments, televisions, phonographs, sporting equipment, and other luxury items. Includes table on U.S. birthrates.

612. Fialka, John J. "Another Baby Boom Seems Near, But Experts Disagree on Its Size." *Wall Street Journal,* 4 March 1982, p. 31.

Provides a discussion of the current trend toward increased births in the United States. Attributes the rising birthrate to the post-war baby-boom women, who are now in childbearing years. Considers this an "echo boom" and indicates that there are divergent opinions on the significance of the new boom. Reviews in some detail the opposing views of Charles Westoff and Richard Easterlin on the current fertility cycle. Focuses on the attitudes and behavior of childbearing women regarding their careers, desire to have children, and family size. Predicts continuing contraction of educational institutions and "Frantic" competition for workers as the baby-bust generation of the seventies enters the labor market.

613. "Finance: The Push Is on to Get Baby Boomers to Save." *Business Week,* April 23, 1984, pp. 94–95.

Explores why affluent baby boomers, labeled "yuppies," typically do not save money. Even though they are better educated and have high earnings potentials, these baby boomers have a "strong streak of self-indulgence" that precludes the establishment of regular savings plans. In addition, many baby boomers distrust advertising and respond best to individual contacts. Consequently, many financial companies are actively soliciting young adults with only minimal amounts to invest in savings. A table details "The Surge in Potential Savers."

614. Flax, Steven. "The Greening of Crayola." *Forbes,* April 12, 1982, p. 190.

Reviews the new marketing strategies of Binney & Smith, producers of Crayola crayons. Points out that historically, Crayola dominated the crayon market and the company was able to handle even the decline of the child-age population between 1967 to 1980. Notes that earnings are up significantly and attributes this in part to the new baby boom, which should produce a 1 percent to 2 percent annual growth. Discusses also Binney & Smith's move to broaden its product line into art kits and activity toys.

615. Fowler, Elizabeth. "Baby Boom Children in Job Squeeze." *New York Times,* 18 November 1981, p. 21D.

> Describes the struggle of the baby boomers as they compete for managerial and administrative positions. Argues that the big problem is not the older managers holding on to positions, but the large number of baby boomers competing with each other. The expectations of this group are high because they are well educated. Asserts that the plight of baby boomers may in part be offset by several factors, including (1) the increase in two-income families, which provides ample discretionary income; (2) the ability to develop new careers; (3) ability to provide for new pension options such as IRAs; and (4) developing mentoring relationships with company insiders.

616. Frazier, Steve. "Homes Wanted." *Wall Street Journal,* 30 October 1979, p. 1.

> Assesses the current impact of high interest rates on housing construction and demand. Notes that housing starts are expected to fall and that mortgage rates should rise to 14 percent. This housing drop will coincide with a pent-up demand created by the post-war baby boomers, whose demand could reach 2 million housing units annually. Argues that this could lead to significant increases in the cost of housing. Discusses the need to increase mortgage capital and reviews some of the new funds to accomplish this, including money market certificates. Quotes numerous builders on current problems in housing and construction.

617. Fuller, Doris B. "Baby Boom Puts Style on Bottom Line." *Los Angeles Times,* 8 September 1983, p. 1.

> Analyzes the impact of the baby boomlet created by the decision of baby-boom women in their thirties to have children. Notes that it's "not so much the number of these women as it is their socioeconomic profile that is so economically potent." Typically affluent and two-income, these families are "willing and able to pay for style and convenience." Examples of couples' shopping patterns are presented and this phenomenon is labeled "the age of the gourmet baby" by one manufacturer. Specific products aimed at these baby-boomer parents are also identified.

618. "Gerber: Selling More to the Same Mothers is Our Objective Now." *Business Week,* October 16, 1978, pp. 192–95.

> Discusses the new optimism at Gerber Products Co. as the market for baby products looks brighter. Points out that the basis for this optimism is the fertility habits of baby-boom mothers, who are now between the ages of fifteen and forty-four and who are in their prime

childbearing years. Notes that births are expected to rise to 4 million annually by 1982. Asserts that Gerber must continue a diversification program because the baby boom is the only factor holding back a 170-year trend toward declining fertility. Reflects also on the possibilities of take-over attempts by other companies.

619. Gibson, Paul. "General Motors Scores Again." *Forbes*, November 13, 1978, pp. 43–46.

Discusses primarily the optimistic marketing forecasts made by Pontiac and Buick executives that run contrary to economists' predictions of a slowdown in the auto industry. Recognizes the problems of large consumer debt and shrinking disposable income, but argues that significant demographic shifts improve market conditions. Notes that the baby-boom generation was entering the twenty-four-to-thirty-four age group and that this group uses its disposable income for big-ticket items like autos. Also points out that the family is changing, with wives working and increasing the capacity for high debt.

620. Gottschalk, Earl C., Jr. "Blocked Paths: Promotions Grow Few as 'Baby Boom' Group Eyes Managers' Jobs." *Wall Street Journal*, 22 October 1981, p. 1.

Identifies the problems created by increased competition among first-level managers looking for promotions. Points out that the underlying cause is the large number of post-war baby boomers. Predicts that frustration and job hopping will result. Notes that the number of middle-management candidates will jump 42 percent by 1990, but the number of new positions will rise only 21 percent. Indicates that additional results of the promotion squeeze may be (1) rising employee militancy and unionization; (2) increased length of job assignments; (3) power struggles between the younger and older employees; and (4) redefinitions of "success" in business. Includes chart on middle-management positions.

621. Gottschalk, Earl C., Jr. "Trendy Dwellings: The 'Affordable' Home Turns Out to Be Tiny and Not Really Cheap." *Wall Street Journal*, 7 December 1981, p. 1.

Examines the reality of home ownership among relatively affluent members of the baby boom. Individuals entering the housing market for the first time have "found that the American dream home has shrunk, even if housing prices haven't. They have had to learn to live in smaller spaces and to pay more of their incomes for the privilege." Remarkably, most home buyers interviewed expressed gratitude for being able to own a scaled-down version of their parents' home. Comments from first-time home buyers in California, Virginia, Texas, and Manhattan are included.

622. Guzzardi, Walter, Jr. "Demography's Good News for the Eighties." *Fortune*, November 5, 1979, pp. 92–106.

Attempts to trace the social and economic impact of baby boomers as they mature in the 1980s. Notes that in the seventies, baby boomers were young and created a disturbing youth culture, accompanied by juvenile delinquency, crime, and youth unemployment. Points out as well that the labor market in the seventies experienced a major influx of women. Argues that in the eighties the work force will age along with the baby boomers and that the workers will, therefore, be more experienced and mature and consequently more productive. Reviews the future structure of U.S. households, prospects for minorities, immigration patterns, and consumer markets. Includes tables on work-force composition by sex and age.

623. Hayes, Thomas C. "Selling Computers Like Soap: Top Posts Go to Marketers." *New York Times*, 27 July 1983, pp. 1D–2D.

Notes that professional marketers are being hired by major microcomputer companies to sell personal computers and video games. Executives with experience in selling soda pop, cigarettes, and soap are joining these high-technology companies to provide expertise in selling to affluent members of the baby-boom generation. One common marketing theme for microcomputer companies is to appeal to "baby boomers who want to be successful in their careers and raise intelligent kids."

624. Hoffman, Marilyn. "The Baby-Boom Children of the Fifties Become Pacesetters for the Eighties." *Christian Science Monitor*, 23 January 1980, p. 15.

Summarizes various demographic studies on "emerging thirties," members of the baby boom in that age group. Statistics indicate that baby boomers will marry later (if at all), have fewer babies, and have many two-career families. Home ownership was found to be a major priority. These "emerging thirties" are considered by Ralph Timm, publisher of *House & Garden*, as "an entirely new breed of self-assured, educated, and discriminating young people."

625. "Housing's Big Boost from the Baby Boomers." *Business Week*, June 20, 1983, pp. 172–74.

Reports on the "explosive" growth in the sales of new homes and asserts that this growth may be more than temporary. Points out that people of baby-boom age (between twenty-five and thirty-four) account for 50 to 65 percent of new purchases. Explains that these young buyers traditionally turn to older homes for first-time purchases, but that these homes are not available at affordable prices because they were often purchased during periods of high interest rates and are not attractive buys. Notes also that new homes have lower maintenance costs and can be financed on the rejuvenated thirty-year mortgage. Includes table on percentage of young people who can afford to buy homes.

626. Hyatt, James C. "Aging Americns." *Wall Street Journal*, 25 October 1979, p. 1.

Discusses the overall social impact of aging in the U.S. population. Points out that the over-sixty-five population will expand significantly because of the baby-boom generation, and that this growth will be coupled with greater life expectancy. Cites among problems (1) greater demand for nursing home and medical facilities; (2) tremendous increases in the federal health budget; (3) increased migration to suburban regions; and (4) psychological isolation and diminished ability of relatives to support older family. Speculates that an aging society may also be a more mature one.

627. "Industry Report: Household Products and Apparel." *Forbes*, January 9, 1978, pp. 162–69.

Analyzes buying habits of baby boomers, especially concerning household goods and apparel. Observes that the baby-boom generation is entering the twenty-five-to-forty-five age group and it is this group that buys major consumer items such as houses and appliances. Discusses in detail the appliance industry, particularly with respect to refrigerators, ranges, washing machines, and dryers. Reviews also the market for food processors, microwaves, hardware items, and moderately priced clothing, especially jeans. Describes the competitive relationships between Whirlpool, Maytag, General Electric, Magic Chef, and others. Includes detailed charts of the profitability and growth of numerous companies in appliances, housewares and furnishings, housekeeping products, apparel, textiles, and shoes.

628. "Jobs, Jobs, Jobs." *Forbes*, January 16, 1984, p. 11.

Summarizes projections of the 1995 labor force made by the Bureau of Labor Statistics. The baby boom will have been absorbed and women will have increased their percentage of the labor force by 1995. Predicts that these future workers will be better educated, more experienced, and older. This will adversely affect the largest employer of young men, the armed forces.

629. Jones, Landon Y. "The Baby Boom Legacy." *Saturday Evening Post*, May/ June 1982, p. 20.

Analyzes the significance of the baby-boom population as it ages. Points out that there have been three major population shifts since World War II: the baby boom, the subsequent baby bust, and the aging of a massive baby-boom population. Among issues raised are the following: (1) baby boomers are better educated than previous generations and will bring with them the social and political expectations of their education; (2) baby boomers will place a tremendous strain on social services and on the Social Security system; (3) women will significantly outnumber men; and (4) the elderly class will be more powerful and healthy and will promote less of a distinction between work, retirement, and leisure.

630. Jones, Landon Y. "Baby Boom: The Generation That Gave Us Space and Rock Now Faces a Brave New Cause: Midlife." *People*, December 29, 1980, p. 123.

Discusses the impact of the baby-boom generation, particularly as it matures. Notes that baby boomers are now between the ages of sixteen and thirty-four and that their consumer tastes have changed. Observes that baby-boomer families are often nontraditional, involving divorces, and that this is reflected in TV programming like *Eight Is Enough* or *I'm a Big Girl Now*. Analyzes the tremendous influence of baby-boom women especially in work-force composition. Contends that baby-boom mothers are creating a baby boomlet as they reach childbearing years. Argues also that the sheer number of baby boomers will create intense job competition and resultant job frustrations.

631. Jones, Landon Y. "The Baby Boomers." *Money*, March 1983, pp. 56–59.

Analyzes advantages and disadvantages of the baby-boom generation. Notes that 74 million people were born between 1946 and 1964 and that this population was raised with high expectations. These expectations were damaged by overcrowded schools, oversupply in the labor force, and shortages in housing. Contends that baby-boom women have significantly affected the work-force composition and altered the family structure. Predicts that by 1990, a third of the U.S. population will be between twenty-five and forty-four and that this population will encourage conservative policies to protect families and support day-care centers.

632. Jones, Landon Y. "The Birthing Dilemma: Baby Boom or Bust?" *Saturday Evening Post*, January/February 1982, p. 56.

> Examines issues surrounding the low fertility rate in the United States, particularly the fertility behavior of baby-boom women, who are in their prime childbearing years. Speculates on why baby-boom women have not borne children. Points out several factors, including (1) increased participation of women in the work force; (2) decline in social pressures to marry; (3) increase in the cohabitation of individuals; and (4) increase in the divorce rate. Discusses the differing predictions of two leading demographers, Richard Easterlin and Charles Westoff.

633. "Jostens: A School Supplier Stays with Basics as Enrollment Declines." *Business Week*, April 21, 1980, p. 124.

> Analyzes the business activities of Jostens, Inc., of Minneapolis, a supplier of class rings and yearbooks to high schools. Notes that the passing of the baby boom has seriously affected high-school enrollment and this has forced major marketing changes. Reports that emphasis is now being placed on high-enrollment areas in the South, in junior high schools and colleges, and in related diversified businesses. Observes that attempts to enter into the library-supply market failed.

634. Kadzis, Peter. "Up from Produce, On to Petticoats." *Forbes*, March 14, 1983, pp. 70–71.

> Reports on the marketing success of Stop and Shop of Boston as it diversified from grocery stores into retail clothing. Notes that many firms that diversified into clothing marketed their merchandise as "discount" or "bargain" products. Observes that, in contrast, Stop and Shop viewed the key consumers as the baby boomers and saw that this group was demanding and looked for quality as well as low prices. Asserts that Stop and Shop displayed their goods creatively and paid attention to fashion. Describes the future earnings and financial attractiveness of the company.

635. "Kellogg: Still the Cereal People." *Business Week*, November 26, 1979, p. 80.

> Reviews the marketing strategy of the Kellogg Co., with particular emphasis on current demographic trends. Points out that Kellogg grew rapidly, marketing its cereal to the baby-boom generation. Asserts, however, that this generation has now matured into the over-twenty-five age group and this group consumes the least amount of cereal. Examines how Kellogg has responded to this challenge through

several courses of action, including (1) new product programs; (2) expansion of international markets; (3) challenges to the Federal Trade Commission's anti-monopoly efforts; and (4) diversification. Discusses also the strategies of companies such as General Foods and General Mills.

636. Kettle, John. "The Big Generation: What's Ahead for Baby Boomers?" *Futurist*, February 1981, p. 3.

Focuses on the future prospects of baby boomers, particularly in Canada. Points out that the major baby-boom countries were Canada, the United States, Australia, and New Zealand. Anticipates that baby boomers will experience intense job competition, a shortage of housing, and severe pension problems. Observes that baby boomers were raised with high hopes for the future and that many have been seriously disappointed, leading to alienation and stress. Examines various options for the competitive work environment, including part-time employment, job sharing, and reduction of the work day. Speculates also on the political impact of a potentially apathetic but substantial segment of baby-boom voters.

637. Kiechel, Walter, III. "Brunch and Crunch on the Fast Track." *Fortune*, May 3, 1982, p. 313.

Notes that the baby-boom generation is now flooding the labor market and competition for jobs will be fierce. Asserts that the lesser-educated baby boomers have already suffered, but the elite is just beginning to feel the job pinch. Observes that the M.B.A. from a prestige school is no guarantee of rapid promotion. Examines the attitudes of baby boomers toward management and reports that they are more nurturing and less authoritarian. Projects a trend toward reeducation and a propensity to make several career changes throughout life.

638. Koenig, Richard. "Will Baby Boomers Lead Cigar Makers Out of Sales Slump?" *Wall Street Journal*, 2 September 1983, p. 1.

Considers what potential impact the maturing baby boom will have on cigar sales. Faced with continuing declines, the cigar industry "is latching on to the only hope in sight—the men of the baby boom generation, now near the cigar-smoking threshold of middle age." However, cigar makers must change to market their products to a younger and more health-conscious generation. Concludes that it will be necessary to change "the status of cigar smoking from dirty habit to respectable vice."

639. Kronholz, June. "Baby Boomlet." *Wall Street Journal*, 29 July 1977, p. 1.

Reports on the fertility behavior of the baby-boom generation. Notes that as these women approach the end of their prime childbearing years, they are considering raising a family. Notes recent increase in the birthrate, following the baby bust of the 1970s. The primary reason for the delay in childbearing was financial. Speculates on the possibilities of a baby boomlet or steady rise in the birthrate. Argues that a significant number of women want to have children, and the only question is when they will have them.

640. "Labor's Big Swing from Surplus to Shortage." *Business Week*, February 20, 1978, pp. 75–77.

Examines the impact of the baby-boom generation on the labor force, especially the adaptations that will be required from management and unions. Notes that baby boomers are now reaching the twenty-five-to-forty-four age bracket, which creates intense job competition with additional burdens for women and minorities. Points out that unions respond to protect their members by tightening rules for seniority or shortening work hours. Asserts that new problems will arise as the baby boomers approach retirement age and put a severe strain on the Social Security system.

641. "Liquor's Thirst for a Younger Market." *Business Week*, April 20, 1981, pp. 114–15.

Discusses the recent trend away from bourbon and blends and toward wine and "white goods." Reviews the effects on liquor companies, noting that for the first time Americans drink more wine than distilled spirits. Attributes this change in taste primarily to members of the baby-boom generation as they move into their ages of maximum consumption of liquor. Noting that these individuals were raised on soft drinks, contends that this produces a penchant for lighter and sweeter drinks in adulthood. Observes that chief beneficiary of this change is not only wine, but vodka, gin, rum, brandy, and cordials; chief losers are whiskey, bourbon, and scotch. Provides a list of sales for major liquor companies in 1979 and 1980, noting their losses or gains.

642. "Looking to the ZPGeneration." *Time*, February 28, 1977, p. 71.

Discusses the continuing decline in fertility rate and indicates that the U.S. population may soon reach zero population growth (ZPG). Makes numerous predictions concerning the effects of ZPG, including (1) a reduction in demands on resources and environment; (2) increased discretionary income to spend on products of interest to an aging population such as art supplies, books, backgammon, and electronic games; (3) increased demand for continuing adult education; (4) demand for smaller living quarters; (5) shift of power to the older American and a refocusing of attention on the care and satisfaction of the elderly; and (6) intensification of competition for promotions in middle-management.

643. Lord, Lewis J. "Delayed Baby Boom: Its Meaning." *U.S. News and World Report*, February 20, 1978, pp. 39–41.

Reports that baby-boom mothers who had postponed bearing children are now having babies. Contends that these mothers and their children will have a significant impact on the labor market, the nation's business, and life-styles. Experts believe delayed childbearing usually leads to wanted children and more stable families. Interviews several individuals concerning their decision to have children and asserts that the current trend toward having babies will not create another baby boom. Argues that job opportunities for women and diminished societal pressure to bear children will keep the birthrate relatively low.

644. "A Love Potion That May Sweeten Perfume Sales." *Business Week*, December 20, 1982, p. 29.

Deals primarily with a new marketing technique in the perfume industry—the use of the allegedly aphrodisiac pheromones as an additive. Observes that Jovan, Inc., introduced a fragrance called Andron containing pheromones and sales jumped markedly for the company. Notes that the perfume industry is not performing well, with sales off 5 percent for the year. Attributes this to the end of the "era of growth" caused by the baby-boom generation.

645. McGrath, Peter. "Learning to Love the Baby Boom." *Washingtonian*, April 1980, pp. 95–103.

Discusses in detail the impact of the baby boom in the past and present and projects potential impact in the future. Makes numerous observations including the following: (1) inflation has been caused in part by the influx of young adult baby boomers, who flooded the market with inexperienced, unproductive, and unreliable labor; (2) crime rates increased in the sixties because of the large number of young baby boomers; (3) baby boomers stimulated the creation of suburbs and new schools; (4) high unemployment in the seventies was caused to a large extent by the influx of baby boomers into the labor force;

(5) the subsequent baby bust is disrupting institutions that had adapted to the baby boom, such as schools and colleges; and (6) there are few good explanations as to the cause of the baby boom. Reviews future markets for consumer items such as housing, appliances, cars, and leisure goods. Discusses also the impact on the retirement system as the baby boomers age.

646. "Madison Ave. Chases the Baby Boom." *New York Times Magazine*, May 31, 1981, p. 55.

Discusses how marketing approaches have changed to respond to the attitudes of post-war baby boomers as they have aged. Notes that by 1990, individuals between the ages of twenty-five and forty-five will account for 44 percent of all households and 55 percent of consumer spending. Reviews the changing strategies of such businesses as Levi Strauss, Gerber, Max Factor and the cosmetic industry, Johnson & Johnson, Proctor & Gamble, Snickers, motorcycles, television, and audio equipment. Observes that baby boomers delayed having children until their thirties and have now created a baby boomlet, which should improve the markets for baby products. Indicates that commercials will use older actors and deal more with the problems of aging rather than marketing toward adolescence.

647. Marcom, John, Jr. "Advances in Contact Lenses Erasing Old Image Problems." *Wall Street Journal*, 25 May 1984, p. 21.

Discusses the prospects for the contact lens and the technological innovations that have broadened the contact lens market. Reviews the types of lens, including hard contacts, soft contacts, and rigid gas permeable lenses. Notes that aging baby boomers will constitute the largest future market for contacts but that as the baby boomers age they will require special adaptations for such problems as presbyopia. Argues that this will create a substantial market for bi-focal contacts.

648. Mayer, Lawrence A. "It's a Bear Market for Babies Too." *Fortune*, December 1974, pp. 134–37.

Tries to understand the fertility cycle in the United States since the post-war baby boom. Points out that the baby bust that followed the boom has been very lengthy. Cites the work of Charles Westoff, who contends that the birthrate has been declining for a long time and that the baby boom is the abnormal feature. Reviews also the theory of Richard Easterlin on fertility behavior. Observes that a baby boomlet should have occurred as the baby-boom women reached childbearing years, but that this did not occur. Indicates that the Census Bureau now surveys young married women to anticipate their fertility behavior.

649. "Merrill Lynch Fund Aims to Nurse the 'Baby Boom.'" *Wall Street Journal*, 3 February 1984, p. 28.

> Announces a mutual fund offered by Merrill Lynch & Co. designed to attract baby-boomer investors. Called "Fund for Tomorrow," this fund requires low minimum investments and is being marketed to first-time investors. Baby boomers are judged to have "evolutionary, sometimes revolutionary, needs." Stocks in the fund are not identified, but a spokesman reports they were selected to allow baby boomers to "invest in their own lifestyles, and in the industries that reflect their tastes and habits."

650. Merry, Robert W. "The Benefit Bog." *Wall Street Journal*, 10 November 1982, p. 1.

> Reports on the current political battles being fought over reforming the Social Security system. Notes that there is a short-term insolvency problem, but the major issue is a long-term problem: the aging of the post-war baby boomers, who will place a tremendous strain on Social Security when they reach retirement. Discusses the political aspects of the newly appointed bipartisan Social Security Reform Commission headed by Alan Greenspan. Explores some of the proposed solutions, including interfund borrowing, expanded coverage to government employees, tax increases, and benefit reductions.

651. Miller, Nory. "Architectural Elements: Baby Boom Architects." *Metropolitan Home*, 15 July 1983, p. 68.

> Provides photographic examples of twelve architectural elements that characterize the tastes of new baby-boom architects. Cites among the elements: use of columns; use of humorous touches; stucco; renaissance tiling; lattice work; high tech; and interior windows. Notes that baby boomers are known for the use of "stucco, wallboard, chipboard, lattice and glass."

652. Miller, Nory. "The Baby Boom Architects: Most Talented and Promising Architects: Chicago." *Metropolitan Home*, July 1983, p. 52.

> Reviews briefly the architectural style of several baby-boom architects from Chicago. Includes the work of George Pappageorge, David Haymes, James Mastro, Claudia Skylar, Ronald Krueck, Keith Olsen, and Joseph Valerio. Discusses how Pappageorge and Haymes have converted warehouses and loft buildings using "diverse architectural detail." Characterizes work of Mastro and Skylar as "light and airy" with pastel ornament and color. Describes Krueck and Olsen as "steeped in contemporary art," which produces a sensual architecture.

Notes that Valerio sometimes is influenced by Mies van der Rohe and describes his own work as "the big bang theory of architecture."

653. Miller, Nory. "Baby Boom Architects: Most Talented and Promising Architects: Connecticut." *Metropolitan Home*, July 1983, p. 62.

Discusses the work of noted baby-boom architects currently working in Connecticut. Reviews briefly the architectural styles of Mark Simon, Stephen Lloyd, Chad Floyd, Robert Harper, and Jefferson Riley. Characterizes Simon as "remodeled bungalow"; Lloyd as "low-key Victorian"; Riley as "New England saltbox and contemporary design"; and Robert Harper as "American Palladian." Includes photographs.

654. Miller, Nory. "Baby Boom Architects: Most Talented and Promising Architects: Des Moines." *Metropolitan Home*, July 1983, p. 56.

Discusses the work of Calvin Lewis, who is noted as a "baby boom architect" working in Des Moines. Observes that although traditionally trained, Lewis was influenced by Post-Modernism. Indicates that Lewis employs different styles, from Corbusier's for a corporate headquarters to Michael Graves's for a Tudor garage. Includes photographs.

655. Miller, Nory. "The Baby Boom Architects: Most Talented and Promising Architects: Houston." *Metropolitan Home*, July 1983, p. 49.

Discusses the work of John Casbarian, Danny Samuels, Robert Timme, Val Glitsch, and William Stern. Portrays these architects as part of the baby-boom generation of designers. Notes that Casbarian, Samuels and Timme, known collectively as Taft Architects, employ a technique that is "vivacious, festive and appealing, with a flair for well-crafted construction and decorative detail." Describes the work of Glitsch as using surprising colors, big windows, wide siding, and oversize block. Characterizes Sterns's work as attention to detail, inspired by older homes.

656. Miller, Nory. "Baby Boom Architects: Most Talented and Promising Architects: Los Angeles." *Metropolitan Home*, July 1983, p. 44.

Part of a series of architectural articles on baby boomers in this field. Discusses the work of Frederick Fisher, Peter de Bretteville, Thom Mayne and Michael Rotondi. Characterizes Fisher's work as "made of fragments—diverse, strident." Views de Bretteville as having a high-tech or factory style, using metal trusses and steel gratings. Notes that Rotondi and Mayne, also known collectively as Morphosis, employ a "childlike charm" mixed with "defense industry technology."

657. Miller, Nory. "Baby Boom Architects: Most Talented and Promising Architects: Miami and Atlanta." *Metropolitan Home*, July 1983, p. 66.

Reviews the work of three baby-boom architects from Miami and Atlanta: Andres Duany, Elizabeth Plater-Zyberk, and Anthony Ames. Characterizes the work of Duany and Plater-Zyberk (husband and wife) as in the Spanish Deco tradition. Describes the work of Ames in Atlanta as influenced by Le Corbusier with white as the dominant color, flat roofs, and cantilevered balconies. Includes photographs.

658. Miller, Nory. "The Baby Boom Architects: Most Talented and Promising Architects: New York." *Metropolitan Home*, July 1983, p. 59.

Reviews the work of several baby-boom architects working in New York City. Includes brief discussions of Tod Williams, Billie Tsien, Henry Smith-Miller, and Susana Torre. Describes Williams's and Tsien's work as both clear and "coordinated detail," and emphasis on color, mood, and experimentation. Portrays Smith-Miller as influenced by Frank Lloyd Wright and Mies van der Rohe with high doorways, low ceilings, and free-standing partitions that also serve as furniture. Credits Torre's work with clear interpretations of whatever mode is current.

659. Miller, Nory. "The Baby Boom Architects: Most Talented and Promising Architects: San Francisco." *Metropolitan Home*, July 1983, p. 41.

Discusses the architectural work of Andrew Batey, Mark Mack, Richard Verneau, and Laural Hartman. Identified as baby-boom architects who "move back and forth among stylistic vocabularies." Portrays Ferneau and Hartman as using color contrasts in a surreal manner. Describes Batey as using "Mexican earthiness" and frontier architecture; Mack is a "concrete block type" using geometrics and hard edges.

660. Miller, Nory. "Baby Boom Architects: Most Talented and promising Architects: Washington, D.C.: *Metropolitan Home*, July 1983, p. 64.

Identifies some of the new baby-boom architects working in Washington, D.C. Includes the work of Robert Bell, Heather Willson Cass, and Patrick Pinnell. Notes that Bell has been involved in conversion and remodeling and enjoys "juxtaposing historical and modern design." Observes that Cass and Pinnell take Colonial and Victorian designs as their influence. Includes photographs.

661. Mingay, Jane. "The Baby Boomers Face Up to Old Age." *MacLeans* January 17, 1983, p. 28.

Expresses concern that when the baby boomers in Canada reach retirement age, the Canadian Pension Plan will go bankrupt. Reviews alternative methods for keeping the system solvent. Focuses on special problems concerning pensions for women. Discusses the advisability of diminishing government responsibility and shifting pension responsibilities to private life insurance companies.

662. Minsky, Terri. "More People Face Career Plateaus: A Relief for Some, Shock for Others." *Wall Street Journal*, 2 August 1982, p. 17.

Examines the problem of managers whose careers end at the middle-management level. Notes that career plateauing is particularly problematical because of the entrance of the baby-boom generation into the labor market. Comments that with the large number of new business school graduates, plateauing can occur at any level. Discusses the psychological effects of plateauing and physiological consequences such as high blood pressure and heart attack. Quotes numerous experts in business.

663. Morrison, Peter. "Beyond the Baby Boom—The Depopulation of America." *Futurist*, April 1979, pp. 131–39.

Presents an extensive overview of the demographic future of society. Projections of fertility are used to predict annual increases in population through the first quarter of the next century. The distribution of this population by age and sex is also considered. The ongoing effects of the baby boom are analyzed and projections made. Notes that "demographic change proceeds slowly, but on a massive scale." Various tables and graphs are included to illustrate various points.

664. Mouat, Lucia. "End of 'Baby Boom' Should Help Ease Youth Job-Shortage." *Christian Science Monitor*, 10 February 1981, p. 6.

Observes that as the end of the baby boom enters the job market, the number of young adults competing for first jobs will decrease. The total group of unemployed youth will decline, regardless of the nation's economy. The national trend toward service jobs may not adversely affect young job seekers. However, unemployment will remain high for inner-city teenagers.

665. Mouat, Lucia. "Private High Schools Flourish Despite Waning Baby Boom: Generous Financial Aid, Greater Discipline Lure New Students." *Christian Science Monitor*, 4 August 1981, p. 7.

Focuses on the increase in enrollment in private high schools, just as public schools prepare to meet the coming decline in enrollment.

While the decline in public school attendance is partially attributable to the end of the baby boom, the record number of students in private schools may be due to the older portion of the baby boom's being financially able to send their children to such institutions. A large amount of financial aid is available, but parents typically both work and have not themselves attended private schools.

666. Murray, Alan. "Growth of Labor Force Slows, Raising Hopes of Lower Jobless Rates: Trend, If It Holds, May Lead to Greater Productivities; How Women Affect Data—Baby Boomers Come of Age." *Wall Street Journal*, 4 January 1984, p. 1.

Predicts significant changes in the civilian labor force, especially in the area of unemployment. The slowdown in the growth of the overall labor force will have significant effects on the economy and is caused by "the aging of the baby boom generation, changing work patterns by women and a larger-than-expected number of workers who are too discouraged to return to the job market after the long, deep recession." Problems in accurately forecasting work-force composition are noted.

667. "New Baby Boom May Be On in U.S." *Christian Science Monitor*, 7 August 1979, p. 2.

Reports American Hospital Association statistics to predict that another baby boom may be starting. Figures for hospital births rose dramatically in the first four months of 1979. While experts are not predicting a new major baby boom, the potential impact of the large generation of baby-boom women in childbearing years is stressed.

668. "The New Democrats Turn Out." *Washington Post*, 19 March 1984, p. A18.

Editorializes that a "new Democratic Party may be emerging" in the early 1984 Democratic primaries. Young voters of the baby-boom generation voted in unexpectedly large numbers, primarily for Gary Hart. In addition, a large increase in black voters was evident. While Democratic Party officials viewed these dramatic increases as "harbingers of good fortune for November," it was unclear whether the Democratic candidates were "inspiring enough of its older adherents to win in November."

669. "New Learning Games Make the Grade." *Business Week*, January 24, 1983, p. 81.

Reports on the increasing development of educational software for home computers designed for children. Argues that the significant success of such software is based on the baby-boom generation, who, as parents, have great respect for education. Reviews the activities of several companies in developing software, including the Spinnaker Software Corporation, Atari, Apple Computer, Control Data Corporation, Texas Instruments, and Tandy Corporation.

670. "New/Trends: Unemployment and the Baby Bust." *Fortune*, March 5, 1984, p. 7.

Points out that, contrary to the Reagan administration's claims, the drop in unemployment rate to 8 percent in January 1984 was due more to demographics than politics. The baby-boom generation "has finally grown up and for the most part been placed in jobs." Therefore, more jobs are being created than individuals entering the job market for the first time. However, many of the new jobs require skills not possessed by older, unemployed persons.

671. O'Donnell, Thomas. "Swapping Rock Concerts for Rocking Chairs." *Forbes*, December 6, 1982, pp. 39–40.

Reports that the savings rate has increased from 6 percent to 8 percent and that this is excellent for financial markets. Notes that the real figure may be closer to 12 percent if unreported income is included. Argues that the increase is a result of the baby-boom population's aging, and that as they age, they recognize the need to save money for the education of their children and for retirement. Reflects that saving is also due to a lack of confidence in the economy and the resulting fear of unemployment.

672. O'Hanlon, James. "Bedlam in Photoland." *Forbes*, February 5, 1979, pp. 35–36.

Discusses the battle between Polaroid and Kodak, primarily for the instant camera market. Notes that Polaroid, which originally had 100 percent of the market, now has only 65 percent, but sales are still strong. Projects that the growth in the instant camera market may continue and points out that Kodak attributes this growing market to the post-war baby boomers. Reviews also the growth and competition in the conventional camera market.

673. Ostrow, Ronald J. "Prisons Experiencing Effects of Baby Boom." *Los Angeles Times*, 25 April 1983, p. 3-I.

Cites prison population statistics compiled by the Justice Department's Bureau of Justice to demonstrate that recent increases in incarceration can be attributed to "the post-World War II 'baby boom' and to tougher sentencing and parole policies." As the baby-boom gen-

eration matures into its thirties, a general decline in prison populations is expected. Notes that twenty-to-twenty-nine-year-old males are
statistically most likely to be imprisoned.

674. O'Toole, Patricia. "Finding Work in Glutted Fields." *Money*, March 1983,
     p. 67.

   Examines the job market for the baby boomers preparing to enter the
   labor force. The work force will grow by 19 percent by 1995, but the
   number of workers, mostly baby boomers, will increase by 52 percent.
   Provides advice to the career-seeking by dispelling eight "myths."
   These are: (1) government information and projections are useful; (2)
   there will be no demand for low-technology jobs; (3) specialization is
   best; (4) there is no security in working for yourself; (5) large corporations have most of the jobs; (6) an M.B.A. means success; (7) traditionally female jobs should be avoided; and (8) writing talent is not
   marketable.

675. "The Outlook: Changing Work Force Will Help Economy." *Wall Street
     Journal*, 15 August 1983, p. 1.

   Quotes Michael L. Wachter, University of Pennsylvania professor,
   concerning future changes in the work force. A significantly slower
   growth in the labor force is predicted, based in part on the "declining
   influence of the great post-World War II baby boom." Problems encountered in the seventies as the economy tried to absorb large numbers of untrained workers are noted. As earnings increase for a small
   pool of entry-level workers, the cost to an individual of remaining
   unemployed will increase. Two slightly negative demographic trends
   are briefly discussed: an increasing percentage of minority workers,
   and a sizeable number of disadvantaged workers.

676. "A Popular 34-Year Old." *New York Times*, 25 March 1984, p. 1F.

   Reports on the attempts of financial service companies to attract new
   investors. Points out that half a million investors have entered the
   market in the last ten years. Quotes Allan D. Grody from Coopers and
   Lybrand, who states that this boom in investors is primarily a result of
   the baby boomers. Reveals that findings of his company's study indicate that the average new investor is thirty-four, female, with an initial
   investment of $2,200. Indicates that the preferred investment was in
   an IRA.

677. "Population Changes That Help for a While." *Business Week*, September
     3, 1979, pp. 180–87.

Examines the potential impact of the baby-boom generation on the society and economy as this generation ages. Reviews the theory propounded by Richard Easterlin regarding fertility behavior among the baby boomers. Contends that several positive events will take place in the 1980s, including (1) reductions in inflationary pressures; (2) increased productivity due to a more mature labor force; (3) reductions in government spending for crime, welfare, and education; and (4) reduced labor force growth. Notes as well that a significant negative consequence of the baby boomers may arise as they reach retirement age and place great strain on the Social Security system.

678. Porter, Sylvia. "The '80s Baby Boom: A Boon to the Economy." *Ladies Home Journal,* January 1982, p. 42.

Assesses the impact a rise in births will have on the economy if a significant number of baby-boom women decide to have children in the 1980s. This "now or never" baby boom may occur as older baby-boom women decide to have babies while they still can. Such births at a later age will result in more natal centers to treat high-risk babies; an increase in school enrollment; a need for additional housing; and benefits to industries that cater to babies and children. A chart details the high cost of raising a baby.

679. Quinn, Jane Bryant, and Deborah Witherspoon. "Baby-Boom Economics." *Newsweek,* June 18, 1979, p. 70.

Contends that "economic demographics" has emerged as a new technique for predicting our economic future. This technique is concerned primarily with the influence of the post-war baby boom. Quotes numerous economists, including Michael Wachter, Dwight Jaffee, Fabian Linden, and Sandra Shaber. Notes that by 1989, 31.7 percent of the population will be between the ages of twenty-five and forty-four and that this age group consumes the most durable goods. Warns that after the baby boom comes a baby bust that will have the burden of supporting the boom as it reaches retirement age.

680. Rice, Berkeley. "The Baby Boom Comes of Age." *Psychology Today,* November 1974, pp. 33–34.

Reports on the findings of Ben J. Wattenberg in his book *The Real America*. Focuses on the marital activity of the post-World War II baby boomers and challenges the assertion that as a group they are more liberated and less traditional. Notes that the number of marriages has increased by 50 percent since 1960 and that the number of "shotgun" marriages has decreased. Asserts also that (1) people are marrying at a later age; (2) pregnancies out of wedlock will decline; (3)

married women will also be part of the labor force; and (4) the average newly married couple will be better educated and be more financially stable.

681. Runde, Robert. "Investing in the Boom." *Money*, March 1983, p. 109.

Reports that by the end of the decade, the baby boomers will account for 55 percent of consumer spending. Analyzes several areas in which investment may prove valuable. Covers the following investment opportunities: (1) housing: notes that market is unstable and recommends investing in related do-it-yourself products; (2) life-style: emphasizes in particular the home computer market; and (3) childrens' products: focuses on infant care. Cites as possible companies Black and Decker, Stanley Works, Apple Computer, Commodore, IBM, Tandy, Gerber Products, and Merrill Lynch.

682. Sanger, Elizabeth. "No More Aluminum Ghettos: Mobile Homes Enjoy New Image and a Pickup in Sales." *Barron's*, 19 March 1984, p. 24.

Predicts a bright future for "manufactured homes," formerly known as mobile homes. Such homes are significantly cheaper, easier to finance, and more affordable than conventional houses. While a good economy will increase sales in the 1980s, the biggest factor may be the demographics of the baby boom: "The baby boomers of the fifties need housing, and manufactured homes may be a logical choice." Reports that in 1983 one out of three new single-family homes was a mobile or manufactured home.

683. Sanoff, Alvin P. "Baby Boom Generation Runs into Reality." *U.S. News and World Report*, September 28, 1981, pp. 57–59.

Deals with the maturation of members of the baby-boom population as they move from their teenage years into their twenties and thirties. Provides brief descriptions of specific baby-boom adults and reports on their attitudes and values. Discusses the change in marketing strategies, particularly of Pepsi-Cola, as the need to attract an older audience becomes important. Notes that as baby boomers turn to raising families, their households frequently involve working wives and nontraditional living arrangements. The political attitudes of baby boomers will also become more important. Includes tables on baby-boom attitudes related to civil rights, environmental issues, nuclear power, ideology, government, and women's rights.

684. Schmidt, Peggy. "1980s Grads: Baby Boom to Job Bust." *New York Times*, 16 October 1983, p. 32.

Reports on the frustrations of college-educated job seekers in searching for positions in their field. Notes that the Bureau of Labor Statistics had predicted this condition, observing that the number of
graduates in technical, professional, and managerial areas would exceed demand. Notes further that the Bureau attributed this to the influx of the baby-boom generation on the labor market. Cites several
case studies, with particular emphasis on individuals trained in
business or advertising.

685. Schneider, William. "Gary Hart's Nonpartisan Candidacy: A Campaign
Geared to Baby Boom Voters." *Los Angeles Times*, 26 February 1984,
p. IV–1.

Analyzes the apparent attempt by Gary Hart to attract baby-boom
voters in his campaign for the Democratic presidential nomination.
Statistics reveal a significant generation gap in the Democratic Party.
Points out that politicians and their advisors clearly recognize the importance of the baby-boom vote: "Any politician who could mobilize
the support of Americans born after World War II—now half of the
electorate—would command a new majority." Unfortunately, baby
boomers have so far shown no inclination to be mobilized.

686. Seaberry, Jane. "A Shifting Population May Help the Economy: Aging of
Baby Boom Generation Among Factors Expected to Ease U.S. Problems in 10 to 15 years." *Washington Post*, 28 January 1984, p. 1G.

Reports on an internal administration study for the Cabinet Council
on Economic Affairs on how population shifts, especially the maturing of the baby-boom generation, will affect the economy in the next
ten to fifteen years. A list of possible impacts, ranging from the need
to increase military wages to the survival of the Social Security system,
is presented. Increased worker productivity is predicted as the baby
boom ages. Some economists even believe these demographic factors
will reduce the overall budget deficit in future decades.

687. Shannon, Martin J. "The Baby Boom Has Already Started for Some Businesses and Elementary Schools." *Wall Street Journal*, 25 June 1981, p. 1.

Reviews briefly the effects of the new baby boom on the toy industry
and education system. Notes that Kaybee Toy and Hobby Shop in
Atlanta are experiencing a 30 percent increase in sales and that the full
impact of the boom will not be felt until the mid-1980s. Also observes
that some schools anticipate increasing enrollment, although others do
not see significant increases for several years.

688. "Some Experts Foresee a Collapse in Prices for Homes and Offices." *Wall Street Journal*, 28 January 1981, p. 31.

> Recounts the opinion of Wes English, publisher of a real estate and investment newsletter. Claims that housing prices will continue to decline significantly and that high interest rates will deter buyers from purchasing homes. Contends that many of the post-war baby boomers have already purchased homes and that demand for housing will continue to fall.

689. "State and Local Budgets Become a Brake on Growth." *Business Week*, October 26, 1981, pp. 172–75.

> Examines the impact on state and local government budgets as the Reagan administration cuts back its aid. Points out that state and local spending increased in the 1950s because baby boomers required strong expansion of local schools and baby boomers' parents demanded hospitals, roads, water systems, police, and fire services. Contends that as the baby boomers age, they will foster a strong expansion of demand for housing and the accompanying new demands for police and fire protection. Predicts increases in state and local taxes that could stifle consumer spending and business investment.

690. Strout, Richard L. "Echoes of the Baby Boom." *Christian Science Monitor*, February 16, 1979, p. 23.

> Summarizes briefly the impact of the baby boom on schools, the labor force, the Armed Forces, age and crime, and houses. The definition and use of the term "cohort" is considered. Notes that the baby boom is finally analyzed in the *Budget of the U.S. Government, Fiscal Year 1980*. Different terms for the baby boom ("age lump," "cohort," and "tidal wave") are also identified. The inability of demographers to accurately predict future population trends is humorously emphasized.

691. Tavris, Carol. "The End of the IQ Slump." *Psychology Today*, April 1976, pp. 69–74.

> Studies the prediction that Scholastic Aptitude Test scores (SATs) will reverse their decline and begin to rise by 1980. The theory of Robert B. Zajonc, professor of psychology at the University of Michigan, contends that "the intellectual environment of a family depends on the number of family members and their age." If this is correct, the decline in test scores occurred because of the larger families produced by the baby boom in the fifties and sixties. Statistics and other studies that sup-

port Zajonc's hypothesis are cited. Concludes that the "decline in SAT scores, in other words, directly reflects the increased family size of the post war years and the students' later birth orders."

692. Topolnicki, Denise M. "Get Off Your Plateau." *Money*, August 1983, pp. 109–16.

Reports on the growing problem of increased competition on management levels as the baby-boom population competes for management jobs. Gives advice on ways in which employees can gain a competitive edge to get promoted, including the following: (1) continue to increase education and training in such areas as computers and public speaking; (2) increase job responsibilities; (3) participate in professional organizations or community organizations; and (4) volunteer for a transfer or demotion if the job broadens knowledge.

693. Trunzo, Candace E. "Living the Good Life." *Money*, March 1983, p. 59.

Profiles six families who have been economically successful as baby boomers. Identifies key characteristics of these families, including (1) a belief that they are better off than their parents; (2) education levels that are higher than those of their parents; and (3) a willingness to work sixty to eighty hours a week. Notes that they are disciplined, organized, selfish, and concerned with the quality of their lives.

694. Tuhy, Carrie. "What Price Children?" *Money*, March 1983, p. 77.

Points out that unlike previous generations, the baby boomers do not see children as a fact of life, but a matter of choice. Discusses in detail the cost of raising children, covering such areas as child care, effect on job security of the mother, educational costs, and medical costs. Reviews various financial strategies for financing a child's education, including gifts of money, Clifford trusts, and Crown loans. Notes that, generally, people feel the cost is well worth the pleasure of having children. A table reflecting the cost of children as they pass through various ages is also presented.

695. "Unions Campaign to Shrink Work Time: The "Baby Boom" Generation Demands More Leisure." *Business Week*, April 24, 1978, pp. 30–31.

Examines briefly two divergent trends: the increase in the mandatory retirement age, and the push by unions to reduce the workweek or work year. Observes that historically unions made only a token gesture to reduce the workweek because workers wanted high salaries, but the 1974–75 recession produced a desire to provide stability and more jobs. Points out also that the baby-boom generation, which dominates the labor force, desires more leisure time. Reports that although the retirement age has been raised to seventy, there is a marked increase in individuals retiring early.

696. Van Slambrouck, Paul. "America's Maturing 'Baby Boom'—Good Economic News for the '80s?" *Christian Science Monitor*, 7 July 1980, p. 1.

Describes the positive benefits from the baby boom as it enters the 1980s. Predicted beneficial effects include lower crime rate, a mature and experienced labor force, increased personal savings, less unemployment, and lower inflation. Potential problems include an eventual shortage of young unskilled workers and an increased tax burden on workers to support the Social Security system.

697. Vartan, Vartanig G. "Baby Boomlet: How to Benefit." *New York Times*, 14 July 1981, p. 32.

Assesses some of the future investment opportunities created by the baby-boom generation. Notes that baby boomers are reaching an age group in which housing and furniture become prime purchases. The baby boomers may also have a significant number of children, producing a baby boomlet. Presents some of the recommendations of Smith-Barney to take advantage of this boomlet, including investment in Eastman Kodak, Polaroid, Fox-Stanley Photo, Proctor & Gamble, furniture, apparel, toys, fast food, and amusement parks. Cautions that the boomlet will probably not compare to the earlier baby boom.

698. Velocci, Tony. "You've Come a Long Way, Baby Boom." *Nation's Business*, January 1983, pp. 52–55.

Discusses the demographic trends that will affect business in the coming years. Notes that the most significant feature is the maturation of the baby-boom generation. Points out that by 1990, the largest population in U.S. history will be middle-aged, creating a demand for nondurable goods. Reports also that more than half the working couples are baby boomers, and that working women in this group will stimulate demand for work-saving services, child care, and financial services such as brokerage houses, banks, and insurance. Observes that the baby-boom family is smaller and that many baby boomers live alone. Asserts that such factors affect housing, public service, and consumer markets.

699. Yardeni, Edward. "Current Yield: Megacyclically Bullish and Demographically." *Barron's*, June 1981, p. 54.

Begins with a brief explanation of the economic theory developed by Nicholas Kondratieff called the "Kondratieff wave." Contends that economic cycles peak every fifty to fifty-five years. Employs this theory to argue that the United States is on the verge of a "structural reduction in inflation." Asserts that in the recent past the baby boomers infused the labor market and caused inflation and high bond yields. Notes, however, that the baby boomers needed more jobs than were available, causing unemployment. Also points out that in attempting to bear inflation, the baby boomers fostered families in which both parents worked. Concludes that as the baby boomers age, there will be less unemployment and a movement toward conservative economic policies, thus reducing inflation.

700. "Yesterday's 'Baby Boom' Is Overcrowding Today's Prisons." *U.S. News and World Report*, March 1, 1976, p. 65.

Discusses the problem of prison overcrowding across the United States. Observes that judges are releasing prisoners because of crowded conditions, and that prison disturbances are expected to increase. Asserts that prison officials failed to take into account the influx of baby boomers who are reaching "prison prone" age. Predicts the prison population will continue to rise to 267,000 in 1985. Reviews what states are trying to do about the problem.

701. "Youth Unemployment: Unease and Black Teenagers as Losers." *Business Week*, October 10, 1977, pp. 64–70.

Explores the problem of youth unemployment, particularly its cause and impact. Identifies three factors that exacerbate the unemployment issue: (1) depth of the recession and slow recovery; (2) expansion of the teenage population due to the baby boom; and (3) the end of the Vietnam War and compulsory draft. Notes that from 1955 to 1974 the number of teenagers doubled to over 16 million and that teenagers' participation in the work force has increased significantly. Discusses the effects of unemployment on young people and the difficulties ahead for the hardcore unemployed. Includes tables of teenage unemployment and joblessness for black teenagers.

702. "Why Savings May Stay High." *Business Week*, September 13, 1982, p. 62.

Discusses the savings pattern of the American consumer following the recent recession. Points out several reasons why savings should remain high, including (1) lower inflation rates; (2) new tax incentives; (3) high real interest rates; and (4) demographic changes, most notably the aging of the baby-boom generation. Notes that as baby boomers age, their rate of savings should increase. Includes table on personal savings as a percentage of disposable income.

Periodicals Cited Index

References are to entry numbers.

Author Index

References are to entry numbers.

Abrams, Bill, 556
Adams, Melissa M., 476
Alden, Alison, 1
Alsop, Ronald, 557
Ancipink, Patricia, 361
Anderson, Joseph M., 2
Anderson, Polly, 447
Andreason, Aaron, 227
Andreassen, Arthur, 167
Arenseon, Karen W., 560

Bakan, David, 478
Baker, Ross K., 65
Baker, Russell, 569
Baldwin, Wendy H., 73
Barabba, Vincent P., 3, 66
Bean, Frank D., 67
Beck, Melinda, 571
Bell, Chip R., 428
Berger, Mark Charles, 4, 168
Berry, Leonard L., 235
Berry, Mary F., 5
Bianchi, Suzanne M., 214
Bienstock, Herbert, 6
Blake, Larry J., 169
Bleakley, Fred R., 573
Block, Susan, 236
Bloom, David E., 533
Blumenstein, Alfred C., 480
Blyskal, Jeff, 575, 576
Bohmbach, Dwight, 335
Bouvier, Leon Francis, 481
Bowman, Robyn, 7
Brackman, Jacob, 577
Breckenfeld, Gurney, 578
Brennan, Denise M., 237
Brenner, Lynn, 363

Briggs, Jean A., 579
Brock, B., 71
Brody, J.A., 71
Brott, Jody, 571
Brown, Arnold, 471
Brown, Barbara I., 482, 483
Brown, Paul B., 581, 586
Brown, Paul E., 582
Browne, Lynn E., 170
Buckley, Jerry, 571
Bulkeley, William M., 583
Bumpas, Larry L., 134
Butler, Robert N., 8, 485
Buyz, William P., 68
Byrne, John A., 586

Caffarella, Edward P., 486
Cain, Thomas J., 364
Califano, Joseph A., Jr., 487, 488
Campbell, Arthur A., 69
Cargan, Leonard, 117
Carlson, Allan C., 489
Carlson, Elwood D., 490
Carlson, Eugene, 587
Carlucci, Carl, 491
Chase, Richard Allen, 9
Chernoff, Joel, 430
Chiang, Cheng-Hung, 492
Christian, James W., 365
Ciccolella, Cathy, 240
Clark, James L., 70
Clark, Robert L., 10
Coates, Joseph F., 588
Collier, David C., 366
Collins, Glenn, 589
Conte, Christopher, 592
Contreras, Joe, 571

Subject Index

References are to entry numbers.

Barbecues, 359. *See also* Leisure-time activities

Baseball, 483. *See also* Leisure-time activities

Batey, Andrews, 659

Beer, 266, 276, 581, 601. *See also* Alcoholic beverages

Bell, John P., 129

Bell, Robert, 660

Benedictine Marketing Service, 557

Benefit plans, 430, 442, 461, 470, 606, 650

Berdis, Bert, 600

Beverages, 581. *See also* Alcoholic beverages; Soft-drink industry

Bibliography, 7

Bicycles, 304, 359, 483

Binney & Smith, 243, 411

Bilt-Rite, 576

Birth control pills. *See* Contraception

Birth dearth. *See* Baby bust

Birth order, 479, 555, 589, 691

Birthrate, 2, 14, 16, 17, 19, 25, 48, 58, 67, 90, 92, 96, 100, 102, 109, 116, 124, 127, 144, 163, 164, 165, 214, 231, 244, 271, 281, 293, 299, 303, 327, 330, 349, 352, 476, 479, 499, 503, 506, 520, 524, 529, 556, 561, 565, 599, 608, 609, 611, 643, 665

Bissell, John, 266

Black & Decker, 411, 681

Black teenagers, 701. *See also* Teenagers

Black unemployment, 207. *See also* Unemployment

Blacks, 3, 207, 238, 701. *See also* Minorities

Bleaches, 582

Blue-collar baby boomers, 574

Blue jeans, 356, 593. *See also* Clothing

Board games, 260. *See also* Games industry

Bonuses, 464. *See also* Benefit plans

Book publishing. *See* Publishing

Boom-bust cycle, 571

Boston, Mass., 36, 281, 341, 493

Bourbon, 557, 641. *See also* Alcoholic beverages

Boys' clothing, 350. *See also* Clothing

Brainard, Alex, 357

Brandy, 641. *See also* Alcoholic beverages

Bread, 330

Bretteville, Peter de, 656

Brookings Institution, 314

Brown-Forman, 306

Budget of the United States Government, Fiscal Year 1980, 690

Buick, 427, 619. *See also* Autos

Burger King, 568. *See also* Fast-food restaurants

Burokas, Cecilia, 464

Business travel, 250. *See also* Travel

Business trend analysts, 326

Butz, William, 166

Buying habits. *See* Shopping patterns

Buying power, 216, 238

CDs. *See* Certificates of deposit

CFCF-AM, 239

Cable TV, 332. *See also* Television

Cadillac, 369, 427. *See also* Autos

Cadillac Cimarron, 369. *See also* Autos

California, 120, 318, 421

Calisthenics, 483. *See also* Physical fitness

Cambridge Research for the No Load Mutual Fund Association, 305

Cameras, 294, 359, 672

Camping, 483. *See also* Leisure-time activities

Canada, 22, 31, 70, 135, 141, 149, 194, 239, 273, 385, 390, 434, 438, 557, 661

Canadian Pension Plan, 661

Car seats. *See* Auto seats

Car sound systems. *See* Auto sound systems

Cars. *See* Autos

Career advancements. *See* Promotions

Career counseling, 38, 469

Career development, 37, 52, 66, 195, 433, 602, 615, 637

Career ladders, 438

Career plateauing, 432, 443, 473, 662

Carpet industry, 321

Casabarian, John, 655

Cass, Heather Willson, 660

Casualty insurance, 397. *See also* Insurance

Catalog sales, 274

Catholics, 165. *See also* Religion

Census figures, 96, 100, 108, 127, 136, 139, 142, 144, 151, 412

Cereal industry, 303, 307, 610, 635. *See also* Food

Certificates of deposit, 607

Chain restaurant, 249. *See also* Fast-food restaurants

Chain Store Age Magazine, 359

Chemical companies, 259

Chevrolet, 392. *See also* Autos

About the Authors

Greg Byerly is an associate professor of library administration in the Kent State University Library, and works as a reference librarian and on-line searcher. He holds a Ph.D. in higher educational administration, an M.A. in library science, and an M.A. in English. Currently, he is president of the Ohio Library Association. He has published three earlier books, including two on incest and pornography (coauthored with Rick Rubin), and numerous articles in professional journals.

Richard E. Rubin was personnel director of the Akron–Summit County Public Library in Akron, Ohio, when this book was being written. He is currently pursuing doctoral studies in library science at the Graduate School of Library and Information Science at the University of Illinois at Champaign-Urbana. Mr. Rubin has published two books (on pornography and incest) and numerous articles.